The History of the British Film 1929–1939

Documentary and Educational Films of the 1930s

The History of the British Film 1896–1906 (with Roger Manvell)
The History of the British Film 1906–1914
The History of the British Film 1914–1918
The History of the British Film 1918–1929
The History of the British Film 1929–1939:
  Films of Comment and Persuasion of the 1930s

The History of the British Film
1929-1939

Documentary and Educational Films of the 1930s

by
RACHAEL LOW

London
George Allen & Unwin
Boston   Sydney

First published in 1979

GEORGE ALLEN & UNWIN LTD
40 Museum Street, London WC1A 1LU

© George Allen & Unwin (Publishers) Ltd, 1979

British Library Cataloguing in Publication Data

Low, Rachael
    The history of the British film.
    1929–39: Documentary and educational films of the 1930s
    1. Moving-pictures – Great Britain – History
    I. Title   II. Documentary and educational films of the 1930s
    791.43′0941   PN1993.5.G7   78–41277

ISBN 0-04-791036-4

Typeset in 11 on 12 point Baskerville by Trade Linotype, Birmingham
and printed in Great Britain by Fakenham Press Limited, Fakenham, Norfolk

Acknowledgements

I would like to express my gratitude first to the Calouste Gulbenkian Foundation, which by a Research Fellowship at Lucy Cavendish College, Cambridge, made the initial research for this and two other books on the British film in the 1930s possible; and secondly to the British Film Institute, which has made annual grants towards the expenses of research since then. Lastly my thanks to the National Film Archive, and to Jeremy Boulton in particular, for endless patience in digging out innumerable small films for me to see, cannot be overstated. I would also like to thank Brenda Davies, Thorold Dickinson and Paul Rotha for their advice and encouragement down the years, and to add a word of tribute to the late Ernest Lindgren, who kindled my early interest in the subject and continued to help and advise me until his untimely death.

RACHAEL LOW

Contents

Illustrations

It is difficult to give any but a sketchy idea of a film when movement, editing and sound are not present. All these illustrations are frames of film, not photographs taken under special conditions by a stills cameraman. Their quality is therefore not that of the "art shot", but they are relevant to the text and give some slight indication of what the films looked like. I would like to acknowledge the assistance of the National Film Archive Stills Department in securing them.

1

Introduction

One of the greatest of the British documentary film-makers has written of the 1930s that, apart from the mainstream of the documentary movement, there is little to say about non-fiction film making at the time.

An artist must be excused for the belief that the group within which he works is the best of all groups, and that little of importance is happening elsewhere. And the historian of art or literature is a retrospective critic, who finds his interest in quality. But, if film is a medium of communication, there is more to its past than the highlights of artistic achievement, just as there have been important and influential books in the past which were written to communicate something, not to create literary masterpieces. It is probably true that the mainstream documentary movement of these years is Britain's greatest contribution to the development of the cinema. But it is also true that during this decade the film was bursting its theatrical bonds and the documentary movement was only one part of a seething mass of activity outside the commercial feature studios, one effort among many to use film as a genuine form of communication not confined to the set pattern of the picture show.

The cinema's birth in the fairgrounds and music-halls has become such a popular piece of nostalgia that the industry's swashbuckling forefathers begin to seem as glamorous as the pirates of the Spanish Main, but the swashbuckling was not without its drawbacks. The cinematograph which had been invented for serious purposes, and had given the world a new means of communication, was promoted almost entirely because its projection on a screen made it a cheap form of theatre, and it was promoted by people who were, at best, of limited experience and imagination, and at worst ignorant and mercenary. They had a new means of communication, but little to communicate. For many years virtually all film production in this country was in a theatrical straitjacket, a fact which was reinforced by the inflammable nature of 35 mm. film, and its use was dictated by what the showmen believed the greatest number of people would pay to see.

By the time the sound film became commercially possible in the late twenties things had settled down into a ritual of "going to the pictures" The ingredients, however good, were limited. The story film, whether main feature or shorter and usually shoddier second feature, the cartoon, the regular newsreel, and sometimes short interest or travel·films made as cheaply as possible as fillers were almost the only films being made, and they were made only if they seemed to have a very wide appeal. During the thirties the spread of Sunday Opening and news theatres, a misnomer for cinemas showing a brief miscellany of short films, was to bring no real flexibility.

But there had always been a few other people trying to use film for some special purpose of their own. Trade and industry, for example, had early seized on the idea of advertising by film. The First World War, too, had led governments to use film for record, propaganda and training. Enthusiasts and cranks had filmed many things from Arctic expeditions to a drop of water under a microscope. There was considerable interest in films for education. The dreaded "health propaganda" films so feared by the film trade, more properly sex-education films, anticipated John Grierson's idea of films made in the service of the community. The film society movement and repertory cinemas, also, were signs of the inadequacy of the institutionalised picture show. In the thirties substandard film became widely used. This was film 16 mm. wide, or sometimes 9.5 or 8 mm., instead of the 35 mm. gauge commonly used in the theatres. This development, together with that of safety film and non-theatrical exhibition, was accompanied by an enormous increase in both the quantity and the quality of films of every type made outside the feature studios.

What else did these films have in common, and is there a less cumbersome way of defining them than that they were made outside the feature studios? There is so much overlapping that rigid categories are elusive. The distinction between commercial and non-commercial production is not particularly helpful. Many were shown in the cinemas, but not all. Many were sponsored, but not all. Many were short, but not all. It is tempting to settle for the term "factual film". At best it is not strictly accurate, as there are many examples here of story films and the use of actors, although the non-studio film did at least tend to use more realistic backgrounds, if only for practical reasons. But in any case the whole question of factual or actuality film and realism is a trap, and it was precisely during the thirties that the nature of this trap became evident. The original division of films into actuality and fiction was in need of re-examination, for imagination is present in the devising of even the simplest record, and in very few films were things exactly what they seemed. Even in John Grierson's own film *Drifters*, we are told, the underwater sequences of the fish at sea were shot in a tank. The trend was towards an ever more elaborate re-creation of the apparently real, with "real" people shown not only in interviews (and none of these, after all, was spontaneous) but even in a sort of re-enactment of themselves, planned and rehearsed. The appearance of reality caught on the wing was used with ever growing deception, and the borderline with fiction became blurred in firms made in places other than the regular commercial feature studios.

For everywhere people were making teaching films, advertising, current affairs and propaganda for everything from the Conservative and Unionist Party to teetotalism, films of exploration, abstract films and many others as well as the documentary as it is commonly understood. But documentaries, advertising films and films of exploration were all used indiscriminately as school films, and natural history films intended for the classroom might well turn up in the cinemas. Even documentary turns out not to be the simple matter it had appeared when the term "the creative treatment of reality" had been coined to describe it. The documentarists themselves became unhappy about the word in the mid-thirties and tried to substitute "realist". But the more the movement spread the more varied became the films within it. Vigorous discussion of the nature of documentary continued throughout the period. The revered pioneer Robert Flaherty was attacked for what was now called his "idyllic-evasive" style. Grierson theorised about the need for an education for democracy, and harangued Paul Rotha for his "impressionism". Rotha and others sought a more specific commitment to social and economic change. And towards the end of the thirties a split developed between those who favoured a more dramatic and humanist approach and those who turned the film into an illustrated lecture in what was thought of then as the *March of Time* style. At the same time films which would have to be included in any reasonable definition of documentary were being made by people not accepted within the charmed circle. It almost seemed that, to some people, documentary films were the ones made by people they liked, and interest films were made by the rest.

The number of these varied films made in the period is, of course extremely large. A *National Encyclopaedia of Educational Films* published in 1937, which embraced anything from amateur films, teaching and advertising films, documentaries and even some old feature films in its very wide definition of "educational", contains between 2,000 and 2,500 titles, and this was certainly not exhaustive. Some sort of classification is necessary, however, in order to thread one's way through this labyrinth. For practical purposes we may distinguish three possible motives on the part of the film maker. He may wish to pass on to other people his own impressions and experience of the world about him in the hope that this will also interest or entertain them. He may wish to improve others by instructing them. Or he may seek to persuade them, whether for commercial, moral or political reasons.

This most basic of all divisions of communication into giving pleasure, informing, and persuading must, of course, be further broken down and it hardly needs to be added that the categories are not mutually exclusive. In the first category, the whole field of the studio entertainment film lies outside the scope of the present study. But among the non-studio films to which we have referred above lie many films of observation, made neither to teach nor to persuade but simply to pass on ideas and information to other people for their interest and pleasure. They include, for example, travel films ranging from commercial travelogues, through expeditions undertaken simply to make films, to true expeditions of which the films were by-products; they include a wide variety of interest films made by people all the way from the commercial shorts merchants to documentarists not in the élite mainstream, and finally many little films made by individual, and even sometimes eccentric, film-makers. News films, whose production, although commercial, was quite separate from the feature studios, were made simply to form part of the entertainment package and may also be classed as films of comment and pleasure, without didactic intention. Consideration should be given to films of current events including the regular commercial newsreels and their occasional special issues, the influence of *The March of Time* and the arrival of television, and certain compilation films on current affairs, especially pacifism and disarmament. Films of persuasion include commercial advertising, but also the promotion of many points of view from religion and many moral and social "good causes" to the politics of both left and right.

All these are described in a companion volume to this book, *Films of Comment and Persuasion of the 1930s*. Here, we confine ourselves to a study of films made with a clear intention to instruct. Our field includes the progress of the educational film with a glance at certain colonial experiments, as well as the documentary movement which was of such importance in the thirties. This was the exclusive Grierson school of documentary, the true documentary boys with all their prestige and self-confidence. In view of its undoubted social and artistic importance it is described in some detail. Grierson's stated aim was to teach a democratic populace about society and their place in it, and in the early thirties he equated both education and propaganda as interchangeable terms applicable to this didactic aim. But, as we shall see, the meaning of words like "documentary", "realism", "propaganda" and many others shifted somewhat during the decade, as did the documentary movement itself, and what began as a didactic movement ended as a tool for propaganda in the modern sense of presenting a case.

The formation of the British Film Institute, which was a practical if confused expression by society of the belief that film was too important to be left to the film-makers, is described in an appendix.

No attempt is made either here or in the companion volume to be comprehensive. Rather, a preliminary survey of the whole field is undertaken and a number of the films are identified either because they are important, or because they are typical, or because they are of some particular individual interest. These examples suggest the many sources and purposes of film making at this time in addition to mainstream documentary, which is no longer seen as an isolated phenomenon. The general picture is one of great vitality and diversification. Universal education and universal suffrage, mass circulation newspapers, radio, the development of advertising and the public relations business were the background against which the film was forcing its way out of the entertainment-art of the studio feature film, to find new functions in society as part of the mass media.

2

The Educational Film

There were extravagantly high hopes for the use of films in education. John Grierson, writing a foreword to W. H. George's *The Cinema in School* in 1935, wrote of using film to teach civics :

> the bringing alive to children of the life and composition of the community as they see it on their doorsteps and under their doorsteps, and as they will see it when they come to work in the mine or stand in the Labour Exchange queue.[1]

And in the same year D. Charles Ottley, in his book *The Cinema in Education*, was rhapsodically blind to the real nature of film :

> The Cinematograph is free from bias; it neither condemns nor condones. It makes no statement, neither does it think; its function is to *record*. The record may be two-fold, comprising picture and sound, or it may be only picture. The record is a record of truth, since neither lens nor microphone can invent. Because the Cinematograph is unconscious of its scholars it favours neither genius nor dunce; because it is wrought of steel it suffers no human ailment; because it is mechanical it more nearly attains to the perfect in teaching than any other medium known to man.[2]

In the introduction to *A National Encyclopaedia of Educational Films* in 1937 it is hoped that "the educational film freely used among children of the world will prove the solvent of prejudices and animosities, and create a better understanding between nations" [3] In the opinion of George H. Green, Lecturer in Education at the University College of Wales and a director of Visonor Educational Films, film would free the teacher from the chore of what he called cramming in the facts, and allow him to concentrate on the "formation of character", "personal contact and frank friendship" and to "inspire effort and self-control".[4] Alas, like international understanding, none of this was as near as it seemed.

Despite these hopes it was still not clear how to use the film in school. What sort of films were needed – general ones to give background and stimulate interest and imagination, or precise films of explanation and demonstration? sound films, with a professional narrator doing the teaching, or silent films, with or without notes for the teacher to introduce, interpolate and discuss afterwards? How long should they be? What subjects lent themselves best to film treatment? Was it a good idea for the teacher to stop the film frequently and comment, or better to rerun the film later? Was dark or daylight projection wisest? Follow-up work? What age- and ability-groups seemed to benefit most? Would children in fact understand and retain lessons better with a film? and what were the pros and cons for the different widths in which film was made?

Many enthusiasts not only used films in the classroom early but even tried their hands at making them. One well-known pioneer was Ronald Gow of the County High School for Boys at Altrincham. Over a period of six or seven years he and his pupils made a number of standard gauge, including some which were rented to other schools. At summer camp in 1926 they made, for £30, a one-reeler showing a day in the life of a boy of the Neolithic Age called *People of the Axe*. Next year came *People of the Lake* about the late Bronze or early Iron Age, and in 1928 a three-reel film for the Scout Movement, *The Man Who Changed His Mind*. Venturing further into the use of film for purposes over and above mere classroom teaching, in 1929 they made a two-reel mediaeval drama called *The Glittering Sword* with disarmament as its theme. Gow also made a short, silent stop-motion nature film called *The Sundew Plant*. Encouraging the boys to make films such as a study of rivers filmed on school outings, he regarded the very production of the films as educational. W. H. George, another pioneer, was a master at the William Rhodes Modern School of Chesterfield, where at his suggestion in May 1932 Stuart Legg was to film the documentary *The New Generation*. George was described in the *Educational Film Review* as "film master", and was responsible for a number of productions – studies of sheep farming and the steel industry, *The Outer Isles* and *Clouds and Rain, Life in Ponds and Streams* and *The Tides*. Uddingston Grammar School in Lanarkshire had two 16 mm. silent films for hire : *Preparatory Class*, which was an anti-war film, and a road safety film called *Safely Across*. These are only isolated examples but they suggest the amount and scope of school filming. The best-known and longest lasting unit was that which flourished under the Elmhirsts at Dartington Hall from 1934, under its leading spirit the geography teacher William Hunter. They made *No Work on Sunday* and *Camp Newsreel 1935* about the school, and later a two-reeler *The Senior School*; *Sheep Dip*, four films on north-west Derbyshire, *Canary Bananas* and later *Farmers of the Fjord, Norwegian Harvest* and *Nomads* were teaching films.

So it seems there were teachers willing not only to use films, but to make them as well. Perhaps this was because there was such a shortage of really suitable films. Yet the idea of films in schools was hardly new. The Cinema Commission of Enquiry set up as far back as 1917 had led to investigations by Professors Spearman and Burt, with favourable results which had been published in 1925 in *The Cinema in Education*, edited by Sir James Marchant. But despite this early encouragement progress was in fact very slow. Most school and educational authorities were reluctant to commit themselves to the expense of providing equipment until they were sure of an adequate supply of truly educational films. Producers, on the other hand, were equally reluctant to embark on large-scale production of these until they were assured of a sufficient and continuing market. The lack of agreement as to what sort of film was most suitable made this vicious circle very hard to break. Instead, throughout the decade, tests and investigations were conducted one after another in a search for real evidence of the teaching value of film.

In October 1928 the Historical Association appointed Frances Consitt to carry out an investigation into the value of films in the teaching of history. Funds were provided by the Carnegie United Kingdom Trustees, and the Film Enquiry Committee received the co-operation of a large number of educational bodies.[5]

The enquiry started in Leeds in February 1929. It was to include children from 7 to 18 years of age in all sorts of school and in both rural and urban areas, and to determine the extent to which film could help at different types of school, different grades, and at different ages, the best way to use film for history teaching and the most suitable types of film, and was also to consider such practical matters as projectors. Formal tests were used with control groups and timed lessons both with and without the use of films; informal tests were also employed, to find out the opinions of both teachers and pupils of the value of the films. These included British Instructional's *Roman Britain* and *Naval Warfare 1782–1805*, both of them re-edited excerpts from feature films, two amateur films including Gow's *People of the Axe*, the four-reel 1926 League of Nations film *The World War and After* and an American film lent by Yale University. It was admitted that the films were a poor collection, but history films were scarce.

After the Historical Association's investigation came the establishment of the great Commission on Educational and Cultural Films. The Association of Scientific Workers, one of the first bodies to see the film's potential value outside the cinema, set up a Scientific Films Committee in 1929. In December of that year, on their initiative and that of the British Institute of Adult Education, the Commission was set up to "investigate the Service which the Cinematograph may Render to Education and Social Progress". This was, in time, to lead to the establishment of the British Film Institute.[6]

Meanwhile Miss Consitt, who was a member of the Commission, proceeded with her own investigation and held a conference at Leeds University in January 1930, at which elementary-school teachers met to discuss the results of film experiments so far held in their schools. It was believed at this time that only about 300 schools in Britain had projectors. The Consultative Committee of the Board of Education in a *Report on the Primary School* in 1931 recommended the use of both film and broadcasting in schools but, whereas broadcasting was to prove a comparatively simple matter, the use of film was not. The Commission, together with the British Institute of Adult Education and the British Association for the Advancement of Science, organised exhibitions of mechanical aids to learning at the London School of Economics in September 1930, and in South Kensington in September 1931. It was hoped by this means to interest local authorities, who by installing projectors would provide a real market for films and thus encourage their production. The Oxford Secretary of Education, A. C. Cameron, who was Joint Honorary Secretary of the Commission, also arranged for experiments to be undertaken on behalf of the Commission by the Oxford Education Committee. Reporting mainly on geography, science and recreational silent films, they concluded that the best available films were American ones such as those in the large Kodak library, as British Instructional films were not yet available on substandard stock. Shortly afterwards another officer of the Commission, the Honorary Treasurer F. A. Hoare, who was also Assistant of the Education Committee of the National Union of Teachers, addressed a conference of the Association of Special Libraries and Information Bureaux, maintaining what was by now becoming a cliché, that films would be of great value in teaching once the vicious circle of production and outlet had been overcome.

With Miss Consitt and the Commission at work, a third important study was set up in 1931, the Middlesex Experiment, sponsored by the National Union of Teachers with the Middlesex Education Committee and the three commercial firms of British Instructional Films, Western Electric and British Movietone. This investigation was specifically to study the educational possibilities of the sound film, of particular interest to both Western Electric and British Movietone. Films were provided by British Instructional and Movietone, and equipment in the shape of a travelling sound-reproduction unit by Western Electric. After this experiment F. A. Hoare, who was as we have seen a member of both the N.U.T. and the Commission, joined the Western Electric company as their Director of Educational Research. Harry Bruce Woolfe of British Instructional was also a member of the Commission, as were Frances Consitt and and Alan Cameron. The Commission was of crucial importance in its influence through this small group of key people.

Late in 1931 all three investigations – that is, the Commission, the Historical Association enquiry and the Middlesex Experiment – made their findings known. The Commission produced a report called *The Film in National Life* in October, published in 1932. Its main result was the establishment of the British Film Institute, described in the Appendix. But the report had a great deal to say about the educational film, and its influence was considerable. Miss Consitt also produced her *Report on the Value of Films in the Teaching of History* in 1931 and later published a *Brief Abstract* of it. The results of the Middlesex Experiment were published as *Sound Films in Schools* in December 1931.

Taking Frances Consitt's report first, she found that the attitude of teachers had changed considerably during the experiment, becoming much more favourable as they found that the use of films made history more interesting and helped the children to assimilate and retain, and also to enjoy, their history lessons. This was especially so in senior schools, and on the other hand in rural or poor urban areas where the standard of general knowledge was low, and also among backward children. It was recommended that teachers should see a film first, give an introduction and make occasional comments, and conduct a follow-up discussion. A one- or two-reel film with reasonably good photography was suggested dealing with social life, biographies, events and causes, with a plea that it should be historically accurate, not mix periods or make confusing analogies, and not contain too many maps and diagrams. It was pointed out that such films would best be produced with co-operation between teacher, historian and producer but, in ominous closing words, were unlikely "to provide adequate financial returns to the producer".

The third report, that of the Middlesex Experiment covering 3,602 children between the ages of 8 and 18, seemed to the satisfaction of its commercial sponsors to be a complete vindication of the sound film in education. It was once more felt, however, that the films used were poor and that England was lagging behind other countries in tackling the vicious circle of production and outlets. It was strongly advocated that teachers and film-makers should collaborate in the planning of suitable films, and that these should be started immediately, without waiting for the spread of equipment. The results of this report were far-reaching. Bruce

Woolfe,'the pioneer producer of serious school films, was later to say that the move towards the educational film really started with the Middlesex Experiment.[7] His work at British Instructional and its transfer to the newly founded Gaumont-British Instructional, and the establishment of Western Electric's educational service providing mobile equipment as well as films for hire, date from this report.

Besides these three important studies there were other signs of action even at this early date. The cinema at the Imperial Institute in South Kensington claimed they had had 290,000 visitors by August 1930, 76,000 of them in school parties. Sir James Marchant and Sir Oswald Stoll, early and impatient protagonists of the educational film, had founded the Cinema Visual Educational Movement in 1929 to make films at the old Stoll studios in Cricklewood, and gave the first Visual Education show in October of that year. And the founding of the International Institute of Educational Cinematography in Italy in 1928 began a struggle to free educational films of import duties which dragged on throughout the thirties.

The International Review of Educational Cinematography published in Rome stated in its first issue in July 1929 that "the Italian Government, under the inspiration of its chief, H.E. Benito Mussolini, proposed to the League of Nations, which willingly accepted the duty", to create an "international" institute of educational cinema which was, however, set up and financed almost entirely by the Italian Government and seems to have been located beside Mussolini's own villa. Despite the ambiguity of this position the Council of the League of Nations approved the Statutes in August 1928. The Institute produced its monthly review in five languages and later initiated the Venice Film Festivals. At first much was hoped of it. It had an international Administrative Council, the British representative on which was G. T. Hankin of the Board of Education, an Inspector of Schools and Training Colleges with a special interest in films. He represented the Board on the Central Council for School Broadcasting, was on the League of Nations Union Film Committee and was Chairman of the Historical Association's Film Enquiry Committee, which had initiated Frances Consitt's work. This Council, however, had little real power and the Institute was later criticised strongly by Dr G. F. Noxon, who had himself been the English representative on the Editorial Committee of the review, and who claimed that it was the personal creation of Mussolini himself with propagandist aims, disguised by its connection with the League.[8]

The League of Nations, and in time our own British Film Institute, treated it as though it were a genuinely international body. A preliminary draft convention to facilitate free trade in educational films had appeared in the Institute's *Review* in June 1930. A League of Nations report on the Institute appeared in 1932 with recommendations on matters such as national and international archives of educational and topical films and the cataloguing of educational films. In October 1933 the League held a congress in Geneva at which a Convention for Facilitating the International Circulation of Educational Films was signed by several countries, including Britain, although this was not implemented here until the Finance Act of 1935. Under it, films were to be certified as educational by the International Institute, for whom the British Film Institute would act in this country as agent, and to whom was given the task of persuading other countries to join. By the winter of 1934 the Convention had twenty-five signatories, although the United States was a notable absentee. Two Italian films were the first to be examined by the B.F.I. late in 1936, but by this time relations with Fascist Italy were becoming strained. The Institute was closed by Mussolini late in 1937 and the Convention lapsed, Italy leaving the League of Nations in 1938. New efforts were made to free educational films from customs duties in 1939, when a conference called by an "International Institute of Intellectual Co-Operation" was attended by Oliver Bell on behalf of the B.F.I. The Prime Minister was questioned about this in Parliament by Geoffrey Mander, an M.P. with particular interest in films, but with the outbreak of war the issue ceased to be of practical importance.

Experiments and investigations continued throughout the thirties, their character changing slightly as the usefulness of the film was generally accepted and people simply sought how best to employ it. The Glasgow Experiment, conducted by the Corporation of Glasgow Education Department among boys and girls of 12 and 13, led to a sub-committee's report, *The Film in the Classroom*, in November

1933. The experiment set out to test the aid to retention by a comparison of carefully matched classes. Unfortunately, although the experiment was very systematic, the films[9] were poor and suffered from being on 9.5 mm., far too small for such large classes. The report concluded that films did aid retentivity, especially in the hands of certain teachers, and that, of course, the better the film the more effect it had. It was felt worth while to carry out further experiments with films better designed to act as lessons in themselves, and Glasgow Education Authority went ahead with plans for a production unit and the provision of school projectors. Carrick Classroom Films was formed as a result by Blake Dalrymple and J. C. Elder.

The Edinburgh Education Committee and the Educational Institute of Scotland also conducted experiments, coming to the now familiar conclusions, which they published in October 1932 in *The School and the Film*. The London Teachers' Association published a pamphlet *The Film in Education Today* in the summer of 1933. And the St Pancras Experiment was held in London between 1932 and 1934. Starting with a few cinema matinées for 1,000 children, they showed documentary and nature films. The following year twelve fortnightly shows for 12,000 children were held, sponsored by the National Milk Publicity Council. The report, printed privately, was said to be well disposed to the use of film, especially the silent film with a teacher-narrator. Later Manchester Education Committee, after issuing a first report in October 1935, conducted an experiment with 16 mm. films between October 1935 and March 1937, side by side with shows of 35 mm. G.P.O. documentaries, to 35 schools in January 1936 and to 15,000 children between January and March 1937. A report was published in June 1937 followed by a programme for the use of film. We hear of experiments at Rawtenstall in 1936, Brentwood in 1937 and Eccles between September 1935 and March 1937, the last of which suggested that more Regional and Central Film Libraries were needed. In Wolverhampton between September 1936 and March 1937, 3,500 children saw 42 films varying from classroom films to G.P.O. documentaries; the report, which came out in September 1937, recommended that there should be more booklets to accompany the films, clearer and slower commentaries and captions, more recapitulation and subsidiary material such as maps. Early in 1936 the London County Council announced a programme of shows, some purely educational and some of mixed entertainment and educational films, to be given as cinema matinées to some 14,000 children in such a way as to tie in with their lessons, in the hope of finding out which form of programme was most effective. The committee charged with the investigation reported to the Education Committee in 1937 and a report was presented in July. As a result the committee recommended the expenditure of £1,000 for more equipment, that more films and film shows should be used, and that schools should put aside rooms equipped for projection. A thousand pounds was hardly generous provision, but the committee added that it would consider a more general extension when formulating its 1938–41 programme.

By now the value of the film in formal education had been widely endorsed. By the summer of 1937 the London Education Committee considered it was fully established.[10] Professor Lancelot Hogben, addressing the N.U.T. Higher Education Conference in December 1936, had mentioned its usefulness in the teaching of maths. Dr Julian Huxley and R. A. Watson Watt, speaking at the Royal Institution in January 1937, also referred to its value in teaching biology and physics and both also co-operated in the production of educational films.

Ways of harnessing all this goodwill were canvassed. One interesting scheme which came to nothing was that of Sir James Marchant, chairman of the 1917 enquiry set up by the National Council of Public Morals, who in 1932 hoped to get the Cinematograph Exhibitors' Association, the Kinematograph Renters' Society and the Kinematograph Manufacturers' Association to support a Royal Institute within the film trade. This would promote its national and international interests and contain an educational section headed by Simon Rowson, a renter known to be keen on the educational film and with a reputation as the statistical expert of the industry. Marchant, who is said to have been behind the publication of Walter Ashley's attack on the British Film Institute,[11] wanted, with Sir Oswald Stoll, to found a Film University. This People's Cinema University in London was to be designed by Sir Gilbert Scott and include a Zeiss planetarium of over 100 projectors,

and was to work together with existing universities to study and
develop the practical application of what were later called visual
aids. Nothing came of this imaginative plan. A rival to the B.F.I.
was quick off the mark. Like J. A. Hoare and Bruce Woolfe, a
third member of the Commission on Educational and Cultural
Films plunged into the practical supply of educational films. This
was the secretary of the Commission, the educationist J. Russell
Orr, previously Director of Education in Kenya Colony, who
became managing director of a new Central Information Bureau
for Educational Films set up towards the end of 1932, with an
information service for subscribers. In June 1933 the Bureau published a paperback a *Guide to Instructional and Educational Films*
available in Britain from forty-nine sources. The second edition in
1935 was a large hardback volume called *A National Encyclopaedia
of Educational Films and 16 mm. Apparatus.* It now included
eighty-six sources of films and had articles by Dr George Green, a
lecturer on Education at the University of Wales, and H. D. Waley
of the British Film Institute. It was accompanied from March 1936
to November 1937 by a supplementary bi-monthly bulletin called
Film Progress, and further volumes were brought out in 1937 and
1938, the latter again with articles by Green and Waley and this
time by Oliver Bell as well. The prompt publication and large size
of these film lists were a contrast to the slower and more cautious
work of the British Film Institute. However, little or no attention
was paid to the suitability of the films for actual classroom teaching,
and the lists included everything which could be even roughly
described as information.

As to production, Simon Rowson, fascinated as he always was by
the juggling of large figures, had calculated in 1931 that the preliminary costs of launching production of educational sound films
on a national scale would be £7,150,000, allowing £1,500,000 for
projectors, £4,000,000 for talkie equipment, £750,000 for
production and £900,000 for prints.[12] In an article in the new
paper *Sight and Sound* published by the British Institute of Adult
Education, Bruce Woolfe in 1932 gave some figures based on his
own experience at British Instructional, and expressed the belief
that only a big professional company could make a success of such
production.[13]

Almost immediately he and Mary Field took their work in nature and other instructional films from British Instructional, now taken over by the big commercial feature film company British International Pictures, to the large combine Gaumont-British Picture Corporation. The company formed two subsidiaries, Gaumont-British Equipments in July 1933 and Gaumont-British Instructional in November, in a double attack on the vicious circle of scarce films and scarce equipment in schools. Shortly afterwards Western Electric, also as a direct result of the Commission and the Middlesex Experiment, set up a road show and film service under Hoare in early 1934.

Thus the various investigations and the publication of the Commission's report in 1932 were enough to stimulate a certain amount of activity even before the long negotiations over the founding of the B.F.I. were complete. When it finally opened its doors many hoped that the way ahead was clear at last. Some of the Institute's first actions, however, were hardly helpful. We have seen its ineffective flirting with Mussolini's Institute. The standardisation of substandard sound film and equipment caused more trouble. In 1932 the American Society of Motion Picture Engineers had published recommendations, one of them being that the sound-track should be on the side of the film nearest to the projectionist. Owing to a misinterpretation which was not noticed for seven months, the so-called D.I.N. standard was published in Germany in 1934 with the sprocket-holes on that side instead, with the result that in an S.M.P.E. projector such a film would appear reversed unless corrected by a special prism. This standard was adopted by the International Institute in Rome, and by its loyal follower the British Film Institute, which published a leaflet on available equipment in November 1934 advocating the D.I.N. standard and apparently ignoring the difficulties it would cause when showing American films. The D.I.N. standard was used by G-BI under Bruce Woolfe. In May a conference was held in Berlin. This was boycotted by most of the industry, which had already taken exception to the anti-Semitic propaganda of the German hosts, but was attended by Bruce Woolfe and J. W. Brown of the B.F.I., who continued to support the German standard. There was furious reaction to this in England and the matter was finally put to arbitration by Lord

Riverdale of the British Standards Institution, as a result of which the S.M.P.E. standard was approved in March 1936 and at last, in October, adopted by the Institute. Considerable expense and delay were caused by this readjustment. Another indiscretion was a well-meant scheme to facilitate the provision of film equipment to schools by setting up a bulk-buying service. This led in 1935 to the founding as a subsidiary of the Institute of a commercial company for educational equipment and supplies. J. W. Brown was to be director of the company whilst still continuing to be the general manager of the Institute. The competitive advantage secured by this arrangement was resented by the film trade and the scheme was dropped, the firm being left in the spring of 1936 to carry on independently. This capitulation confirmed the belief of many critics that the Institute was dominated by trade interests.

Not everything the Institute did was so tactless, however. The magazine *Sight and Sound* was taken over from the British Institute of Adult Education in the winter of 1933, and a *Monthly Film Bulletin* was started in January 1934. Both contained much useful information about the educational film, although after a while more general film interests became important. The reviewers of entertainment films were allowed to be somewhat idiosyncratic, but the criticism of educational films in the *Monthly Film Bulletin* became quite severe. An Educational Panel was started, to get teachers, experts and film makers together to discuss the kind of film that was needed. Cataloguing of educational films proceeded slowly and early in 1937 publication began of a series of careful reports and selective catalogues of the highest quality films available for teaching. The first of a series of annual summer schools to interest and instruct teachers was held in 1935. At a congress of the World Federation of Educational Associations held at Oxford in August 1935 a Visual Section was provided by the Institute.

By 1935 the prospects looked good, and an *Educational Film Review* was founded by a commercial publisher. Several books on the film in education appeared in the mid-thirties, including one, *The Film in the School* in 1935, edited by J. A. Lauwerys, who was Lecturer in Education at the Institute of Education in London. This included a list of some ten main libraries, estimating that between them they had over 1,000 films. Not all these libraries produced their own films. Some handled each other's work or farmed out production to the many small companies making not only educational but also publicity and interest or documentary films. Sometimes, too, companies might acquire stock material and tailor it to their own ideas of what educational films should be.

The first company to strike a distinctively educational note, back in the twenties, had of course been British Instructional Films, largely the creation of Harry Bruce Woolfe. Incorporated in 1927, with the novelist John Buchan also on the board and with a studio at Welwyn Garden City, by the early thirties it had installed the German Klangfilm sound system and had a capital of £230,000. Its reputation was for serious realistic and patriotic feature films as well as for the famous *Secrets of Nature* short films. Bruce Woolfe and Mary Field became famous for the latter, more famous in fact than the patient, skilful experts and cinematographers who made them, including the remarkable Percy Smith, whose work was mostly anonymous. Nine sets of six *Secrets of Nature* were registered between the end of 1929 and the end of production early in 1933. The first to use sound was *Bathtime at the Zoo*, shown in November 1929 and made by Arthur Woods, and *Kine Weekly* described its "running commentary with the speaker unseen", noting that this technique, later referred to as "voice-over", had already been used in the American *Spotlight* series.[14] They were informative, well-made, single-reel films on insects, plants, birds and animals. Clear pictures with musical backing taken over from the silent cinema were accompanied by clear decorous upper-class voices, delivering cool commentaries with a touch of lightness and whimsy here and there. Zoo films were thought to be good for a smile. More varied subjects were tackled later. The final set included two physics films on *Surface Tension* made by Louis Anderson Fenn and *A Mediterranean Island*, a film about Cyprus made in collaboration with James Fairgrieve and the Royal Geographical Association. Other films included one called *The Flag* about the development of the Union Jack, directed and written by Mary Field, the accuracy of which caused considerable controversy. More successful were two language films, *Forty-eight Paddington Street* on phonetics and supervised by Professor A. Lloyd James, and *King's English* a year later in 1933. This last film, made with the co-operation of the

1 The bedder comes and goes, but the undergraduates sleep on (*Cambridge*, 1932).

2 The salmon leap (*Upstream*, 1931).

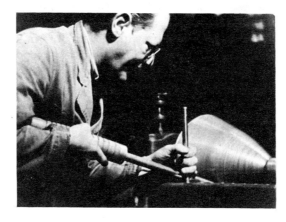

3 "The Parts are Nearly Ready" (*Aero Engine*, 1932).

B.B.C., showed the radical difference between French on the one hand and the various dialects of Britain on the other, all of the latter sharing the same basic rhythms and therefore intelligible to people from different parts of the country. Considered by many to be a documentary rather than a school film, it is representative of the best of their film making and suggests why many people admired British Instructional and later Gaumont-British Instructional films so much, and even preferred them to those of the mainstream documentary movement.

The company had, in fact, a number of contacts with the documentary movement. To begin with the film work of the Empire Marketing Board was loosely connected with British Instructional and its distributor New Era, and Walter Creighton's sound film *One Family* was recorded at Welwyn and put out as a Pro Patria film. The early E.M.B. maintained this link until after attempts had been made to get theatrical distribution through British Instructional's contacts and later, with the Imperial Six films, through G–BI. Paul Rotha, also, had connections with the two companies.

The idea of sponsorship was not developed with imagination by Bruce Woolfe as it was to be by Grierson. But British Instructional did make sponsored or "contract" films as well as its much publicised educational films, among others for the Admiralty, War Office, Ministry of Agriculture and the Central Electricity Board. Many straight record films made for private electrical companies, and some in a more popular style, were virtually publicity films. *Reyrolles and the National Grid* is an example, a short silent film about circuit-breakers at Northfleet, which could just as well have been a lantern lecture with its long informative titles and its static, flat shots. Nevertheless they had a way of turning up in lists of education films, as did those made for the British Social Hygiene Council and other social bodies. Films like *Deferred Payment* and *How to Tell* were socially motivated and are best described along with the "good cause" films elsewhere. *The Mystery of Marriage*, made in 1931, was more ambitious. Made in sound, it was followed by a theatrical version called *The Changing Year* in 1932, and combined compilation film and acting. Directed and written by Mary Field with a commentary and music, it drew on material from many different nature films and some specially shot scenes of a young human couple, in order to draw parallels between human, animal and insect behaviour in courtship, marriage and family life. This was an interesting idea for such an early film but was marred by a slightly coy approach as well as by the messy appearance of ill-matched sequences, and did not receive the welcome which it probably deserved. Another part-compilation film about this time was their two-reel film of flying from Icarus to the 1931 Schneider Trophy, which secured registration for cinema showing as quota footage, *Conquest of the Air*.

Cambridge was not a true British Instructional film. It was made by Stuart Legg and G. F. Noxon as an impression of Cambridge life from the undergraduate's point of view in 1931, after Legg had already directed an amateur four-reel story film called *Varsity* for the Cambridge University Film Society. *Cambridge* was shot silent with music and effects and non-synchronous speech recorded afterwards at Welwyn, and the British Instructional cameraman Jack Parker is given the credit for cinematography. It is an amateurish "day in the life" impression which starts with Cambridge waking up, undergrads rising reluctantly, a gibberish lecture, an explosion of life and sport outside the lecture rooms, then peace on the river and the coming of evening. Using the conventions of the silent film as well as its sound-track, it seems somewhat dated. Its appearance as a British Instructional film suggests that Bruce Woolfe was still hankering, as he had in the twenties, to attract the young university graduates who were beginning to come into film production. From now on, however, they were to turn to Grierson for leadership.[15]

More characteristic of Bruce Woolfe was *England Awake*, a three-reeler, again a combination of compilation and acting, which was made in 1932. This patriotic saga is said in the film credits to have been directed by Bruce Woolfe and John Buchan, with Legg as assistant director, but according to *Sight and Sound*[16] it was directed by Legg. However, it is unmistakably Bruce Woolfe's idea, and Legg found himself a more congenial home thereafter with Grierson. Planned as a morale booster in November 1931, during the economic depression, it shows British achievements in engineering, science and industry since 1815. It mixes clips from travel films, the war and some industrial sequences, and theatrical reconstruction of historical sequences. With breath-taking absurdity, a brisk tour of the modern Empire is conducted by a double-exposure Duke of Wellington, who gives a commentary worthy of a newsreel editor. The film is marked by old-fashioned technique, with minimal sets, contrived situations and dialogue, and stilted acting, a reverential attitude to the Empire and nostalgia for what is seen as a golden age of happiness for all before 1914. With such phrases as "Thank God we did not falter" and "We shall have our reward, if we show ourselves worthy of it", it is a mixture of naïve patriotism and insensitive film making, yet for some years it was one of the few films considered suitable for history teaching, and is a perfect example of what Bruce Woolfe believed a documentary film to be.

After British Instructional was taken over by B.I.P., and later A.B.P.C., they ceased production and their very large library of factual and educational films was distributed by Pathé. After resigning in August 1933, Bruce Woolfe made an abortive move in the direction of sponsored documentary. Forming a unit of his own, British Independent Pictures, he got Rotha, with B.I.F. cameraman Jack Parker, to make a two-reel film *Roadwards* for the B.S.A. and Daimler car companies.[17]

This experiment did not continue, and Bruce Woolfe joined the new educational unit set up by Gaumont-British. Writing at the time that the new company was to make documentaries, he defines these most curiously as films depicting the life and work of "our people", presumably the British, and helping us to understand each other and thus "definitely doing a good work and making a contribution to our national effort".[18] He also somewhat speciously hinted that Rotha would be working with them, although the latter, who wrote later in his autobiography that he was engaged on a "menial fee basis", was a far from willing member of the team. This toying with the new documentary idea, of which he had no real understanding, and with Rotha, to whom he was personally antipathetic, shows Bruce Woolfe striving to remain in the forefront of the factual film movement. It must be emphasised that he had given a very early lead in this after the First World War with his war reconstruction films, and tried to keep high professional standards alive under very unpropitious circumstances. His contribution to the development of the cinema must not be underrated. But he was completely antagonistic to the type of young man now entering the Grierson school of production, temperamentally uncongenial and in politics more closely allied to the conservative leadership of the newsreels and of the British Film Institute than to the Grierson élite. Films expressing any political or social opinions, like the egregious *England Awake* or later *The Gap*, were so ingenuous that they hardly helped the cause they were meant to support. His real field was the school film, which he made valiant efforts to develop, and his leadership in this cannot be questioned. Some of these films were of wider scope and were classed as documentaries by many people. But by the end of 1933 he had lost his brief interest in sponsored documentary and turned back to the school film.

Thus he, Mary Field, their *Secrets of Nature* work and even their tenuous and uncomfortable link with Rotha moved over to the new unit formed by one of the biggest film combines in Britain, Gaumont-British Picture Corporation, with its distribution outlet Gaumont British Distributors. The two new subsidiaries Gaumont-British Equipments and Gaumont-British Instructional had interlocking directorates under the chairman Maurice Ostrer. They planned to make sound films for classroom use, while the equipment branch expanded the market for them by selling projectors to schools. They opened an information department, G–BI Films Bureau under Margery Locket, which together with the Film Institute and the Central Information Bureau was expected to help teachers find their way through the labyrinth of equipment and films on the market. Eventually a small London studio of 2,800 square feet in Cleveland Street, off Tottenham Court Road, was opened officially in March 1935. Although the aim was to tackle the non-theatrical field on a large scale, their experience had led them to believe that this would only be economically possible if a large proportion of the films were prepared not only in school versions but in more popular versions for entertainment shows as well. The old *Secrets of Nature* became G–BI's *Secrets of Life*, and British Instructional's two language films *Forty-eight Paddington Street* and *King's English* led on to two French teaching films.

The French "U" and *La Gare* were both directed by Mary Field and shot by Charles Van Enger. The first contained animated diagrams showing the correct conformation of the mouth and a demonstration by M. Stephan of University College, London, and the B.B.C. Others in the summer of 1934, in what *Sight and Sound* referred to as the first group of classroom films to be issued in Britain, were *Shakespeare*, a one-reeler directed by J. B. Holmes and supervised by Dr G. B. Harrison about Shakespeare's bio-graphical and historical background, and three physiology one-reelers, *Breathing*, *The Blood* and *Circulation* directed by Donald Carter. Early in 1935 the first nature films, now renamed *Secrets of Life*, were *Roots* produced by Percy Smith, edited by Mary Field and supervised by Professor F. Salisbury and *The Thistle*, also directed by Percy Smith and edited by Mary Field.

They plunged into the production of scholastic one- or two-reel sound films with the help and supervision in biology of Dr Julian Huxley and in botany of Dr Salisbury, and with the co-operation of various official and scientific bodies. These films, with such simple factual titles as *Annelid Worms* or *White Flies and Tomatoes*, were greeted with approval on all sides. *The Sea Urchin*, a two-reeler made by H. R. Hewer and cameraman Frank Goodliffe under Huxley's supervision at the Scottish Marine Biological Station, won the Prix Alberteum for the best scientific film at the Brussels Exhibition of 1935. *The Blowfly* and *The Amoeba* by the same team both received Medals of Honour. Their two-reeler *The Earthworm* was even to receive fulsome praise from the literary magazine *Life and Letters Today*.

But despite the high quality of the films difficulties were soon encountered. Not only did comparatively few schools have pro-jectors, but also the majority of these were silent. Some of the films were therefore put out later in mute versions, some re-edited and adapted as silent films with titles. Theatrical versions of the films were also prepared and offered for cinema distribution. No possibility, 35 mm. or 16 mm., sound or silent, was neglected. Throughout 1935 and 1936 simple school films with titles like *The Frog, How Plants Feed* and *Wood Ants* would turn up at Gaumont British Distributors with catchy cinema titles like *He Would a-Wooing Go, Queer Diet* and *Community Life*, and from 1937 many had special commentaries by the popular G–B news commentator E. V. H. Emmett. School versions accompanied by booklets, maps, diagrams and reading lists provided the educational service through

G–BE. For the next few years Mary Field, Donald Carter, J. B. Holmes and Andrew Miller Jones, with such cinematographers as Charles Head until he died in 1938, Oliver Pike, Frank Bundy, George Pocknall and Frank Goodliffe and later B. G. D. Salt and R. Jeffryes, who both specialised in animation, turned out films on plant and animal life which acquired a very high reputation. Later favourites included *Kings in Exile* about king penguins made in Edinburgh by G. W. MacPherson and shot by Pocknall. *The Tough 'Un*, one of the most famous, about dandelions, was made in 1938 by Mary Field and Percy Smith with an Emmett commentary, and was shown at the New York World's Fair. Their first catalogue was published in 1936, in which year they, like the British Instructional films now handled by Pathé, had to convert from the D.I.N. to the S.M.P.E. standard for their 16 mm. prints. The fact remains, however, that despite general approval for these films their popularity amongst exhibitors was limited because until the new quota legislation of 1938 they did not count as British quota footage.

Not all their films were nature films. They had several early ones on cooking for the Inspector of Domestic Science in Leeds, and science and industry were covered in varying degrees. By June 1935 they had films on biology, hygiene, botany, geography, history, languages, and physical training and sports. Starting in 1934 with two *Physical Education* films, one for girls and one for boys, they eventually had a large number of them including six one-reelers on *Lawn Tennis and How to Play It* featuring the tennis star Dorothy Round, and a series of soccer films made under the aegis of the Football Association. Further detailed films appeared in 1936 including two on *Physical Training – Infants* and in 1937 on swimming. Longer than many G–BI films, the PT productions owed much to the instigation and co-operation of the Film Institute's advisory panel and the Central Council for Recreative Physical Training, and some of them were made to illustrate the Board of Education's 1933 syllabus for PT in elementary schools. Also made in 1937 were a series on hygiene and health education, following the appearance in 1936 of Andrew Miller Jones's *The Red Army* on the bed bug, although this was rather outside the narrow definition of school films. They also made a historical series called *Eminent Scientists* for the National Physical Laboratory, and films of Lord Hirst of Witton speaking on the electrical industry and Lord Rutherford on the atom.

Perhaps the best of their work was a number of remarkable history, geography and weather films, some films about the English countryside which to some extent overlapped geography and history, and a few scientific films. *Wheatlands of East Anglia* was a 1935 two-reeler directed by Mary Field and shot by George Pocknall and was followed by one-reelers *Fruitlands of Kent* and *Hoplands of Kent*. Four reels on farming seasons in East Anglia appeared in no less than three different guises in 1935 and 1936, in an effort to use the film material to the utmost. *Town Settlement* was about the geographical factors leading to the development of the Suffolk town of Saxmundham. *This Was England*, directed by Mary Field and shot by Pocknall and Bundy, showed the continuity of agricultural tradition in Suffolk from the Stone Age to the twentieth century, and the two-reeler *The Farm Factory* late in 1936, also shot by Pocknall, showed how a Suffolk farm built in 1810 was still functioning efficiently over 125 years later. It was in 1936, also, that J. B. Holmes made perhaps the most famous of them all, *Mediaeval Village*. This two-reeler shot by Bundy and Goodliffe was planned by H. L. Beales, the London University historian, and R. S. Lambert of the B.B.C. and the Film Institute. It was an imaginative film which examined the village of Laxton in Nottinghamshire where farming still followed the mediaeval system of strip farming in common fields. It used animated maps and various techniques to show the village as it was in the thirties and how it had been centuries before. This was an experimental approach to the making of history films which was widely praised. *Progress* was about the development of the mechanical sciences from 1910 to 1935, especially aeronautics, radio and shipbuilding, but two other history films at the same time as *Mediaeval Village* caused even more of a stir. In *The Expansion of Germany* produced by Mary Field, who had once been a history teacher herself, and directed by Andrew Miller Jones, the cinematography and diagrams by R. Jeffryes used new techniques from Europe which animated not only maps and diagrams but picture symbols. The art of communications was advancing, and with it the purveying of statistics. The method of Dr Otto Neurath of Vienna, illustrating social and economic statistics with symbolic pictorial diagrams, had been the subject of an exhibition in London early in 1933 and had been demonstrated by Dr Neurath himself at a talk under the auspices of the B.F.I. in November of that year. The introduction of picture symbols or pictographs to express statistical information, with its decorative rows of little stylised men and half-men, sacks and half-sacks, ships and half-ships, was doing much to brighten and clarify the mass of statistics now being disseminated. *The Expansion of Germany* and its companion by the same team, *The Development of the English Railways*, successfully and delightfully made their subjects palatable with an adaptation of the system, with such devices as little trains chugging along the railway map. *Changes in the Franchise* in 1937, also by this team, dealt with electoral changes in Britain since 1812. Films about climate included *Coast Erosion* and *Water in the Air*, which explained factors in cloud formation both by laboratory experiments and by normal and stop-motion cinematography, and the most famous, *Story of a Disturbance* in 1936, which used the same techniques to trace the passage of a weather disturbance over Britain, explaining isobars, fronts and other weather terms by diagrams, cross-sections, ordinary and stop-motion filming.

As well as these narrowly scholastic films there were other productions, some of them on heavy industries and some about Scotland, some on more varied subjects. Among the most interesting were the films made in 1937 by Julian Huxley about heredity in animals and man, films which were made in co-operation with the Eugenics Society and which were rather more than mere educational films, and are more suitably described with other films of social causes. A number of heavy engineering films were made. *Aircraft Design* and *Hull Design* were made in 1935 in collaboration with the National Physical Laboratory in Teddington, and a number of short films about shipping appeared from 1934 to 1936, partly as a result of Rotha's films in the shipyards. *Steel* in 1934 was directed by Rotha and *Dry Dock* was made from off-cuts edited by his erstwhile assistant Stanley Hawes in 1936. There were other films such as *Propeller Making*, *Shipcraft*, *Streamline* and *Heavy Industries*. Films about Scotland included *Raw Materials* about the industrial midlands of Scotland, and *Power in the Highlands* in May 1936 was apparently the theatrical version of Hawes's film about hydro-electricity in the Grampians, *Waterpower*. *Scotland for Fitness* was made in 1938 by Brian Salt for the Films of Scotland Committee, but the big Scottish film was a two-reeler made by Mary Field and cameraman George Stevens in 1938, *They Made the Land*, also made for the Films of Scotland Committee. This was handled commercially by an American company after the new legislation of 1938 had introduced a shorts quota. It is nice to look at, a slow but clear semi-educational or loosely documentary film, with a leisurely if slightly portentous Emmett commentary. It shows Scottish farming over the last three hundred years, wresting a living from an unwilling soil, waging war on peat, bog and heather, with hand ploughs on the hills and the reafforestation of sand dunes, the rearing of sheep and eventually the prosperous farms of some hundred years before. The film, in fact, has something in common with the earlier rural pictures of England, and is documentary in style. Another of the best G-BI films of these years was a 1936 two-reeler called *The Mine*, with its non-theatrical version *Coal*. Made with the Safety in Mines Research Board by J. B. Holmes, shot by Bundy and with diagrams by Jeffryes, it was about a modern colliery in Warwickshire. Again, it was a documentary rather than a teaching film, and greatly admired by many who disliked the Grierson style, as well as being awarded a medal at Venice in 1936. There seem to have been other mining films, *Some Aspects of the Coal Industry* produced by Mary Field and directed by Andrew Miller Jones in 1937 with diagrams by Jeffryes, *Black Nuggets* made in 1938 in connection with the Safety in Mines Research Board and *Buried Treasure* with the Coal Utilisation Council.

These latter films suggest that the company was giving up hope of making the purely classroom film economically viable, and adopting a form of sponsorship for films of general knowledge. At the same time, Bruce Woolfe himself made a three-reel documentary in his own style. This was the Territorial recruiting film *The Gap*, made in collaboration with the Army Council and Air Council. A dramatic representation of what might happen in an air attack because of the gap in ground defences, it included a faked air raid. It was directed by Carter, shot by Pocknall, and was given the full G–B treatment with an Emmett commentary and musical direction by Louis Levy, with reliable if not outstanding actors playing the Service chiefs. On the whole it was taken seriously as a documentary by people not connected with film making; but to the documentary film makers its failure to show the reality of an air raid and its general feel of faking were deplorable. Even as propaganda, William Farr in *Sight and Sound* pointed out that, if all that stood between us and destruction was the recruiting of Territorials, our forces must indeed be in a bad way.[19]

These films, classroom teaching and documentary and combinations of the two, in all their versions, represent the unit's best years. By 1938 it was running down and, although the nature films continued to appear and by the outbreak of war were beginning to be made in Dufaycolor, other teaching films were fewer. Some on the food industries in various parts of the Empire seemed to be taking over the promotional role of the old E.M.B., but with cute cinema titles like *Kernel Nutmeg* and *Grappling with Grapefruit*. The company also struck out in a new direction with religious and moral tales and a film by Vernon Sewell about venereal disease, *Test for Love*. Two late films which show the opposite extremes of their style are *Plan for Living* and *The Welsh Plant Breeding Station, Aberystwyth*.

Plan for Living, a film made by Donald Carter about 1939 for the British Commercial Gas Association, is quite an ambitious attempt to explain in a light-hearted way the importance of a balanced diet. The B.C.G.A. was, of course, the sponsor of some of the most outstanding and enlightened mainstream documentary films and did not usually work through G-BI. Starting with the usual explanatory desk lectures facing the camera by Julian Huxley and the Parliamentary Secretary to the Board of Education, Kenneth Lindsay, M.P., we go on to some pleasing animation with the relevant foods, the letters of their written names collapsing into figures personifying such characteristics as "body building" and "body protecting", with cartoon sequences on how they work; next there is an extremely poorly executed pantomime sequence in which the amateurishly costumed "foods" dance out their functions and sing

> We stand for food production,
> We can make you fit and fine,
> But planning is what you need. . . .

After a rhymed act between an experienced housewife and a girl wearing a learner's "L" plate, and a talentless tap dance by the foods on a huge table-top, the film ends with final words from Kenneth Lindsay and Huxley.

The Welsh Plant Breeding Station at Aberystwyth had been the subject of Arthur Elton's early film for Grierson in 1931, *Shadow on the Mountain*. The G–BI film, although a complete contrast, is serious and interesting and, unlike *Plan for Living*, can stand comparison with serious documentary. Shot and directed by the biologist J. V. Durden, it is about the production of new strains of grasses to enable better use to be made of cold and barren Welsh hills by sheep farmers. The technique and approach could hardly be more different from the other film. The young and still romantic Elton had been concerned to show how and where the new grasses were needed, and set the work of the Station against images of hills, sky and sheep, some of them beautiful, some rather self-conscious. Durden concentrates quietly on the work in the Station itself, now much more modern than in the earlier film, and includes cinemicrography of the pollination, making a virtue of clear no-nonsense photography. With comment from time to time but no direct speech, the film performs its function perfectly and does not claim more. It is easy to see why many people preferred this understated style to the variable results and more sophisticated aims found among the mainstream.

But it had to be faced that despite high quality and considerable financial and distributive backing, and despite ingenious multiple use of the material shot, educational film production was still not a commercial proposition. It has been calculated that by 1939 G–BI had made some 240 teaching films.[20] Mary Field, highly educated and articulate, had spoken and written on behalf of the educational film as Grierson had done for the documentary. But her personality and approach, and those of Bruce Woolfe, did not generate enthusiasm and devotion as Grierson did, nor were she and Bruce Woolfe interested in the wider possibilities of commercial sponsorship. Thus their early initiative in the field of serious factual film passed to Grierson and his young men. Between the two groups there was considerable coolness. The Association of Short Film Producers was formed late in 1938 under the chairmanship of Bruce Woolfe to represent the British short film industry. The mainstreamers were already organised in their own Association of Realist Film Producers and Film Centre. To Bruce Woolfe the others were extremists, left-wing bohemians, arty and pretentious; to them, his idea of documentary production was tame, commercial and without social significance. Yet to many educated people films like *The Mine*, for example, seemed not merely as much a part of the documentary movement as the films of the mainstream, but even better. Arthur Vesselo in *Sight and Sound* actually preferred *The Mine* to the G.P.O.'s experimental *Coalface*, which used a new sound technique of orchestrated voice-over with music by Benjamin Britten and words by W. H. Auden, on the grounds that it was so much more clear.[21] He also defended Emmett's "humorously interpretative" commentaries to the *Secrets of Life* against the charge often made that they were condescending and laboriously facetious. *The Gap* was praised by Graham Greene, not often a kind critic of British films. And the literary review *Life and Letters Today* unfailingly supported G–BI's straight approach against the more imaginative film making of the others, which it attacked at every opportunity. The strength of the G–BI films, in fact, lay in their capacity to simplify, clarify and explain, which they did supremely well at school and student level. Had it been economically possible for them to stick to school films, even if theatrical versions with quota eligibility had been necessary to make it pay, they might well have contributed more to the cause of an educated democracy, in an unspectacular way, than all the G.P.O. films put together. Sadly, the larger commercial interests of Gaumont-British and the lack of effective action by the Board of Education or the Film Institute to promote the use of school projectors made their almost single-handed attack on the double problem hopeless.

However, although their effort to tackle equipment and films at the same time was unique, there were other firms also trying to remedy the shortage of suitable films. One of these was Visual Education. We have seen how quickly Sir James Marchant, with the help of Oswald Mitchell and Sir Oswald Stoll, got to work. Their *Visual Education: A Catalogue of Educational and Cultural Films* came out in 1931. The old Stoll studio at Cricklewood was used, with its Visatone sound system, and a large number of short films, mostly natural history and geography, were put out. A vast amount of acquired travel and natural history footage was edited by L. H. Gordon, previously a writer and editor for the Stoll company, and Christopher Radley, who became manager. The plan was to compile films and fit them with sound-tracks under the approval or supervision of experts in various fields, Professor L. W. Lyde for geography, Sir Charles W. C. Oman for history, Professor D. M. Blair for physics; a number of early natural history films had been put together with shots of the late Sir J. Arthur Thomson of Aberdeen University as lecturer. But despite their desire to maintain a strict classroom standard a large proportion of their material was simply adapted travel film. History was a problem, and excerpts, with diagrams and archive stock added, from a number of old costume films were used. *Thomas a'Becket* (*sic*), for example, was part of the old Stoll silent film with Sir Frank Benson. Nevertheless some of the films were attractive, informative and lively, a few with unexpected signs of their foreign origin, like the hives in *Honey for the Queen. The Orange Tip Butterfly*, a one-reeler registered in 1931, is said to be by the early nature cinematographer Charles Head, who had been used by Bruce Woolfe for the *Secrets of Nature*, but his name is not on the film, which has been re-edited and combined with shots of Sir J. Arthur Thomson. The result is a charming if odd little film, the bushy moustache and the slow precise Aberdeen speech of the teacher almost a parody of the unworldly professor, some flittery music in the background giving way to the final "We end as we began, with the dainty orange tip butterfly having little feasts of honey, and making love".

A few sports films and general scientific films were included as well as earlier material by the other nature cinematographers, Frank Hurley's New Guinea films and carefully chosen items like Frank Smythe's *Kamet Conquered*.

Radley and Eric Spear made a number of films, also, mostly tours of historical interest, which were handled about 1933–5 by their associated distributor Zenifilms. By 1935 Visual Education had one of the largest libraries of school films in the country.

Another film of some importance by the mid-thirties was that of Ronald Steuart and his wife Isla, Steuart Films in Chelmsford. With animation facilities, they specialised in scientific, mathematical and technical production both on their own account and for others involved in commercial or educational production. Although the number of Steuart films was small, their quality and reputation were high. Examples were *Electricity*, which explained molecules, atoms, protons and electrons by diagrams; *Milling Machine*, by Alex Francis of the Poplar School of Engineering; *Mensuration*, which explained the calculation of area and volume; *Precision* was about accuracy in machines in industrial use. In addition they handled a large number of short loop films on maths, electricity, physics, engineering and individual scientific or technical processes made by Dance Kaufmann Technical Films. This unit, based in Liverpool, was run by Max Kaufmann and H. E. Dance and among other things made many films for Dryad, for the teaching of handicrafts. Among their early subjects from 1929 onwards were such items as the generation of ellipses, electrostatics, the theory of alternating currents and many others. Steuart also made a few films which were more documentary in character. In 1933 *Where the Road Begins* directed by J. B. Holmes and shot by Jimmy Rogers showed car manufacture from the blueprint stage to the road, and was a public relations film for Humber-Hillman. In the same year *Success*, also by Holmes and shot this time by Steuart himself, was about vocational training possibilities, made on behalf of the Juvenile Employment Bureau in order to show to parents and school-leavers. Steuart also made a few scenic films but did not go further into the idea of industrial and social sponsorship.

These were the most important producers of school films. But the fields of educational and publicity films were intertwined, and a large number of small companies were prepared to undertake either educational or commercial production on contract, some of them specialising in animation or other special processes such as cine-micrography. Revelation Films, with C. A. Cochrane and R. A. Newton, was one of these. Science Films in Kensington and later at Letchworth used cameraman Frank Goodliffe in the latter half of the decade, making films containing animation, optical printing and cinemicrography for commercial, scientific and schoolroom films. Visonor Educational Films, like so many firms, seems to have selected or edited school films rather than produced them. For Carrick Films, J. C. Elder and J. Blake Dalrymple made some fifty films on geography, natural history, domestic animals, farming, transport and industrial processes as a result of the interest and co-operation of the Scottish Educational Film Association and the Glasgow Education Committee, and they also seem to have filmed a long journey on the River Amazon in 1936. Commercial and Educational Films, with a studio at Red Lion Court from the early thirties onwards, despite its name made public relations or training films rather than school films. And C. E. Hodges Productions, which advertised "dramatic, interest and industrial" films, had an enormous list of travel films which found their way into geography lists despite suspiciously flippant names like *Dallying on the Danube* and *The Land of Cuckoo Clocks*.

A few more sophisticated and advanced teaching films were made later in the period, usually as a result of individual effort. Professor Polanyi's *An Outline of the Working of Money* was a twenty-five minute silent diagrammatic film outlining the monetary system, made in 16 mm. in 1938. *Rate of Change*, another silent diagrammatic film, was made by A. D. Segaller to explain the first principles of differential calculus for schools, and was distributed in substandard by Visual Education. Four silent animated diagrammatic maths films, all about five minutes in length, were made about 1937 by the professional film-maker Brian Salt, *The Equation $X+X=O$* and *The Equation $X+X=A$ Sin Nt* both made in collaboration with Robert Fairthorne in a new notation devised by him, and *Euclid. I, 32 (Angle Sum of a Triangle)* and *The Theorem of Pythagoras* by Salt alone. In an interesting article called "Abstract Films and the Mathematicians" Fairthorne pointed out that these films, expressing abstract relations in terms of shape and motion, were the true abstract films, rather than the animated films of concrete shapes which were commonly called abstract.[22] Films made by the B.F.I. Technical Officer H. D. Waley with James Fairgrieve and J. A. Lauwerys in 1933 were also silent experimental diagram films : *Illustration of Elementary Functions, Movement of Air in a Circular Cyclone Crossing Britain, Movement of Rain in a Thunder-*

storm and several under the title *Harmonic Motions*. Fairgrieve, who was a Fellow of the Royal Geographical Society, was chairman of a committee of the B.F.I. which was responsible for the preparation of certain geography films. The 1938 catalogue of the National Film Library included two silent 16 mm. films about the Hunza shot by a Lt-Col. D. L. R. Lorimer and specially edited by this committee, another using stock film on China edited for the committee to show rice cultivation, and *Cocoa from the Gold Coast*; this last was supervised by the Geography Committee and provided with a teachers' guide, and was compiled from the large stock of film held by Cadbury Brothers, who had been making some of the more enterprising publicity films for years. Odd films made from time to time because of some personal interest were frequently called into the service of education. Maurice Browne, the dramatist and theatrical producer, in association with Western Electric made a two-reel film in 1934 on the Domesday Book and the New Forest, called *Domesday England*. *Bassetsbury Manor* made in 1936 by Cyril Jenkins about a seventeenth century mansion found an unexpected welcome as a history film, as did two by A. Moncrieff Davidson in 1935–6. The first, *The Mystery of Stonehenge*, was about the building of Stonehenge and included diagrams and aerial photography, as did his second, *White Horses*, about hillside rock carvings. His clear unfussy style was much admired and *Life and Letters Today* went so far as to call him the best "fact-film director working in this country". It would appear from two later films, however, that his interest was simply in making very cheap films about historical and monumental stonework. It is also tempting to include the two-reel 1935 film *High Hazard*, made by the Chief of the British Mountain Guides about rock climbing in Cumberland, as educational. Indeed, it was often treated as such, but here we are crossing the borderline into general interest or documentary films.

The borderline was, in fact, frequently ignored, especially by the Western Electric School Hiring Service. There were now a number of services, including Gaumont-British, prepared to hire mobile units and complete programmes to schools. By late 1934 Western Electric was giving performances which included music films, industries, travel, nature, current affairs, religion, physics and sports films, almost all general knowledge rather than syllabus teaching.

This brings us to the central problem of the use of films by schools, and that is the continuing shortage of suitable films. Some producing companies had tried to make them, but they were still extremely few. The optimistic compilers of catalogues of educational films from Lauwerys in 1935 onwards tended to include everything remotely suitable and much that was not. The *National Encyclopaedia* listed a very wide range of films, which included large numbers of commercial travelogues and interest films, especially promotional films from the Dominion governments; advertising, public relations and training films; all the Empire Marketing Board films, which were useful for geography lessons, and also the G.P.O. documentaries which were good quality and informative, even if rarely relevant to school work. All the British Instructional films, even their work for industrial sponsors, were there, as were those of Visual Education and Gaumont-British Instructional. In particular there were large numbers of nature films. But there were also many amateur films, specialised medical and dental demonstration films, religious films and socially motivated propaganda of every possible sort. There were even many musical items and sports films from purely commercial firms like Butcher's Film Service and British Lion, as well as the unique Pavlova film *The Immortal Swan*. The occasional improving feature occurs, like *Windjammer*, *Tell England* or *Kameradschaft*, as well as a rather scratch lot of silent films representing literature, an early *Lady Windermere's Fan* and *The Vicar of Wakefield* and even, supreme oddity, a silent *La Traviata*. Films often appeared in several versions or with different titles, and the material shot by one company might well appear later in other films. It is also very noticeable that many productions were of such an imprecise nature that they appeared in catalogues in several different categories, classed for example as geography, history and industry. Yet the *National Encyclopaedia* made no attempt to assess the quality or suitability of this mass of material. The British Film Institute began in late 1936 to bring out recommended lists which were, of course, more rigorously selected. Lists of history films appeared in April 1937 and June 1938, science in March 1938, geography in March 1938 and September 1939, and physical education in November 1938. But their first list was one of medical films, hardly relevant to schools, and in June 1939 they produced a list of religious films. As they did not produce films themselves apart from the few sponsored by the Committee, they could only list what was available, and it is clear that most school subjects were poorly served. But when their Annual Report in June 1938 estimated that some 2,250 educational films were at the schools' disposal, and two years later brought this figure up to 2,800, it appears that like everyone else they tacitly accepted the rag-bag of informational films masquerading as education even if they did not include them all in their own lists. This is confirmed by their breakdown of these films into 600 geography and travel films, 455 science, 400 "civics, commerce, engineering and industrial", 400 medical, veterinary and vocational training, 170 physical education, public health and hygiene, 140 agriculture and a mere 80 history and the arts.

Although doubtless these films were educational in the broadest sense, the very small proportion of them which could usefully be connected with the school syllabus was not enough to tempt most schools into an outlay that was, after all, not trivial. From the mid-thirties onwards there was on the market a range of up to forty 16 mm. silent projectors costing between £17 and £129, and about twenty 16 mm. sound projectors from £75 to £300. Screens, film hire and perhaps special rooms added to the cost. Even with a grant from the Board of Education, at the price levels of the day these figures suggest that if a school was to use films to any real advantage it had to be prepared to spend quite a lot of money. But the thirties were a time of financial stringency and many schools were poorly equipped with even basic amenities.

Thus the hopefulness which still existed in the mid-thirties, with the Institute, the International Bureau and the Gaumont-British information service doing their best to promote the idea, gradually waned. It turned out to be more difficult than anyone had supposed. The *Educational Film Review* optimistically founded by the publisher George Newnes in 1935, edited by Percy Harris assisted by Colin Bennett, seems to have misjudged the market and ran for only six months. Late in 1937 a memorandum by Bruce Woolfe, Mary Field and John Grierson maintained that a company making educational films could survive financially only if it was able to show them theatrically as well as to schools. The current quota system was against this. By the later thirties the parent company of G–BI, Gaumont-British, was in disarray and the Ostrer brothers were anxious to move out of production. Their difficulties were reflected in the subsidiary company, whose production decreased and changed in character. It seemed that the vicious circle had not been broken yet.

In 1935 Lauwerys had estimated that there were only about 1,000 projectors in use in our 32,000 schools, compared with 9,000 in France and 20,000 in Germany. The Board of Education made a grant of 50 per cent towards the cost of film apparatus for Secondary Schools and 20 per cent for Primary Schools, and in early 1937 the new edition of their *Handbook of Suggestions for the Consideration of Teachers and Others Concerned in the Work of Public Elementary Schools* contained, for the first time, recommendations for the use of film in schools, a fact which was regarded as a welcome landmark by the B.F.I. But in February of that year J. B. Frizell, Edinburgh Education Officer, was said to have repeated the charge that only some 1,100 British schools used the film. The Institute set out to discover the truth. When the results of its investigation appeared in May they caused consternation. Although the census was not complete, it was calculated that out of 32,000 schools and colleges in the United Kingdom, projectors were used in only 669 schools and 69 colleges, although 74 local educational authorities also had them for hire. This was compared with 17,000 schools out of 55,000 in Germany, 9,400 school projectors in France, and 10,097 projectors in 82,297 schools in the United States.

While the Institute was at work on the survey, it sent a deputation to the Parliamentary Secretary to the Board of Education, Geoffrey Shakespeare, in April 1937. Professor Lyon Blease told him on the Institute's behalf that it was concerned at the small use made of films in Britain and considered it essential that the number of school projectors should be increased if the production of educational films was not to die out altogether in this country.

Mr Shakespeare replied, according to *Sight and Sound*, that the Board was deeply interested in what he strangely called "this supreme method of unconscious teaching". Later the new Secretary,

4 The Iron Duke's
guided tour of the
modern world
(*England Awake*,
1932).

5 Martin the
shepherd's help is
needed (*O'er Hill and
Dale*, 1932).

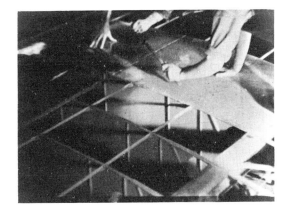

6 The making of a
wing (*Contact*,
1932–3).

Kenneth Lindsay, and several other M.P.s made public statements on the need to promote the use of films in school. The Board of Education grant to Primary Schools was now brought up to the 50 per cent allowed to Secondary Schools. At the end of June an informal conference was held at the Institute, which was attended by a number of Directors of Education, three officers of the Board of Education and a couple of representatives of the Institute, to discuss what should be done. A short, late and very small course on visual aids had been held by the Board in Bristol in the summer of 1937, attended by a mere thirty teachers, and the Board brought out a pamphlet called *Optical Aids* in 1938. Whether because of these measures or not the number of projectors rose, according to the B.F.I. annual reports, to 916 teaching establishments and 126 local authorities late in 1937, to 1,490 and 200 respectively at the end of 1938, and 1,546 and 195 at the end of 1939. But such a rise was disappointingly slow. To put it into perspective, perhaps, it should be compared with the use of school broadcasting. As early as October 1935 the *Educational Film Review* had remarked on the fact that over 3,500 schools in England, Wales and Scotland were registered as listening to the B.B.C. school broadcasts.

Why were the early hopes not fulfilled? The key to progress lay with the teachers, and the contrast to school broadcasting is not without significance. It was easy for a teacher to plan a radio lesson, which was organised centrally with full back-up services and advance information, helping them to fit it into a school curriculum. Compared with this the educational film world was chaos, and expensive chaos. The difficulty of finding out what films there were and where to get them, for whatever equipment you might happen to have, and planning for the regular use of films in such a way as to make sense with the rest of the course was hardly being tackled at all. It was increasingly felt that what was needed was a network of libraries, both centrally, regionally and school based, where a film relevant to the day's lesson could be obtained as reliably as a textbook. The teachers needed far more help if they were to be convinced. It may have been true, as some suspected, that a few teachers saw the film as a threat to their profession but it was far more likely that they just did not know enough about how to get the films, how to project them and still control their classes, or how to integrate into their courses the chancy selection offered by the multiplicity of sources. The feeble efforts to interest and instruct teachers lay at the very root of the problem. If the Institute or the Board of Education had mounted a campaign to convert not individual teachers but the teacher training colleges, a new generation of teachers could have been produced able to use truly educational films as they were made.

A footnote to the educational film is the passing thought that was given to providing special films for the peoples of the Empire, as it then was. In all the lively discussions about the film's potential for teaching, hardly any attention was given to what it might achieve in backward countries until at last, in 1939, the Colonial Film Unit was formed.

In 1929 the Colonial Office Advisory Committee on Native Education sent Dr Julian Huxley to East Africa to report on the teaching of biology in African schools, and on the value of nature conservation there. He went in August, and it was on his own initiative that he took a cine camera and a projector with three films secured through the good offices of the Empire Marketing Board. With these he conducted a small but influential experiment. The films comprised one on cotton-growing in Nigeria which he took because the subject was familiar to the audience; one called *Fathoms Deep Beneath the Sea* shot in Plymouth Aquarium was taken for the unfamiliarity of its content; and *The Life of a Plant* which, with its stop-motion cinematography, would present the audience with totally new concepts. It was, he believed, the first time films had been used as an adjunct to formal education in Africa. The boys were asked to write about what they had seen. Huxley was favourably impressed with their interest and understanding and in 1930 wrote a *Report on the Use of Films for Educational Purposes in East Africa*, recommending it and suggesting that the E.M.B. might be asked to make suitable films and act as a clearing-house for them. The following year he wrote a book about his experiences, *Africa View*. Nothing came of the E.M.B. idea, which was perhaps too peripheral to attract Grierson, but the book was read by one Major Notcutt, who as a planter had already tried showing films to East Africans as early as 1926. He was interested to find his belief that films could be used in their education confirmed by Huxley, and was later to take part in the important Bantu Educational Experiment.

Before this took place, however, there was some activity back in London, although with little result. A widespread but vague idea of using film to educate the "natives" became confused with the anxiety felt by many people lest an undesirable impression of the Sahib might be given by the unrestricted showing of commercial films to colonial peoples. It was not only the British Board of Film Censors with its tabus, so easy to mock, which feared this. A noted liberal authority on India, Edward Thompson, with his deep knowledge and love of the country, was known to feel that films shown in India left little respect for the Western way of life. In *Close Up*, too, a biting attack on the Leslie Fuller comedy *Kiss Me, Sergeant* with its ignorant and contemptuous disregard of Indian feelings represented another point of view. At the same time there were many in the film trade who sought a bigger market in the Empire. These people of differing interests now came together in a strange collaboration. A Colonial Films Committee was appointed in March 1929 under the chairmanship of Sir William Brass, with the Government Film Adviser E. Foxen-Cooper and, representing the Federation of British Industries Film Group, those wily operators Simon Rowson and Harry Bruce Woolfe. Its terms of reference were "the use of the cinematograph as an instrument of education; the supply and exhibition of British films; and censorship". In less formal terms, it was to examine films in the colonies, protectorates and mandated territories and see how to improve them with special reference to two things – the political and economic desirability of showing British films, and the film's potential as education in the widest sense.

It reported over a year later recommending a central organisation to acquire and distribute educational films and equipment, which it rashly considered financially possible; and also a central organisation in London associated with the F.B.I. to select and supply British feature films censored, or at least selected, in such a way as to avoid the danger of "demoralising" films. A minority report by Sir Hesketh Bell, however, maintained that films for the education of primitive people would in fact require far more care and special techniques than was realised and that this would not in fact be economically practicable for the film industry. In this he was undoubtedly right. But it proved to be irrelevant, as the only interest the colonies had for the trade was as a captive market for feature films. Bell warned of the harm likely to be done, in his view, by films "representing criminal and immodest actions by white men and women". It was still possible, in 1930, for him to write: "The success of our government of subject races depends almost entirely on the respect which we can inspire."

The Secretary of State communicated with the governors of colonies. And the film industry went ahead with what, to it, seemed less a measure of self-censorship than a new trade opportunity. At the end of 1931 a body was formed, British United Film Producers Ltd, which looked rather like a sort of high-minded moneymaking concern and which, not unexpectedly, was under the chairmanship of Simon Rowson. The General Manager and Secretary was Neville Kearney of the F.B.I., and the film trade was further represented by Bruce Woolfe, the high-powered John Maxwell of B.I.P. and C. M. Woolf of Gaumont-British, as well as S. W. Smith of British Lion, a quota producer of poor quality films whose search for easy markets had already led him to investigate exports to Canada. Official members were appointed by the Colonial Office, but with this line-up of heavyweights idealism was unlikely to carry any weight whatever. The intention was to distribute suitable films from all British producers, but to secure the best terms for its own members. From time to time it was announced that films had been sent to such places as West Africa and the West Indies, and B.U.F.P. claimed that it had sent well over a million feet of film to the colonies by the end of October 1932. But despite frequent protestations that all was well the company made a loss and was in fact taken over completely by Gaumont-British after a couple of years, disappearing from view thereafter. No more was heard, in any case, of its censorship function and there is little indication that there was ever any machinery to ensure that the films sent were not "undesirable".

On the question of the educational film, however, the Colonial Films Committee had recommended that an experiment should be undertaken in some suitable area to discover what form the proposed expansion of its use should take. It was found that films were used for little more than some medical and agricultural instruction to adults in certain areas.[23] For children, very limited use for background education occurred in Nigeria, the Federated Malay States and Kenya, and in Kenya also the Agriculture and Veterinary Departments had tried producing their own films. Apart from this, it seemed, nothing was being done. The Colonial Office was in favour of the proposed experiment, but for the time being no money was forthcoming.

Meanwhile something more constructive was being done outside official or film trade circles. In 1932 the Department of Social and Industrial Research of the International Missionary Council sent a commission under J. Merle Davis to Northern Rhodesia and the Belgian Congo, to study the effects of heavy industrialisation on native life. It noted the divorce of rural and urban communities, the undermining of the tribal structure and the barren recreational life of the uprooted communities. The I.M.C. was anxious to do something about the situation with the help of the Colonial Office, several colonial governments and others. Merle Davis spoke of "building the Kingdom of God on earth",[24] and a strong religious motive was the mainspring of the resulting Bantu Educational Cinema Experiment of 1935–7, which began as a study of how the film could help tribal society. Set up in March 1935, it had an Advisory Council chaired by Lord Lugard, who was also Chairman of the International Institute of African Languages and Cultures; Vice-Chairman T. Drummond Shiels, who was Chairman of the Dominions, India and Colonies Panel of the British Film Institute; and members from academic, colonial, missionary, Y.M.C.A. and B.F.I. circles. Oliver Bell, William Farr and Miss Locket were members. The general direction was under Merle Davis, and Major Notcutt was made Field Director with G. C. Latham as Educational Director. Notcutt and Latham went out to east Africa in June, taking camera, sound and projection equipment and operators with them. They made and showed thirty-five films with commentaries in English and various dialects, finding out how films could reinforce ordinary educational methods, how they could help Africans to adapt to changed conditions and preserve what was best in African traditions, no doubt from a Western standpoint, and how they could provide recreation.

Their experience confirmed Huxley's good opinion of African peoples' interest and understanding of films, and in addition they found it possible to produce films there for local consumption. Their report came out in 1937, called *The African and the Cinema*. After all this work and backing from the Establishment it is perhaps not surprising that the purpose as now stated in the book, to see if the cinema would be useful in the education of backward races, seems somewhat far from the original aims of helping tribal society and founding the Kingdom of God. Highly detailed recommendations were given for setting up centralised and standardised sound production in the colonies and dominions, with local production units and the interchange of films, using them for inter-racial understanding; propaganda was recommended for improvements in health, social conditions and agriculture, for instruction, civics, missionary work, anthropological research and the expansion of Empire trade; entertainment was also mentioned, but only to warn that the tribal peoples should be taken in hand before "their taste is vitiated by unsuitable films".[25]

3

The Documentary Movement

(i) Early Stages

The main facts of the documentary movement in Britain in the thirties are so well known that they are in danger of becoming a modern legend, a sort of "Grierson Story".

It has been told again and again how John Grierson, son of a Scottish schoolteacher, was brought up in a strongly Calvinist tradition, studied moral philosophy at Glasgow University, served on naval minesweepers and loved the sea, taught at Durham University after the war and went to America in the early twenties for research in the social sciences on a Rockefeller Foundation Grant; here he reached the conclusion that people needed to be better informed if democracy was to work; experience in editing the silent Russian films for English-speaking audiences taught him about film technique and enabled him to make a brilliant short silent film for the Empire Marketing Board, *Drifters*, which was an instant critical success; on the basis of it Sir Stephen Tallents at the E.M.B. and Grierson himself launched a film unit which grew into a "movement"; the keen, talented, highly educated and socially conscious upper-middle-class youngsters he gathered around him, artists by inclination but schooled by Grierson to remember that they were also public servants, developed a system whereby not only official bodies but also large commercial firms and groups began to put up the money for films, some of them about social problems and of no direct commercial gain to the sponsor; and the reputation of these films and their makers stood, and still stands, as being the finest

British contribution, some would perhaps say the only one, to the development of world cinema. Names like *Nightmail, Song of Ceylon* and *Housing Problems* leap to the mind.

So often has the story been told that images of the chief protagonists in the legend have become clear to us, clearer and more caricatured, no doubt, at each telling. Harry Watt's enjoyable autobiography, in particular, gives us such vivid pictures it is hard not to see the people through his eyes, especially Grierson, "an extraordinary little Scots visionary", "grey-faced" with eyes which "were piercing and bored into you. There was a tremendous feeling of suppressed energy, almost of fanaticism".[1] On a B.B.C. programme about the great days Watt, again, spoke of Grierson's "dynamic eyes", Basil Wright spoke of him as a talent spotter and "a hard task master", Norman McLaren described him as a catalyst who drew the best out of people; Stuart Legg, less generous, said he was "very tough indeed" and "hit below the belt". Erik Barnouw's book written many years later even used the words "brutal" and "tyrannical",[2] but there is no doubt that he also had the capacity to arouse hero-worship, and to have had such a strong personality that he quelled open revolt in at least one who deeply resented his treatment. It took the courage and iconoclasm of Paul Rotha to embark on a career in documentary outside the umbrella of Grierson's talent for fixing. We read about the characters in the play until we feel we know them: the brilliant and intellectual member of the Cambridge inner circle and the art world; the Chinese New Zealander with his revolutionary and invigorating approach to the visual arts; the handsome, sad-eyed Brazilian from the French film industry who brought to the group high professional standards and imagination, especially in the use of sound; the funny, bonny, ambitious and roistering anti-intellectual; the dark, intense and loyal friend with his quiet facility for savouring the world around him; the information men, skilled at choosing just that angle, event, movement to analyse and convey; the passionate incautious loner who was his own worst enemy; and all the others, down to the "loyal factotum", an undeservedly belittling tag in such a bunch of *prima donnas*, and the first-class professional cameraman with his fatal weakness for drink.

They were an élite, and a highly articulate élite, and it is easy to read them writing about each other and imagine we know them better than we do, even to fictionalise these lively stereotypes and fabricate theories about them. The personality of Grierson himself, especially, a hero to some and more recently a suitable subject for debunking to others, is complex and intriguing. But let us set the events in order and try to trace the evidence of the movement as it developed through the thirties.

The creation in January 1930 of the E.M.B. Film Unit by Grierson and Tallents itself suggests an interesting partnership. These two practical men made use of each other over a period of years in the pursuit of quite different aims. Grierson was far-sighted enough to see that democracy would not work if ordinary people were not able to understand its complexities. But in this he was not alone.

A subject then called "civics" was being introduced by progressive educationalists in the hope of producing a new generation educated in the functioning of society. Grierson's contribution was the idea of clarifying the workings of society by dramatising them on film. Two points spring from this. One is that dramatising did not for him, ultimately, mean going as far along the road to actual anecdotes or even stories as it did to some of his adherents. What he had in mind was interesting exposition, using all the skills of film making to hold the attention. Without making too much of the strictness of his upbringing, it must be admitted that theatrical distribution and eventually the story-film documentary both lost his support. Secondly, he certainly wanted to teach common people how to operate society so that the democratic nature of the state could survive, however large and involved. Plenty of quotations can be found from his voluminous writings to prove his devotion to democracy. In *Searchlight on Democracy* he wrote of the importance of arousing interest, initiative and standards in vast communities of ordinary people; and of helping people to knowledge and understanding of the things that concern them in order for democracy to work. "By the mere acceptance of democracy we have taken upon ourselves the privilege and the duty of individual citizenship, and we must organize all communications which will serve to maintain it."[3] Thus, although at many points he seems interested only in serving the State, it is clear that it was a democratic state he had in mind and his democratic roots cannot be questioned. Nevertheless it is also true that unlike many of his followers he was a conformist rather than a reformer and the desire to improve social conditions was not in the forefront of his mind. His picturesque vision of the working man as a somewhat heroic figure exemplifying the dignity of labour can perhaps be taken as a sign of some complacency. Nor does his loyalty to democracy seem to have shown itself, even during the critical years of the thirties, in any concern with international affairs.

Thus it came about that the unit he formed and which attracted to itself young men and a few young women, mostly university graduates, who frequently showed a combination of artistic creativity and critical social sense and who were far from conformist, was first harboured by such an unlikely body as the Empire Marketing Board, ostensibly concerned with the marketing of food-stuffs grown within the British Empire. It was a time when the structure of the Empire was undergoing great, and it was hoped triumphant, changes and when free trade, protectionism and Imperial Preference were live issues. Sir Stephen Tallents, a bene-volent bushy-moustached Establishment figure with an appreciation of the value of good propaganda rare in British governing circles, was as great an opportunist as Grierson. At this stage of their association their joint avowed aim was "to bring the Empire alive".

Much has been made of a beautifully produced pamphlet consisting of an essay by Tallents called *The Projection of England*, about the "new art – the art of national projection". The need to publicise and promote the things in which England excelled, the need in fact for propaganda, is discussed. Then, rather as a minor issue, the "greatest agent of international communication at the moment is unquestionably the cinema". America uses it. "A foot of film is worth a dollar of trade," he quotes. But only the Soviet Union is "setting itself to express its point of view and its purposes seriously".[4] The E.M.B. gave Grierson a chance to remedy this as No. 45 of its 45 departments; but most of the pamphlet, which was in any case not published until 1932, by which time the Film Unit was well established, was in fact devoted to other forms of com-munication, above all to exhibitions.

Writing in the summer of 1933 Grierson indulged in a little

rhetoric which usefully obscured the two different mainsprings, education for citizenship and Imperial trade, papering over the join with talk of changing the "connotation of the word 'Empire' ". "I give you this conception of the E.M.B. as a world force, without apology."[5] Perhaps the best thing about their rather impoverished existence as a minor part of the E.M.B. was the enlightened and tolerant attitude of Tallents himself to the question of propaganda, which needed time and experiment before it could show results.

The story begins with the two films made at the end of the twenties, Grierson's *Drifters* and Walter Creighton's *One Family*. Right away a difference of approach was evident. Creighton, no longer a young man, was the son of a bishop, had a public school and Cambridge background and had been introduced to the project by Rudyard Kipling. Much more conventional than Grierson, he had experience of exhibitions and tattoos but not of films. He decided to make a feature-length sound film for cinema showing, containing a strong narrative element. Taking many months to shoot, his fantasy of a little boy's Empire tour featured the statuesque actress Phyllis Neilson-Terry and a number of titled Society ladies as personifications of parts of the Empire, and was finally finished in full talking sound film at Welwyn in February 1930. It was handled by Pro Patria on behalf of British Instructional, acting as a business front for the E.M.B. The long production time caused many Questions in Parliament and the M.P. Harry Day finally elicited the information that it had cost £15,740 to make and had received only 54 theatrical and 21 non-theatrical bookings, plus the Canadian rights, yielding a return of £2,865.[6] A one-reeler about the South African fruit harvest made with offcuts called *A Southern April*, also in sound, was described by Rotha as a nice little film and was later highly praised, especially for its poetic commentary phased to the visual image, which was considered to have been before its time.[7] But nobody was pleased with Creighton's expensive failure to storm the cinemas and, although he had some subsequent success in publicity film production, no more was heard of him in the documentary movement.

Grierson, on the other hand, aimed at the second feature slot in the cinema with his famous *Drifters*, economically made as a silent film in three and a half reels and handled by New Era for the

E.M.B. A *tour de force* for a new film maker, it showed the work and background of the herring fleet with beautiful photography by a professional cameraman, Basil Emmott, and overwhelmingly effective cutting which was modelled on the Russian silent style with which Grierson was familiar. It was shown at the Film Society in London in November 1929 where it was a great success and established a lasting reputation for its maker. It is clear that at the time Grierson was aiming at the cinema public, and in an article in *Kine Weekly* he specifically recommended second features of up to four reels.[8]

The unit now began to assemble. According to Rotha the first to join was professional cameraman J. D. Davidson, followed by Basil Wright and then the very young John Taylor, whose sister Margaret married Grierson in 1930. Early in 1931 Rotha was employed for five months during which he and Donald Taylor, who joined slightly later, made "poster films", short loop films advertising some Empire food products. Neither remained long as a member of Grierson's inner circle; in fact, according to his own account Rotha was sacked in September 1931. More amenable were Canadian woman journalist Evelyn Spice, Arthur Elton, Edgar Anstey and Stuart Legg. All these young people were between 20 and 25 except John Taylor, who was only 16. Wright, Elton and Legg had all been up at Cambridge, Elton and Legg both at Marlborough before Cambridge, while Wright had been to Sherborne. Rotha, an art student, had been at the Slade School at London University and as a film enthusiast had already published a book on the subject, *The Film Till Now*.

The earliest works of this expanding group were modest compilation films of acquired footage with titles like *Australian Wines*, *Plums that Please*, *Netting Millions*, *Axes and Elephants* and many, many others. Large stocks of film were available from various parts of the Empire, especially from Canada, where the Government had long been interested in promotional travel-interest films. One of the only films with a production credit was *Conquest*, a silent three-reeler of 1930 described on the film itself as "constructed" by Grierson, assisted by Basil Wright. Primarily a school film, it showed how the wilderness of North America, peopled rather hilariously by primitive man as portrayed in old silent feature films, was conquered by the use of tools and eventually by transport and power. Using stock film from the Canadian Government, the railways and old features it relies heavily on titles. No masterpiece, nevertheless it was shown at the Film Society, which by now was backing the new unit whatever the films were like. Basil Wright also made a one-reel film called *Lumber,* compiled from Canadian footage about lumberjacking and registered in December 1931 with a synchronised commentary. This was criticised by *Kine Weekly* as highbrow and what they called rather "B.B.C.".[9] In 1932 a new, longer and hopefully more popular version, *King Log,* was made with a bright and breezy commentary about "old King Log, a merry old dog with a heart of oak, deal and pine." Wright's first real chance to shoot a film was in 1931, with *The Country Comes to Town.* The theme that the countryside, however picturesque, is really a food industry supplying the town gave Wright and his professional cameraman the chance for some lovely as well as practical photography.

The interesting thing about this mild little film is that the great Robert Flaherty accompanied Wright and, according to the latter, "He (as it were) lent me his wonderful eyes".[10] He also, it seems, lent his usual disregard for expenses and shooting schedules.

Temporarily without work, as he so often was, this pioneer of the documentary film had come over from Germany and in 1931 spent some time loosely attached to Grierson's group. There was an amateurism about them despite their use of good professional cameramen, and Grierson, in his way as great a contact man as Alexander Korda, felt that his lively young people could learn much from the master. As far as Wright is concerned, when in 1932 he made his first entirely personal film *O'er Hill and Dale* about the work of a border shepherd in the lambing season, it is hard to say if he had needed any such lesson. Commentary and music added later are conventional, but the evocative images of the rolling Cheviot Hills, the sure and confident handling of the subject suggest he had no need of Flaherty's eye; his own style, cool and fastidious yet savouring all around him, was already emerging.[11]

Meanwhile Grierson naturally wanted to prise a Flaherty film from his distinguished visitor, which he did with rather mixed results. In 1931 it was decided to spend some £2,500 on a film about craftsmanship in industry. Flaherty set off, initially to film the steel bridge at Saltash, and characteristically became fascinated with his material. Reel after reel of "tests" began to come back to London from various parts, but no script. The lordly prodigality of this way of working was impossible for the E.M.B., where every foot of film counted, and indeed was irreconcilable with Grierson's very different temperament. In London there was eventually a stormy scene between the two of them, and this unlikely collaboration ended. But a film called *Industrial Britain* was later made using Flaherty sequences, notably of pottery making at Stoke-on-Trent and of glass blowing, but filled out with sequences of waterways and flying boats by Basil Wright and of coal mining by Elton. Edited skilfully by Edgar Anstey, the historical transition from gentle rural scenes and old country crafts to the modern world of powered industry is accompanied by undistinguished musical backing and a "Griersonian" commentary rather over-delivered by the actor Donald Calthrop, bearing the message that even under modern conditions individual craftsmanship is necessary and that it still exists in Britain. This combined effort was shown in 1933, described on the film itself simply as produced by Grierson and Flaherty. Considering the history of its production it was a creditable and even an influential film, but it was certainly no Flaherty film.

Others, too, were learning to make films more important than the mass of Empire compilations. Arthur Elton, who had previously worked for a short while at Gainsborough Studios, began to make a film in the autumn of 1931 about Professor Stapledon's experiments to find strong and persistent grasses for the bleak Welsh mountains which would increase their suitability for sheep rearing by providing winter fodder. Referred to simply as *An Experiment in the Welsh Hills*, its sequences at the Welsh Plant Breeding Station at Aberystwyth are preceded and followed by lyrical shots of the lonely hills, the sheep and the skies, overhead shots of the lower-lying land, and after the fertilisation of the grasses there is a lovely joyful sequence of the sun and the ripening grass. The style is clearly based on Russian silent films and relies heavily on dynamic titles, the building up of shots and similes, and even uses waves of sheep flooding on to the screen in superimposed all-over coverage. Production was not finished, but the film was roughly ended with four enormously long explanatory titles. Like *Industrial Britain* it was later finished and given a synchronised sound-track, and was retitled *Shadow on the Mountain* in 1933. Elton next made a film about salmon fishing in Scotland called *Upstream*, again making full use of the gorgeous visual possibilities of dazzling white fishing cottages under the dark hill, the sea and the nets and a famous sequence of salmon leaping the waterfalls, which was later shown separately as *Salmon Leap*. Again the influence of the silent Russian films is seen in the selection of significant detail; fishing boats lying sideways on the ground on the Sabbath, shorts blowing on the lines to dry, the nets and lines waiting. The commentary synchronised later, spoken by Andrew Buchanan, with its glorification of "these sturdy fighters" making a living from the "reluctant deep", has a touch of the Grierson view of the heroic workman and ends with a hurried account of the salmon's life cycle after the visually climactic leap; and the choice of music, switching from Mendelssohn to "Over the Hills to Skye", is rather routine. It was in mid-1932, however, that Elton made his own first contribution to sound, *The Voice of the World*. This was a three-reeler about the manufacture of radios and their social implications, and used the sound-track with some imagination, ending with what was described as a finale of Malcolm Sargent conducting the radio factory to the music of the London Symphony. Still concentrating on rhythm and montage, Elton's treatment did not stress the social significance or the heroic element sufficiently to please Grierson, who admitted "it puts Elton first among the documentary directors of this country" but, in a review of curious detachment about a film on which he himself is credited as producer, slammed Elton in an often-quoted passage as being "possibly unappreciative of radio's social significance", adding that this affects "almost all the tyros of documentary. Too damned arty and post-war to get their noses into public issues".[12] The film, however, is of unusual importance as the first of the mainstream documentaries made with backing from a commercial sponsor, in this case the Gramophone Company and H.M.V. Although an E.M.B. film, it was officially put out through the firm of New Era. It was shot by George Noble, a professional cameraman who was to film many of the best mainstream documentaries in the next few years.

It was in 1932, also, that sponsorship by another outside body led to a film with even more social content. In May and June, Stuart Legg's film *The New Generation* was produced for the Chesterfield Educational Authority. About 1928 Chesterfield had reorganised its educational system so as to turn out young people with the capacities and skills needed by the community. The idea for a film on the subject came from W. H. George, assistant master at the William Rhodes School and a film enthusiast. Grierson was instrumental in getting the commission for Legg, who was already at work in Welwyn for British Instructional, and the film was officially a New Era film shot by a cameraman from Stoll's, Gerald Gibbs. Costing only £250, it was a silent film. Robert Herring wrote in *Close Up* "It is a pity, but perhaps natural, that it is based on the Russian technique", and mentioned dynamic subtitles;[13] and Basil Wright, whilst welcoming it as straightforward and unpretentious, complained of a certain self-consciousness which he called "the Welwyn style".[14] Legg was now taken into the E.M.B. fold, and the team of Grierson, Legg and Gibbs were to make several nore films in the next few years. The last of them under the E.M.B. set-up was one made for the Post Office, *The New Operator*. This was about the training of girl telephone operators and was still very much the silent film, with titles, shots of hurrying feet, and long-held glances.

By about 1932, several things were becoming apparent. Although the stream of short, anonymous compilations about Empire produce continued, the wider possibilities of alternative sponsorship for more interesting film-making were now evident. Also, and most important, the question of how and to whom the films were going to be shown began a division of opinion which was to have lasting results. In mid-1933 Grierson made an arrangement with Gaumont-British whereby the six main films, *Shadow on the Mountain*, *King Log*, *The Country Comes to Town*, *Industrial Britain*, *Upstream* and *O'er Hill and Dale*, were given the synchronised commentaries and musical backing that we have discussed. The films were to be presented as a package, known as the Imperial Six, for showing in the cinemas as supporting shorts distributed by Gaumont-British Distributors. We have seen that the imposed sound-tracks were of a character rather different from the films themselves.

The little anonymous E.M.B. films became less important and Grierson's young "tyros" began to emerge as real film makers. *Aero Engine*, made with the eye of an artist and the technique of a perfectionist, established Elton as a master of the film of technical explanation. A long silent film on the manufacture of aeroplane engines made for instructional purposes, with shorter versions for less technical audiences, it was beautifully photographed by George Noble. It demonstrates its material with images, compositions, angles and lighting all superb if somewhat static; Elton still leans heavily on the Russian style, with the dedicated hands touching the shining surfaces, the noble faces of the intent workers, simple titles reminiscent of many a Russian film :

> The Parts are Nearly Ready
> At every Stage, Tests.

It ends with the planes starting one after another in an elaborately edited take-off sequence that is exciting to watch.

Meanwhile, Anstey, also, was making his first solos with two films shot for the Admiralty, *Eskimo Village* and *Uncharted Waters*, filmed in 1932 on the *Challenge* Expedition to survey the coast of north Labrador. Thus official as well as commercial sponsorship began in the same year, 1932. Parts of the Flaherty material were made into shorts for the Travel and Industrial Development Association, or T.I.D.A., which was to become a regular factor in the documentary world. More films were made with an eye to theatrical distribution, which was attempted again in 1934. *Spring on the Farm* was made by Evelyn Spice with a Visatone sound-track and registered by New Era. *Spring Comes to England*, made for the Ministry of Agriculture and Fisheries, was directed by Donald Taylor. It was a longer film about how the rationalisation of market gardening brings fruit, flowers and vegetables to the English markets; also in sound, it has some unsuitable music trilling away sweetly in the background and is not as impressive as some of the other films.

The most interesting of the productions when the unit was still officially under the E.M.B., however, are Grierson's only other personally made film, *Granton Trawler*, and some films made by Basil Wright.

Granton Trawler, made in 1933 but not trade shown until the end of 1934, was a companion piece in sound to *Drifters* and also about deep-sea fishing. Like the other it is a lovely film, if somewhat cold, interested in man as a worker rather than as an individual. In view of the difficulty of deciding who contributed what to many films of the documentary movement, it is worth describing this film and its production in some detail.[15] It begins with a dark screen and the sound of a mouth organ. We see the prow of a trawler, the *Isabella Grieg*, rising and falling gently. The changing rhythm of this rise and fall is felt throughout the film. We see the funnel, hear a couple of blasts, a shout, and the unobtrusive beat of the engine. Once at sea, on a gentle swell, men quietly get on with their work with mouth organ, rhythmic clatter and half-heard voices, the creak of cleats and the rattle of chains, the cry of gulls in the background. There is some similarity to *Drifters*. The shots are lovely but not self-indulgently so, always justified by the accumulation of detail to build up the atmosphere of absorbed work. The seas get up, the wind blows, the gulls scream and wheel, and we are surrounded by the sounds of a violent sea. Finally, after getting the catch in, the men sit absorbed as they gut the fish. Evening falls, and with the darkening sea and sky comes peace again, and the mournful sound once more of the mouth organ.

Grierson, who had his name on many, many films as producer even when the director or cameraman was anonymous, is always said to have made only two personal films, this one and *Drifters*. According to his own words in the interesting series of interviews taped so many years later by Elizabeth Sussex, he said:

> We could all edit well. We could all write well. There was no part of it we couldn't do, even camerawork. The one credit I was absolutely insistent on was putting my name on as a cameraman on one picture, and it's still there. I'm very pleased with that, having my credit as a cameraman on *Granton Trawler*, I had to put my name on because there was nobody else on the picture except me. It was a solo effort.[16]

He was old and ill when he said that, and on the copy described, at all events, he is not in fact credited as cameraman. *Sight and*

Sound at the time of the film's production actually lists J. D. Davidson as cameraman,[17] although this is not verified anywhere else. But, according to Anstey in the same series of interviews, Grierson had been seasick and his camera had fallen over, and on his return he had thought so little of the material that he did not bother to edit it. Anstey is said to have done this between 10 p.m. and 4 a.m. one night, and thus the structure of the film, so important to its success and so much like a more sophisticated and modern application of the Russian style used in *Drifters*, was a contribution actually made by Anstey. He also said that he had created the effect of a much more violent storm than had actually occurred, partly by using the film taken as the camera fell. Small wonder that Richard Barsam credits Grierson with only one film and ascribes this one to Anstey.[18] When the film was mentioned in *Sight and Sound* later it was described "editing : Grierson-Anstey" and said to be silent.[19] So, and perhaps even more important, the sound-track was added after Cavalcanti's arrival and was in fact probably one of his first contributions to the Unit. The film was trade shown and registered as a New Era film in the autumn of 1934. The importance of the sound, with its oblique approach and its atmospheric power, is incalculable. How could Grierson possibly regard this film as a solo? It has always seemed strange that one who could film and edit as well as he had seemed to do in *Drifters* could afterwards be content to produce rather than to make personal films. The story of *Granton Trawler* only makes the mystery deeper.

Meanwhile in 1933 Basil Wright was off on his travels making films which were entirely his own, shot, edited and made by him directly. First he went to the West Indies, making on the way *Liner Cruising South*, a silent film for the Orient Line on one of their cruising ships.[20] For the E.M.B. he made *Windmill in Barbados* and *Cargo from Jamaica*.[21] The latter shows in neat, quiet, well-ordered fluidity of shots the bananas growing, being cut from the tree and finally loaded by a snaking line of Jamaican porters on to a cargo ship; a later sequence of mechanised unloading in London was one Grierson had shot and not used, and replaced a scene of coolie labour at the docks which Wright had planned to use in order to underline a theme of exploitation. It ends rather oddly with a close-up of a bunch of bananas. It seems that in the change-over from the E.M.B. to the G.P.O. Film Units it was not fitted with a sound-track as planned. But it is perfectly comprehensible without titles and was highly praised by B. Vivian Braun in *Film Art*[22] as "poetic cinematicism", not a phrase to appeal-to Grierson, but kindly meant. The style is noticeably different from the mounting pressure of varied detail that characterised the Russian influence. *Windmill in Barbados,* upon which we find Cavalcanti credited for the first time as "sound supervisor", was even more successful and was in some ways a forerunner of *The Song of Ceylon*. It was put out after the change from E.M.B. to G.P.O. as a New Era film. Beginning with an old map, it ranges quietly over the island, skies and clouds, sailing ships, white breakers and beaches; fields of sugar cane with their workers, oxen and an old windmill with its lovely sail; the goods train, and finally the beaching of a small boat with billowing sails. These exceptionally beautiful visuals are accompanied quietly by occasional comments in a local accent, with local music and singing. Food production, a beautiful and unfamiliar country and local sound are employed most ingeniously to make a small jewel of a film out of a commission to popularise Empire food products. After this Basil Wright embarked on his trip to Ceylon for the E.M.B. and Empire Tea Marketing Expansion Board, which resulted in one of the best and most loved of all documentary films, *The Song of Ceylon*. Whilst he was at work on it, however, the whole scene changed and the unit became attached to the General Post Office.

Meanwhile, as we have seen, Rotha had left the Unit. Although remaining very much part of the movement, he was in future to pursue a separate though parallel path, an individualist and a personality of great directness. More generous and loyal in later years than some who had long continued as Grierson's close associates, Rotha has said little about the separation. But the two men were totally different in character. Both were very articulate people whose writings were important to the movement, but their outlook was different. An artist, Rotha wanted to make personal films from the start, and his style was what Grierson repeatedly called impressionist rather than informational. He consciously sought to humanise documentary and, whereas Grierson wanted to make democracy work, Rotha was committed to social change. He was to remain a loner, and was rather like Flaherty in being a round peg in a square hole whenever he tried to fit into anyone else's team, as in his reluctant association with Bruce Woolfe and later his abruptly ended stay with Strand. To judge from anecdotes in his own autobiography, he was capable of carrying his refusal to toe the line to the length of offending the pretentious and powerful, and he evidently lacked that small element of submissiveness necessary to make life possible with the dominating Grierson. Looking back, he can be seen as the third considerable figure in the movement along with Grierson and Cavalcanti, pursuing a gallant if somewhat peppery course of his own.

Having made short trailer films in his time at the E.M.B., this somewhat arrogant young theorist now started his film career in earnest with *Contact*, designed as a film impression of the conquest of time and space, especially by air transport. He has told the story of its somewhat inauspicious production at length in *Documentary Diary*. He raised sponsorship of £2,500 from Shell-Mex and B.P. through their enlightened publicity director Jack Beddington, and the co-operation of Imperial Airways, thus making it the second film, after *Voice of the World*, to get commercial backing for a film made as prestige publicity rather than as direct advertising. Cast out by Grierson, his necessary production basis became British Instructional, which forced him into a relation with Bruce Woolfe which lasted for several years, full of contempt and suspicion, possibly on both sides. It left him with the feeling that the facilities accorded to him were second class and that Bruce Woolfe was always ready to take credit where none was due. With a good British Instructional cameraman, Jack Parker, for early sequences in England, and another, Frank Goodliffe, at the latter end of production, to his disappointment most of the film was shot by the older and more sedate Horace Wheddon who, although technically proficient, was unimaginative and personally antipathetic to the aspiring artist.

The first part of the film shows how an air route is planned and planes assembled, and the second part is an air journey. This clear separation of a film into different parts was to prove characteristic of Rotha. A three-month tour by air as far as Karachi in the east and Capetown in the south between October 1932 and January

1933 was studded with difficulties about equipment, film supply and customs regulations. A camera fault made much of the film they shot unusable. Seeing the film today, his greatest handicap seems to have been that he was not allowed to mount the camera on the outside of the plane and that his filming was thus restricted to shooting through a small window, and shots from the ground of other planes, but not his own, landing and taking off. From what he has called his "high falutin' outline" about "The Poetry of the New World of the Air", this was down to reality with a bump. On his return he cut it in Welwyn between February and May 1933. His desire to have a special score by composer-conductor Clarence Raybould was thwarted, and Raybould had time only to compose a modernistic "fugue" for the first part, accompanying the rest with some highly irrelevant Rossini, Mozart, Tchaikovsky and some pseudo-Eastern effects. The sound-track consists only of music and effects, and Rotha writes that he decided to have no commentary, but "where absolutely necessary a minimum of sub-titles, very short ones".[23]

The result of all these difficulties and theories was a long string of short, broken titles with excellent illustrative shots carefully edited in the manner of the silent film, clear and concise but lacking the warmth and passionate intensity of some of his later films. The copy available in the National Film Archive is apparently that distributed by Wardour and widely shown in the cinemas, which was 2,644 feet, whereas Rotha has said he wanted a forty-five minute film. On the assumption that he achieved something like this length, the copy available can only be a partial guide to his original. Bearing this always in mind, therefore, we still find the narrative conveyed in sentences broken up into some seventy-six titles, many of them of one or two words only. The accompanying shots, directly illustrating the titles, show in the first part plane construction and ground organisation and a plane's departure, and in the second ground shots of the various countries intercut with a few aerial views of some planes, a few aerial shots of the ground and of clouds, and a great many uses of an aerial close-up of the propeller. Even in this copy the editing rhythms and titles are carefully designed to give variety and shape to the film, and it ends with the plane's return and landing. The opening sequence, incidentally, is a little historical prologue: "for a long time" . . . shots of the tide's edge, breakers . . . "road" . . . we see a road . . . "and rail" . . . and we see rails . . . "have been highways for traffic" . . . the cutting of close-ups speeds up the pace . . . "Now . . . air" . . . the music changes and bottles of ink, hands, plans and instruments introduce us to the sequence about plane construction. These introductory résumés of the past were to prove another Rotha characteristic.

During its production British Instructional had been taken over by British International Pictures, and the film was distributed by Wardour and had considerable success at the cinemas, with 1,500 bookings. To Rotha's disgust it was nominally produced by Bruce Woolfe. Although Rotha claims that Arthur Dent of B.I.P. hated the film, it was shown at a gala put on by Gaumont-British for the World Economic Conference in July, and was warmly welcomed even by *Kine Weekly*, which recommended it as a "very good short attraction".[24] It was certainly no run-of-the-mill travelogue. Critical as well as commercial reception was good, and Grierson took it seriously enough, as Rotha's début, to review it in *Cinema Quarterly*.[25] His description of it as a cold and cerebral film, if apt, was rather harsh in view of the difficulties attending its production. As a beginner, Rotha's aims had probably been too high. Nevertheless this first film established him as a force to be reckoned with. While the E.M.B. Film Unit metamorphosed into the G.P.O. Film Unit, Rotha continued in uneasy alliance with Bruce Woolfe.

Before we proceed, a few remarks on the volume of production, on distribution, and on dates and credits are necessary.

·In this chapter we are concerned with the films of a small group of people, the E.M.B. and later the G.P.O. Film Units and their offshoots, and Paul Rotha, who together form what is always thought of as "the British documentary movement". To disentangle the story, we must remember that it was the Empire Marketing Board itself which began the whole thing by constructing a cinema at the Imperial Institute in 1926 to show films of Empire life and work. Many films were contributed by the government authorities of Canada, Australia, New Zealand, South Africa, India and various colonies as well as the later Ministry of Agriculture and Fisheries and certain commercial sources, and these were the

7 The new luxury cruises (*Northern Summer*, 1934).

8 Moholy-Nagy's light display machine (*The Coming of the Dial*, 1933).

9 Vigorous ceremonial dancers (*The Song of Ceylon*, 1933–5).

foundation of the E.M.B. Film Library, a stock of films available free to schools and educational authorities. When the E.M.B. Film Unit was formed, much of its first film-making consisted of the use of this material in re-edited versions or compilations before they took to filming their own material. The 1932 E.M.B. Film Library catalogue lists some 176 films. In 1952 a list of Crown Copyright films was compiled under the auspices of the British Film Institute which claimed to be as full and accurate a record of official documentaries as any prepared up to that time. As only about 40 of the 176 films in the 1932 catalogue are included in this 1952 list it seems fair to conclude that it was these 40 which had been in some sense "made" by the Unit. Most of these seem to have been simply put together from bits of films from various parts of the Empire. *Axes and Elephants*, for example, is a six-minute "composite" film of lumber footage from New Zealand and from Burma; *Children of the Empire, Irrigation* and many others are built on a similar plan. If *The Conquest of Natural Barriers* is typical, the standard was pretty crude, relying on titles to convey the message with unmatched illustrative shots taken from any old source. "Man," says a title in this one, and we see a primitive man's head, "faced by natural barriers of mountain ranges" which we see, "rivers hemming him in" and we see rivers . . . and so on, through bridges, camel trains, railway building, to end with a symbolic radio pylon radiating animated zig-zag lines. Little sign of the grand Russian style here. Others also in the 1952 list seem to be re-edited material from one country only, like *Furry Folk* about the Canadian beaver. The films are anonymous and it is noticeable that neither Grierson's *Drifters* nor Creighton's two films are in the catalogue, although there are two shortened versions of the former, *Our Herring Industry* and *Drifting*. But we know that the compilation *Conquest* was made by Basil Wright, and there are signs of the 1931 filming by him, Elton and Flaherty in short films on salmon fishing, lambing in Scotland, glass blowing and pottery making. The films in the Library were all silent versions except one. The catalogue also includes twenty-two "film posters" made by the Unit. It is interesting that there is a long film in two parts called *Port of London*, tracing its history from Roman times and showing its work in the early thirties. In the Sussex tapes Grierson says that after *Drifters* he was given £7,500 for a film on the Port of London but that, although he did a few shots, including the sequence used by Basil Wright in *Cargo from Jamaica*, he used this money as the basis on which to set up the Unit. He even refers to it as "this mythical film that I kept on pretending was going to be made", and Wright also calls it "the film he never finished". Nevertheless a lot of film under this name features in both their own catalogue and in the *National Encyclopaedia of Educational Films*. Whoever actually made it, it was clearly not a film Grierson wished to be associated with and in any case certainly did not use the whole of this sum, if in fact his recollection of it is correct.

When the British Film Institute was formed, and in 1933–4 when the E.M.B. Film Unit was transformed into the G.P.O. Film Unit, there was some argument over who should act as custodian of the Film Library. It would appear that the E.M.B. Film Unit had by then made about a hundred films of its own. This figure is borne out by the 1952 list, my own film-list, and an article by J. B. Holmes in *Sight and Sound*.[26] But as the Library included films other than its own it was eventually decided that it should remain at the Imperial Institute.[27] To mark the Royal Silver Jubilee the Empire Film Library was inaugurated on 14 June 1935 at the Imperial Institute cinema by the Duke of Gloucester, and included both E.M.B. and G.P.O. films. The figures for borrowing during this period are interesting, showing as they do that, although the G.P.O. figures increased far more rapidly, they were still small compared with those of the E.F.L.:[28]

	G.P.O.	E.F.L.	Total	Borrowers
1934	898	13,652	14,550	1,500
1935	3,555	13,946	17,501	1,900
1936	6,624	16,161	22,785	2,500

The second edition of the catalogue in 1937 lists 348 titles, claiming it has acquired 63 of them since the first edition in 1935, which would indicate it began with 285. It includes a few Gas Association and T.I.D.A. films as well as the G.P.O. and purely E.F.L. films. During the war this collection was taken over by the Ministry of Information and after that by the Central Office of Information, who were responsible, with the B.F.I., for the important 1952 list which makes it possible to trace the earliest work of the Unit.

To anticipate, after 1935–6 the movement began to split up, members of the group making films for other sponsors, especially the British Commercial Gas Association, Shell and T.I.D.A. Donald Taylor in a letter to *Kine Weekly* wrote that 150 people were engaged in making documentary films and that about 100 films would be made in 1937.[29] *The Factual Film*, on the other hand, later asserted that by 1939 about 60 people were involved in documentary. Clearly it all depends on your definition of what is a documentary film and who were members of the mainstream movement. Paul Rotha has said that from 200 to 300 films were made by the documentary movement in the decade, and my own research bears it out that these films, and the people who made them, do indeed constitute what is usually meant by the "documentary movement" in Britain in the 1930s. Beginning with *Drifters* and ending with the first weeks of the war, over 210 films can be traced to members of the élite group, and to these must be added the film posters, the more or less anonymous early editing jobs at the E.M.B., and later some smaller and uncredited films of the G.P.O.

The way these films were distributed changed during the decade, and the changes led to differences of opinion in the movement. Grierson started, as we have seen, with the idea of films up to four reels in length occupying the supporting slots in cinemas. This view was clearly stated in the article by him in *Kine Weekly* in 1930 mentioned before in which he criticised Creighton for making *One Family* of feature length. Both *Drifters* and *One Family* were registered with the Board of Trade for theatrical showing, being handled by New Era. We have seen that as he formed the E.M.B. unit he became associated with free school distribution of acquired footage at and through the Imperial Institute, but the films shot by the Unit itself were intended for the cinemas. A determined effort to make an attractive package and establish a brand image was made in 1933 with the "Imperial Six". Despite what Grierson remembered as a great commercial success,[30] theatrical distribution did not in fact prove the answer. The growth of the double feature programme worked against it and, while an exhibitor would probably prefer an advertising film which he was paid to show, the public might well prefer the "and so we say farewell" travelogue, or a variety turn, to a documentary. The quota legislation, also, was against the maker of serious short films in Britain. No quota of British short films, as such, was required by law. Films wholly or mainly of news or current events, natural scenery, commercial advertisements, educational, industrial processes, or scientific films did not require registration with the Board of Trade, and so could not be treated as quota footage. A few early documentaries were actually registered as available for quota. For example *Drifters* and *One Family* both had a "Br." registration number, which meant they could be used as part of the exhibitor's obligatory British footage. But by 1933 almost without exception the few documentary films which were registered at all received an "E" number, which meant that they were British but did not count for quota. Meanwhile commercial products like *Don Bradman on "How I Play Cricket"* and some of John Betts's sports films were being registered as Br., to say nothing of the rubbishy products of some very unscrupulous operators. At the same time the excellent British Instructional *Secrets of Nature* films as well as the fringe documentary-dramas *Black Diamonds* and *Men Against Death* and others were also always given an E. With the dice thus loaded against outsiders, the industry and the Board of Trade forced Grierson to think again. The question of the quota legislation and its effect is discussed more fully in the companion volume to this.

It is not always easy to say exactly when, or by whom, the E.M.B. films we have discussed, and the G.P.O. and others we are about to trace, were made. People's memories prove unreliable and contemporary written evidence at the time of production is scanty. When a feature film was being made, of course, its occupation of the studio floor was noted in the trade journals, and when it was finished trade show and registration dates are a matter of record. But with documentary films things were rather different. As most were not destined for showing in the cinemas until the end of the thirties very few were registered with the Board of Trade at all, and even then it was often long after production and might be in altered versions or even with changed titles. After the 1938 Quota Act more of them were registered, but a lot of these had been made earlier. Press shows and presentation at the Film Society in London, a favourite showplace, likewise were sometimes after production and give only a later limit to the date. Production was always on a shoe-string and the films borrowed from each other, shots and sequences sometimes turning up in later films. Dating in later published sources has sometimes not helped. Autobiographies and taped memoirs are not always accurate and when compared with contemporary records such as catalogues and the Board of Trade registration lists are sometimes found to have films in the wrong order. Further complications are introduced in some cases by changes made in later versions.

But there are even more painful confusions and doubts than those of dating. These concern the question of credits. In the feature world the struggle for screen credits was cut-throat, yet even so the story behind some of them reveals anomalies and injustices. While the audience yawns and protests at these lists of names, it does not realise that they are the film maker's proof of his work, his references or *curriculum vitae*. In the documentary movement they were, to begin with, rather amateurish and casual about it all. Units were small and flexible, most producer-directors devised rather than wrote their own films and, as we have heard from Grierson, most of them could turn their hands to anything. The dividing line between production and direction was not so clear as it was in the feature world. Thus credits might well be imprecise. At the time no one seemed very interested. Also, there was a lot of borrowing of material, re-use of stock, taking over of productions and helping out. Grierson encouraged this casualness. To him it was the body of production and its social impact which mattered, and he fostered the idea of group production. He also believed that if you could direct films it was your duty to become a producer and teach others to direct, thus enlarging the circle. This is what he had done himself, and his belief in it amounted almost to evangelism. Indeed, it was the way in which many trained recruits moved on and founded new units which made British documentary a movement. But as individual skills improved personal differences of style and talent became more obvious, and with each film the very real contributions of different people more important. Although many of the well-known productions like the B.B.C. films, *Pett and Pott* and others were co-operative productions of the whole unit, many others were personal creations, like Basil Wright's *Song of Ceylon*. Some dedicated people might continue to sink their identities in a co-operative achievement; but some quite naturally wished to build a reputation of their own and to carry on as established film-makers in their own right. Harry Watt was one, Rotha another. Grierson's casual and sometimes fanciful attribution of credits was not always felt to be fair. Worse still, in years to come when some of these films, especially the early G.P.O. ones, became classics the inaccuracies which seemed unimportant at the time were to cause some resentment.

As we shall see, significant films like *Coalface*, *Nightmail*, *Housing Problems* and *B.B.C. – The Voice of Britain* had creative contributions not fully recognised in the film credits. Less important films like *Cable Ship* and *Men of the Alps* also present problems. The question of who did what on *Granton Trawler* has already been discussed, and it has been said that Grierson's own name as producer, richly justified as it usually was, was rarely omitted. But it has also been mentioned that on that particular film the contribution of Cavalcanti, of crucial importance, was overlooked by Grierson. Maybe this is also characteristic. Alberto Cavalcanti joined the Unit when it transferred to the G.P.O., coming at the age of 37 from the French film industry where he had worked for some years. His explanation in later years was that, at a time when he was chiefly engaged in making routine French-language versions of imported films, he preferred to accept a comparatively lowly position at a small wage with Grierson for the freedom it gave him to experiment with the new possibilities of the sound film. Certainly at the G.P.O. the use of sound was revolutionised, and leadership in the use of sound was one of the outstanding characteristics of the documentary movement. Others, notably Harry Watt, have maintained that "Cav"'s influence on Grierson's young amateurs was to raise their professional and artistic standards in a way that Grierson could not have equalled.[31] Grierson, however, later gave many people the impression that Cavalcanti had wanted to get into the British feature industry and was simply marking time in documentary, even suggesting that he was not particularly anxious to have his name associated with anything experimental. This is certainly believed by many, including Rotha, to be true and may well have been so when Cavalcanti first came over to England. But it seems unlikely that an established film director would have remained outside the British feature studios for seven years, as he did, if he had actually wanted a job in them, especially at a time when the trade unions were complaining that all you needed in order to get employment there was to be a foreigner. When young, he had made important experimental films in France. It really seems more likely that as an artist, and considerably less gifted at public relations than Grierson, he became genuinely absorbed in what he was doing and was as careless about screen credits as Grierson expected everyone, except himself, to be. The time was to come, however, when the high reputation of the films made creative responsibility for them a question of real pride, and in his old age Cavalcanti felt himself neglected and spoke about it with bitterness.

(ii)   The Middle Years

To get back to the chronology of events, in the summer of 1933 it was announced as a result of the report of the Imperial Committee on Economic Consultation and Co-operation that the Empire Marketing Board was to be disbanded.[32] Sir Stephen Tallents was now the Public Relations Officer of the General Post Office, under the Postmaster-General of the day, Sir Kingsley Wood, and his protégé, the Film Unit, was transferred with him to the Post Office Public Relations Department in the autumn, moving from 37 Oxford Street to 21 Soho Square and acquiring a small studio at an old art school in Bennett Park, Blackheath, in January 1934. A sound system, Visatone, was acquired.[33] Things appeared to be looking up and, with the movement still in one group apart from Rotha, they could now experiment with studio work and sound film. Location recording, requiring the hire of a sound van at a cost of some £200 to £300 a day, was still a problem. Silent film had lingered in documentary as it had in the educational film because of costs, but it had been a barrier to theatrical distribution and much was hoped from the acquisition of their own sound facilities. However, as it turned out, in the absence of a shorts quota Grierson now became convinced that non-theatrical distribution offered greater opportunities. By 1935 the G.P.O. had started road shows and by 1937, although outstanding films were shown at cinemas wherever possible, they had six projection units and showed at big exhibitions and trade fairs as well as lending their films to non-theatrical groups of all kinds. Thus the acquisition of sound and the arrival of Cavalcanti, both making the films more suitable for the cinema, more or less coincided with Grierson's conversion to the idea of non-theatrical distribution.

The end of 1933 began more than a year of busy production and experiment in the G.P.O. Film Unit. After this the whole scene changed, for reasons which will emerge, and the movement dispersed into separate units. Taking the films of 1934–5 as the work of the early G.P.O. days, we find tremendous vitality. A number, like *Cargo from Jamaica*, were taken over from the E.M.B., given sound-tracks, and usually put out as New Era films. All but a few minor items used sound film now, and in some the experiments in its use were remarkable. Walter Leigh and later Benjamin Britten were introduced as composers and poetry specially written by the young W. H. Auden was used with great originality. Sound was synchronised in the studio but recorded scraps of vernacular were introduced in two films, *Under the City* and *Six-Thirty Collection*. Working there at about this time, in addition to the new arrival Cavalcanti, were Grierson's two chief allies Basil Wright and Stuart Legg, the latter sometimes producing and sometimes directing; John Taylor was cameraman and assistant, Grierson's sister Marion and Evelyn Spice made some films, the former making simple travel films for T.I.D.A.; Alex Shaw made some telephone films and also four films for the Orient Line; Arthur Elton produced and directed, Edgar Anstey directed and Harry Watt began to do so as well. Cameramen included professionals like Bill Shenton and George Noble, A. E. Jeakins, S. Onions and J. D. Davidson, as well as youngsters from the G.P.O. staff, trained by the Unit, F. H. Jones and Chick Fowle. Sound recording was by E. A. Pawley and John Cox but, of course, the important influence here was that of Cavalcanti. The foundations were laid for later disagreements over film credits.

Under the new name, a number of films begun under the E.M.B. were completed, of which the most notable were the group shot in Ceylon by Basil Wright, chiefly of course *Song of Ceylon*. The

Empire Tea Marketing Expansion Board had wanted four one-reel films of Ceylon, and in 1933 Wright had gone there with young John Taylor as assistant, and in seven weeks shot 23,000 feet of silent negative.[34] The film grew into a single four-reel film of a more elaborate nature. He got back when they were moving to Black-heath and cut it during 1934. Sound was added, and with it the imaginative encouragement of Cavalcanti. As Wright wrote at the time, the sound-track was going to need "solid experimentation"[35] and musician Walter Leigh wrote that the film was actually cut with the sound in mind.[36] Dancers were brought over for the synchronisation. Four modest and anonymous single-reel films were also made for the E.T.M.E.B., silent except for a short sweet *Dance of the Harvest*, which may perhaps show signs of Wright's "camera eye". *Song of Ceylon* was shown at the Curzon as a second feature in October 1935 and received the Prix du Gouvernement for the best film from all classes, and first prize in the documentary class, at the International Film Festival in Brussels. It marked a new level of artistic importance and is probably one of the loveliest films of the movement as a whole, and of Basil Wright in particular. It was also one of the few documentaries to be registered as available for quota.

As a legacy of the original intention to make four films, it is in four parts. Part I, "The Buddha", begins with breathtaking pans and dissolves of vast fan-like palm leaves, ancient forests, dancers, and a procession of pilgrims as they climb a forested peak to Buddha's legendary footprint in the rock, and is full of movement from the winding procession upwards to the long pans after a soaring bird down, down from the mountain over forest and plain to the sea. Sinhalese singing, the priests' bells and the quiet, thought-ful and slightly accented voice of Lionel Wendt reading a seven-teenth century traveller's account of Ceylon accompany this. Part II, "The Virgin Island", shows the island and the people about their everyday tasks: the dhobi, the training of ceremonial dancers, the grinding of corn and, best of all, a stunning sequence of a fisherman casting his nets; these lead to Part III, "The Voices of Business and Commerce", in which a medley of phone conversa-tions, stock prices, bills of lading and the sounds of radio introduce the modern world of commerce but as an aural background only, accompanying the visual images of traditional life, the gathering of coconuts, the working elephants, and all the ancient ways. Part IV, "The Apparel of a God", starts with a famous sequence of huge Buddhas cut in the rock, with offerings made by a solitary worshipper, and builds through the dressing of the dancers and the assembly of the people to the climax of the dance. The clang of gongs takes us back to whirling pans over the fan-like leaves of the jungle.

Apart from its memorable visual beauty the film was outstanding for the skill with which the visual and sound images were edited to blend with and comment on each other, from detailed juxtapositions to the underlying theme. The use of a seventeenth century description of Ceylon with the visual evidence of an unchanged way of life, and virtually restricting the existence of modern commerce to a busy sound-track of voices from outside, still accompanying scenes of traditional life, transform what could have been simply a picture of an exotic life-style into a comment on its durability. It is the sound-track which achieves this, and the importance of the spiritual element in the structure of society is conveyed by implication and with great subtlety. Walter Leigh discussed how the "sound-score" used Sinhalese voices, singing and talking, drumming, a Western orchestra in a combination of European and Sinhalese idioms and even the commentary itself as sound effects, orchestrated to add an element not contained in the visuals. One well-known piece of ingenuity is that of a swinging microphone used beside a gong which had just been struck. But this is only one effect in what was an extremely intricate and elaborate film. Lyrical, beautiful, quiet and reflective as the film is, it is described aptly by its title, as a song of joy and praise for the beauty and spirituality of Ceylon. In view of its subsequent fame it is surprising to learn from Marie Seton, writing at the time, that it was received with indifference,[37] but certainly many greeted it with enthusiasm. Time has more than vindicated it, and it is one of the best known and most enjoyable films of the movement. By the time that it was finished it had benefited from creative contributions of several members of the Unit and it was put out as produced by Grierson; directed, filmed and edited by Wright with Taylor as his assistant; written by Grierson, Wright "and others"; with music and musical direction by Leigh, and "sound supervision" by Cavalcanti. From what we know of the experiments going on in the Unit at the time we feel that "sound supervision" gives a somewhat rough-and-ready picture of Cavalcanti's function, and from Leigh's article one may feel that he, too, was more involved in the whole conception of the sound-track than is suggested by the conventional term "musical direction". Wright himself would acknowledge the overall importance of Grierson. Nevertheless it is pre-eminently Basil Wright's film.

Song of Ceylon was one of the high points of the documentary movement in Britain during these years. But there was plenty of more humdrum activity to keep the Unit busy. During this early period at the G.P.O., Grierson's sister Marion made some unremarkable silent travel films of Britain which were used by T.I.D.A. Flaherty fragments, also, such as *The Glassmakers of England* and *The English Potter*, were put out as T.I.D.A. films in 1935. Marion Grierson did some filming in London with camera-man Bill Shenton in 1933 which appeared in various productions and versions, finally being used by Strand Films in May 1935 after the foundation of this company by Donald Taylor, whom she was to marry. Taylor, at the same time, had been filming in Lancashire for T.I.D.A. under Grierson's auspices and with George Noble at the camera. This material also appeared under various guises for both T.I.D.A. and Strand.

T.I.D.A. production was financed meagrely by a grant from the Department of Overseas Trade, with assistance from some local authorities and industries. Under L. A. de L. Meredith and A. F. Primrose it continued to be farmed out. A number of pleasant travel and scenic pictures of the country by good cameramen appeared, but they found as Grierson had done that single films were hard to market. They sponsored Marion Grierson in her silent *Edinburgh* in 1934 and its later sound counterpart *The Key to Scotland*, and the silent *St James's Park* and its sound counterpart, this time directed by Alex Shaw, *Heart of an Empire*; *Beside the Seaside* was made at the same time, and the silent *Cathedrals of England* with its sound counterpart *For All Eternity*. Perhaps the best of an undistinguished bunch by her and Taylor, *Britain's Countryside*, was a silent short film with a pleasant eye for detail. Later T.I.D.A. films included one on Bath called *Of All the Gay*

Places by Taylor and yet another London film by Marion Grierson, *London on Parade*, both of them taken by American companies now that there was an obligatory quota of British short films. One of the last pre-war T.I.D.A. films was that produced by former feature director George Pearson to promote British craftsmanship, *British Made*. But the films were extremely conventional and the only one which was interesting or imaginative was *Around the Village Green*, made in 1937 by Marion Grierson but this time with Evelyn Spice as co-producer and co-director, G.P.O. cameraman Fred Gamage, and music by Benjamin Britten. The theme was that mechanisation of farming was changing life in the English village in order to meet the needs of the town, and commentary by John Watt about the structure of village life accompanied rural scenes shot in and around Finchingfield, Great Bardfield and Steeple Bumpstead, three beautiful Essex villages preserving much of their mediaeval character, with an undercurrent of comment in local voices.

Evelyn Spice made *Winter on the Farm* and then graduated to *Weather Forecast*, another carry-over from the E.M.B. with some beautifully chosen shots further embellished by a sound-track showing the influence of Cavalcanti. Music, commentary and the sound of the sea, the winds, gulls screaming, dance music on the radio, a soft background of women's voices as they relay storm warnings complement the visuals of the cat on the window-sill, the long grasses blowing, the lady gardener hearing the radio warning, paper blowing about on a deck. The storm brews to a crescendo with the sound of the wind and the thump of heavy seas under the pier; and after a climax of wild seas round the lighthouse the film ends with the sky and countryside at peace again. This modest but satisfying little film, although neglected later, was a pioneer of free cutting of the sound-track and made with considerable style, and when shown at the Film Society was praised by Rotha for adding a new dimension to the cinema.[38]

Cavalcanti did some preliminary work about this time for a possible film on the Radio S.O.S. Service. He also made his début on the screen credits with *The Glorious Sixth of June* and *Pett and Pott*, two humorous departures from the Grierson style. The first was a short film in celebration of new lower telephone rates, treated as an elaborate joke about "the Papers" which are stolen from the G.P.O. Special Messenger Albert Goodbody, and was rather on the level of amateur charades. Cavalcanti was credited as director. The second, shot in the summer of 1934,[39] was a deliberate experiment made in order to acquire experience in the use of sound, in which the sound-track was recorded first. Produced by Grierson, it was put out as directed, written and edited by Cavalcanti, with other members of the Unit including Basil Wright, Stuart Legg, John Taylor and Walter Leigh credited in various ways. It was in fact an example of Grierson's ideal of group production, but in style and content, both of which were a complete departure for the Unit, it shows the unmistakable hand of Cavalcanti.

It is a whimsical fantasy to show how useful the phone can be in the lives of neighbouring suburban families, the sensible Petts with their phone and the horrible Potts who prefer "a maid, not a phone" and are dominated by their sluttish servant. When a burglar attacks the latter, the Pett child is able to phone for the police, and in the final court scene the judge interrupts a serious summing-up with a friendly word to the audience recommending the telephone. The film is full of comic fantasy. Commuters sway in harmony in the train to chanted news about a burglary, and as we watch this intercut with the train the woman in it screams, and this scream, turning into a train whistle, is the sign for the commuters to alight. As Mrs Pett orders her groceries over the phone, with item after item on the sound-track the picture accompanies foolish phoneless Mrs Pott lumbering up the hill carrying her own parcels; at one moment of exhaustion she plods up in slow motion to the accompaniment of drum-rolls. As Mr and Mrs Pett converse on the phone the screen wipes across phone lines with birds sitting chirruping. Exaggerated apache music accompanies the fight with the burglar. There are many other flights of fancy and it is obvious the Unit had fun making the film, and no doubt learnt a great deal from it. Herbert Read made much of its technique in a weighty discussion of *Experiments in Counterpoint*[40] but as a frolic it is not to everybody's taste. The Unit had always taken itself very seriously hitherto; the film was a harbinger of the changes which Cavalcanti's arrival was going to bring.

More early material of the Unit was, about this time, turned into another highly experimental film called *Coalface*. This has generally been considered, in later years, to be a Cavalcanti film, although there has been argument about the actual screen credits.[41] The most likely story is that earlier filming on coal in Britain had been edited by Legg, other sequences were now shot by others such as Watt, the young Humphrey Jennings and Basil Wright, some of Flaherty's discursive filming was cut into studio shots by Cavalcanti and the film was put together, with its sound-track, by him. This was heightened by the earliest film work of two great artists, then both young and untried, W. H. Auden and Benjamin Britten. Here again, the likely truth seems to be that it was Grierson who found Britten by the simple expedient of asking at the Royal College of Music for a promising young composer, and that Auden approached the Unit himself through a friend, Basil Wright.

The result of all this was a short film, ostensibly a clear, neat and informative account of the coal industry in Britain, its importance, by-products, distribution and uses, with a Welsh choir and some extremely interesting music by Britten on the sound-track for a madrigal by Auden which begins :

O lurcher-loving collier, black as night,
Follow your love across the smokeless hill.

One sequence, which is strangely moving despite poor recording and lighting, is that in which the shift marches into the tunnel stating their names and jobs in an ascending litany to music by Britten. This interesting little film was shown at the Film Society, but was not widely considered important. Vesselo writing in *Sight and Sound* and playing safe as usual even described it as "incoherent in conception and ineffectual in execution".[42] However, it also received a medal of honour at Brussels and increased in importance as the years went by. It was hardly about the work of the G.P.O. or even Empire foodstuffs, and was put out by Grierson as an "Empo" film, which he later claimed was his brand name for experimental films, although this was certainly not consistently so at the time. At all events, clearly he regarded it as unusual. The programme credits at the Film Society in October 1935 ran : "Produced by John Grierson of the G.P.O. Film Unit. Sound recording, William Coldstream, Stuart Legg and Benjamin Britten, under the supervision of Cavalcanti. Verse by W. H. Auden." Under the circumstances this would seem somewhat cursory. In later years it has been claimed that early copies of the film did not mention Cavalcanti at all, but the Film Society programme does not bear this out. However, it is true that in *Sight and Sound* at the time it was described as having been directed by Grierson.

The Orient Line was already film-minded. It had secured short lengths of film of the launch and maiden voyage of R.M.S. *Orontes* in 1929, and like T.I.D.A. had been an early client of the E.M.B., with Basil Wright's silent film of 1933, *Liner Cruising South*. Tommy Tallents, the public relations head of the company and brother of Stephen Tallents, was now responsible for four films made by Grierson's Alex Shaw and Evelyn Spice and, more important, Rotha's next film *Shipyard*. Cruising in the Mediterranean and northern waters, Shaw and Spice made the films with George Noble in 1934, music by Raymond Bennell being synchronised later. Promotion for the luxury cruises so popular in the thirties among those who could afford them, the films received little attention at the time but are pleasant and imaginative exercises in the creation of mood and setting by the selection of visual and sound detail, especially *Sea Change* and to a lesser extent *Northern Waters*. *People and Places* tried the experiment of replacing commentary by a conversation between an unseen man and woman, but they were rather stilted and this interesting idea did not altogether succeed. But the films, from the stewards lining up to meet the boat train, the purser in his cage, the ship's wake and the smokestack, the ship-board routine of deck games, the morning cup of beef tea, sunbathing and dancing, the boat drill and the climb down to the waiting launch, alternate the lazy and ritualised life on board with the exotic places visited, all accompanied by an indistinct buzz of casual fragments of chatter, instructions and the nostalgic sounds of a ship at sea; the music, also, departs from the meaningless background continuum of the commercial travel film and plays its part in the sound picture. But the films were not likely to appeal to the earnest young documentarist and Rotha, writing when they came out in 1935, was snide about "preconceived ideas of 'orchestrated' and 'imagistic' ideas of sound".[43]

Most of the G.P.O. films were much more sober than this. Grierson, Legg and Gibbs carried on the collaboration begun at the

E.M.B. with *Telephone Workers, The Coming of the Dial* and *Introducing the Dial*. The style of these films, with excellent photography and restrained commentary, is typical of the first class information films which constituted the bulk of the Unit's output. *Telephone Workers*, in showing how the phone system was extended to new towns and villages, incidentally gives us a rare picture of ordinary England in the thirties, the countryside being linked by arterial roads and the spread of "ribbon development" housing. *The Coming of the Dial*, on the other hand, is marked by the rather awkward inclusion of a short piece of Moholy-Nagy's film of his Light Display machine, the rights to which Grierson, with his usual opportunism, had acquired. Used here to suggest science and research, it makes an irrelevant prologue. *Conquering Space* was a compilation produced by Legg and edited by Shaw, who also directed a film produced by Elton about the mass of underground tubes, cables and pipes beneath London called *Under the City*. Films about the Post Office Savings Bank included Elton's story of a young couple and a summer holiday, *John Atkins Saves Up*, as well as *Banking for Millions* and *The Savings Bank* made by the author Raymond Spottiswoode. An early film *Cable Ship*, shot for the G.P.O. in 1933, was made by Legg with Alex Shaw, and leant heavily on the commentary.[44] *Air Post* by Elton was directed by Geoffrey Clark. Legg also made *C.T.O. – The Story of the Central Telegraph Office*, about the installation of teleprinters, slightly later in 1935. These films, some competent but dull, some poor, along with even more anonymous ones with titles like *How to Tie a Parcel*, were the staple of the Unit.

An abstract trailer for phones made in 1934–5 may be described in some detail in order to give an idea of the style of these short films, which were an E.M.B. and G.P.O. standby. An animated drawing looking down on two drum tops being beaten by drumsticks is accompanied by rhythmic banging on the sound-track; a rolling title

Tom Toms warned
primitive man

rolls down the screen; a diagonal title "Geese warned" rolls diagonally up right, both of these titles being over a drawn silhouette of geese heads with their mouths clacking, to the sound of quacking; the title "Bonfires warned" rolls up and "the Middle Ages" rolls down, in front of shadowy flames and waving flags; a four-line diagonal title "The Telephone warns the modern world" appears word by word as a shadowy phone behind them moves diagonally down right; a drawing of an upright phone standing over jagged spikes which jerk up and down to represent fire; title "Fire" grows in front of this as a bell rings on the sound-track. And so on. The film is just over 200 feet and consists entirely of this use of titles, with various combinations of position, timing and movement, stylised drawings, and very little on the sound-track. It ends with a two line title

Speak to the World –
Get on the telephone

over a multiple-image representation of a dialling hand, with a foreign voice speaking on the sound-track; the title "Use – your – own – telephone" appears word by word over a moving multiple image of phones, with a burst of military music on the sound-track. Ingenious, cheap and effective, it is fast and to the point.

Meanwhile interesting work was being done by Edgar Anstey and Harry Watt. During and just before the change-over to the G.P.O. a film about Western District's London postal sorting office, *Six-Thirty Collection*, was directed by Anstey with Watt as assistant, and finished by Watt on his own when Anstey left to form a film unit for Shell. They are given screen credits for co-direction, and the film is interesting and unpretentious. It is noticeably economical in its use of material, interesting in view of Watt's account in his autobiography of how he was forced to cut and cut the original greatly to the eventual benefit of the film.

Watt next took over another subject on which Anstey had been working since 1932, a film about the establishment of a radio transmitting station made for the B.B.C. and called *B.B.C. – Droitwich*. Anstey's name is not on the film[45] and nor is Cavalcanti's, though Watt writes of how the film was lifted out of the ordinary by the latter's suggestion that a *mélange* of broadcast sound should accompany the climax when the huge dynamos are switched on, rather than the sound of the dynamos themselves. Relying a good deal on the commentary in B.B.C. announcer Stuart Hibberd's carefully modulated tones, it is informative and competent. Watt was learning.

The following year a second B.B.C. film, *B.B.C. – The Voice of Britain*, five reels long and with a quota registration, was one of the Unit's major productions and another example of teamwork. Given a medal of honour in Brussels and widely shown in the cinemas, it was solid and capable rather than brilliant, and was liked by the public and the film trade rather than by the more highbrow critics, who did not consider it fresh and exciting. Yet in fact it has an outstandingly elaborate sound-track in the group's new counterpoint style, to use the term adopted by Herbert Read, and the underlying concept of a panorama of one day's life in Britain as it was affected by the many activities of the B.B.C. was imaginative and gave the film tremendous scope to interweave visual and sound elements, and yet maintain a basic unity. Like the other B.B.C. film it had hung over from the E.M.B. days and it was a long, troublesome and expensive film to produce, at £7,500 the Unit's most costly film so far.[46] Credits on the film itself[47] mention Grierson as co-producer with Legg, but direction, writing and editing by Legg "and others". These included Evelyn Spice, who directed a sequence on one of the regional stations, but it has been generally accepted that the whole Unit took a hand. Cavalcanti's influence is obvious, and it is strange that his name does not appear, at least on this copy. Legg organised and unified the whole and, though it is his film, the collaborative nature of its production and what some saw as a rather prosaic subject denied him the acclaim as an artist that some of the others were beginning to receive. Unfortunately some of the acting is stiff and stilted and fragments of casual chattering somewhat false. Nevertheless the camera, cutting and sound-track keep this mass of material moving with great facility. After the arty self-consciousness of his early work, Legg had settled down to make intelligent and informative films skilfully put together.

From the *In Town Tonight* signature music behind the credits we are introduced to Broadcasting House and the Reverend Dick Shepphard's daily radio service, tilting down from a cloudy sky through a mix of Union Jack, radio mast, townscapes with a choir singing "Oh God, Our Help in Ages Past". As he speaks we see vista after vista of the towns of Britain. Narration of the daily work of the B.B.C. in its many facets is broken up by the voices of people seen and unseen, and a world of sounds cut and overlapped, mixed and superimposed, is maintained throughout the film. The idea of a confused, busy atmosphere is ever present, both in the narration and in the people we see, as well as in the technical chat and incidental bleeps and buzzes and sounds of radio, with many ingenious sound bridges. The aerial pandemonium lies over peaceful countryside and towns alike. Many B.B.C. celebrities are seen moving about their work at Broadcasting House, the hiss of the tea-urn merging with the lift indicator. Val Gielgud, John Watt, Brian Michie, Eric Maschwitz, John Sharman, Stuart Hibberd, Henry Hall and the B.B.C. Dance Orchestra in rehearsal shirt-sleeves, Christopher Stone trying out a record; sound effects are tried; comedians rehearse, tap dancers practise and their clattering feet merge into the sound of the presses printing the *Radio Times*. The Boat Race commentary, Children's Hour, Stephen King-Hall's famous "Here and There" talks on current affairs to children, ending invariably with the advice to "be good, but not so *frightfully* good that someone at once says to you '*Now* what have you been up to?' " – all are seen or heard through their listeners throughout the country, people running along the Thames towpath, rich children listening in their lovely garden, poor children gathering round the wireless on the kitchen window-sill as mother hangs out the washing. As evening comes Adrian Boult conducts the B.B.C. Symphony Orchestra straight through the first movement of Beethoven's Fifth Symphony. Throughout Britain there are people listening and people not listening, night workers, people out walking against the evening skies. A trawler receives an S.O.S. message; a link-up with Montreal is effected, and transmission from Paris; H. G. Wells gives a talk on Russia; commentary is given as the *Queen Mary* is launched; various artistes give their acts, and all the time there is a changing tide of listeners. In the last reel we see politicians talking while a cymbal-like sound-track and Hibberd's voice accompany them. Famous commentators David Low, J. B. Priestley, G. K. Chesterton and Bernard Shaw sit at the microphone and deliver their broadcast talks, at last giving way to Henry Hall and his orchestra, now elegant in evening dress for the performance.

10 The commuters sway to the sound of the track (*Pett and Pott*, 1934).

11 The idyllic rural past (*The Face of Britain*, 1935).

12 The working man speaks for himself (*Workers and Jobs*, 1934–5).

They play "Piccadilly Riot" to an impression of London at night, from the bright lights to the humble road-gang with their "Road Up" sign. To the tones of "Sweetmeat Joe the Candy Man" people go home. A father worries about a daughter out late. She is seen home by her boyfriend, and the film fades out to Hibberd saying "Goodnight, everybody, goodnight" as the camera moves up towards the sky and a last shot of Big Ben. A busy day for the B.B.C. is over.

Both these B.B.C. films had been started by request before the Unit had been transferred to the G.P.O. Morale was high and the sky was the limit. For the next few years the group was to attract young men of high calibre. Not only were Auden and Britten occasional contributors, but William Coldstream, later to have a distinguished career as an artist, was also working as a junior member. He had cut *Coalface*, and now directed his own film *The King's Stamp* in 1935. This, a part-Dufaycolor film about the Jubilee issue designed by Barnett Friedman, although slow and not outstanding, also had music by Britten. Humphrey Jennings, who also worked with the Unit at this time, was a young man whose all-round intellectual brilliance and connections with the academic and artistic worlds were something new to the circle. Besides helping generally, for example appearing as the G.P.O. Special Messenger in *The Glorious Sixth of June*, designing sets and appearing as the grocer in *Pett and Pott* and contributing shots for *Coalface*, he made three short sound films of his own, which were an early attempt to impart movement to still material. *Post-Haste* in 1934, made with the help of the Postal Museum in Tottenham, is an edited compilation of documents, prints, books, paintings and contemporary quotations used to build up a history of the postal service. *The Story of the Wheel*, also edited, included models from various museums as well, and on *Locomotives* he is credited with direction for the first time. Some existing copies have final shots of pouch collection by mail train which may have been made before the famous pouch sequence of *Nightmail*.

From 1935 onwards the situation was to change radically. It has been seen that the E.M.B. Film Unit had on occasion made films for official or commercial sponsors. It was a time of great interest in the power of the press, radio and film; in fact the power of what were later to be called the mass media was beginning to be realised and to be used to popularise everything from Fascism to Ovaltine. The word "propaganda" had not yet acquired the sinister overtones of falsification and indoctrination which it was soon to have. An article by Grierson in 1933 defines propaganda as "the art of public persuasion",[48] and he speaks of the disillusion with democracy to be found in the work of such modern commentators as Walter Lippman. Along with his social and moral motivation Grierson had all the gifts of the public relations man – the diplomatic tongue, the eagle eye for useful contacts and matters of mutual advantage, all of which he used with great skill. Commercial concerns on all sides were using the educated, the tactful and the socially acceptable for this new type of prestige advertising and contact making. A number of literary men, financially not very successful, even earned their living as publicists for the bigger film companies.

But it was not considered the duty of an official film unit to make public relations films for all comers. Even by the time of the move to the G.P.O. there had been some restlessness in the film industry and elsewhere about this tendency. After a meeting in November 1933 the Film Producers' Group of the Federation of British Industries had written to the Board of Trade expressing anxiety about the new arrangements. It was felt that if the Film Unit, subsidised by public money, were to produce not only for the G.P.O. but also for other public, semi-public or even commercial bodies, or to advise them on choosing a producer, the competition would be unfair on the film industry. Post Office Estimates for 1934 included £12,000 for film production. It is certainly true that there were commercial firms which would have liked to have the opportunity to make such films, and indeed a number did so, but they were mostly very small firms and were not highly organised and certainly had no influence on the Federation of British Industries, with the single exception of the recently formed Gaumont-British Instructional managed by Bruce Woolfe. Thus it may well be true, as some believe, that G-BI was the Unit's chief antagonist, and instrumental in getting its functions curtailed. The British Film Institute, also of recent formation, had been as unhappy as G-BI. As R. S. Lambert said on behalf of the Governors, it should be for the B.F.I. to "co-operate with the industry in sponsoring the making of certain types of cultural films rather than that a Government Department should enter the field of commercial enterprise".[49] It is true that this was among the functions that had been envisaged for the Institute, as was custodianship of the film library, which had been another bone of contention between it and the E.M.B. There were Questions in the House of Commons and the matter was considered by the Select Committee on Public Estimates early in 1934, producing a strong and hostile report in the summer.

This report, among other things, queried the Unit's method of calculating costs of production, its lack of provision for overheads, and the absence of any system whereby orders were put out to tender. Recommendations followed that the G.P.O. films should be confined to advertising postal services or instructing postal workers; that the Unit should not advise or produce for other bodies; that H.M.S.O. should continue to keep the war films but the E.M.B. films, now kept at the Imperial Institute at a cost of £3,400 a year, should be found a more suitable home; and that a government policy on the use of film should be evolved.

Thus almost from its beginning the G.P.O. Film Unit was subject to severe restrictions. As we have seen, a number of films started under the E.M.B. were successfully carried over and finished during these early years. In particular the B.B.C. films, *Song of Ceylon* and even *Coalface* were made despite their irrelevance to the Post Office. But if the movement was going to spread and film other subjects it would have to find some other backer than the G.P.O.

Undoubtedly the existence of an official film production unit sheltering in the Post Office was an anachronism. It was a historical accident which had occurred because of the expediency of Grierson and Tallents, those two men of action who recognised a chance of survival when they saw it. The fierce defence of the Unit by its adherents was more because the work it was doing was good than because there was any logical reason why a film unit financed by the Post Office should have the right to film whatever it chose. The idea of official propaganda was not yet acceptable and there had been no intention to set up a film unit for it. It is understandable that the film industry should have resented it and, once the matter was raised, that the Select Committee should have seen the situation as illogical and untenable. But the decision of this committee decisively changed the course of events. Grierson had already given his brand of film-making the impetus of a movement by insisting that his young directors should extend their operations by becoming producers. There were plenty of far-seeing public relations men in large commercial and semi-public bodies who saw the possibilities of film for a new form of prestige publicity, bigger and better than the little old "industrials". Tommy Tallents at the Orient Shipping Line, Jack Beddington at Shell, the Australian S. C. Leslie now working for the gas industry and C. F. Snowden-Gamble at Imperial Airways were all interested. From now on, besides the work of the G.P.O. Film Unit itself, members of the group diversified their activities and carried on production from outside the Unit for a growing number of sponsors. Still remaining a close personal network, and still guided by Grierson himself, they operated in various ways. Individuals might be commissioned by outside bodies to produce a film; an industry might ask them to set up a film unit for it; or a commercial documentary film company might be set up ready to undertake commissions. From now on all these forms of activity are to be found as well as bodies set up to co-ordinate them, first the Association of Realist Film Producers in 1935 and later Film Centre.

The first documentary unit to be formed by an industry, and in fact the first sign that the documentary movement was spreading, was the Shell Film Unit, which actually pre-dated the Select Committee's report. After Rotha's *Contact* Jack Beddington of Shell-Mex B.P., on behalf of Shell International, sought the advice of Grierson on the establishment of a unit. On his recommendation, his own protégé Edgar Anstey joined them in 1933 and set up the Shell Film Unit. The first production was *Airport*, a two-reel study of Croydon made in 1934. This has the reputation of being a dull film, but had a good press when it was shown in 1935. Anstey, however, left the Unit fairly soon and for a while it, with directors D'Arcy Cartwright and Grahame Tharp, cameraman Stanley Rodwell and animation facilities set up by engineering draughtsman Francis Rodker, was managed by a member of the Shell staff, Alex Wolcough. The technicians who joined at its formation also became members of the Shell staff, and were joined in 1937 by Geoffrey Bell from Cambridge. In 1936 it was decided that the Unit, although still housed at Shell, should be run on a consultancy basis by Arthur Elton from the Association of Realist Film Producers, and later from Film Centre. Simple, clear, technical films were made, not only for internal use but also as direct public relations, including a Shell *Cinemagazine. Power Unit* in 1936 was an easily understood explanation of the internal combustion engine. *Lubrication of the Petrol Engine* is a brilliant short film explaining with crystal clarity how lubrication prevents friction, using examples as far apart as a child's trousers as he shoots down a slide to a ship's slipway to show the principles involved. Reference is made in *World Film News* to Elton's *The Diesel Engine*, one of his most successful films of machinery, made with Beddington's co-operation. A slight departure was the 1935–6 puppet advertising film *Birth of a Robot*, made not by the Unit but by Len Lye and described elsewhere. Some film about gliding shot while Geoffrey Bell was still up at Cambridge was used and put out as a "Savoy" film by D'Arcy Cartwright assisted by Bell, and called *Prelude to Flight*. Shell films were beautifully made and photographed, lucid films on mechanical and scientific subjects rather than true documentaries. But because the people concerned were personally very much involved in the documentary movement the Unit itself is always considered part of it. Many years later Elton's colleague Anstey said :

> It was Arthur Elton's contribution to bringing alive the wonders of technology. He discovered an aesthetic of scientific and technical exposition. Not simply in order to persuade people to buy more goods and consume them, but to give man a sense of his present achievements and possible achievements in the future.[50]

This social purpose seems to have been bestowed on these glossy and brilliant films with hindsight, but they need no such justification.

Individuals also received commissions, usually through Grierson. For example, although still at the G.P.O., Elton produced and directed a film independently for the Ministry of Labour, with sound recording and camerawork by outsiders, called *Workers and Jobs*. As it was shown in March 1935 it was probably made about the turn of the year. About the work of Labour Exchanges, this small and touchingly optimistic film is of considerable historical importance for its introduction of some unemployed men and officials at Poplar Labour Exchange in London in a pioneering use of direct speech recording on location. Two other Ministry of Labour films were also "diverted" by Grierson to help to start the Strand Film Company, as we shall see. And the gas industry through the British Commercial Gas Association and the Gas Light and Coke Company commissioned Elton and Anstey personally, early in 1935, to make a number of films which included two of the most important of the decade. Hiring a studio at Merton Park but not forming a company, using some members of the Unit and some outsiders, in 1935 they first made a short, beautifully clear *How Gas is Made*, and *Men Behind the Meters*. The latter uses speech by the workmen, but is apparently post-synchronised. In 1936, also, two films featuring the celebrated London chef Marcel Boulestin promoting gas cooking were of interest in the cinemas, *A Scratch Meal* and *Party Dish*. There were other minor films. But two of the films made now, *Housing Problems* and *Enough to Eat*, were outstanding and indicated an entirely new direction for documentary.

By this time Elton and Anstey were feeling their way towards letting people, the ordinary people and workers who were the usual subjects of the documentary, speak for themselves directly on the sound-track during filming. Hiring the cumbersome mobile sound recording equipment by the day was expensive, and the G.P.O. sound experiments hitherto, however enterprising, had been in studio techniques. The frivolous tendency of some of these was worlds apart from the great step into direct location recording of speech which these two more serious-minded young men were about to take. In view of the connections, real and imagined, between the new style and the *March of Time* technique, it is important to get some dates straight before we describe these films. *Workers and Jobs*, with its modest introduction of direct location recording of speech, was shown in March 1935 and, as we have said, probably made about the turn of the year. *Housing Problems*, a landmark in interviewing, was shown at the Film Society in late 1935, presumably having taken several months to make, and

Enough to Eat, carrying the changes in technique further into social investigation but away from location interviewing of ordinary people, was made in 1936. *The March of Time* was first shown in America in February 1935 and not shown in Britain until autumn, by which time *Housing Problems* was finished. Anstey went to work for *The March of Time* after these films were made. The *March of Time* use of interview, frequently faked in the studio, with the narrator-journalist carrying the message in a commentary with illustrative visuals, was to influence the movement in Britain in the new few years. But it does not seem to have had any responsibility for *Housing Problems*, which broke new ground of its own following Elton's *Workers and Jobs*.

Housing Problems, for the British Commercial Gas Association, was about slums. It was novel in two ways: first in this use of interviews and second in the sponsorship by an industry of a film about an issue of social importance which contained no direct promotion of its own product. Slum clearance was an important question at the time and our film makers were able to persuade the gas people that, as the provision of modern housing would incidentally increase the use of gas, a serious film on the subject would not be a waste of money. As we see elsewhere S. C. Leslie was already in favour of the documentary approach. The first part of this short but remarkable film introduces us to some slum dwellers who, in marvellously clear, free and confident talk, tell us of rats, bugs and lack of water as they sit in their peeling, dripping, cracked homes, collapsing stair-wells and dank courts. A woman says without emotion "It gets on yer nerves. I'll tell yer, I'm fed up". The second part shows them installed in flats which would be considered barracks by later generations, but in the optimism of 1935, hoping to clear all the slums in ten years, the bathroom seems "very beautiful" to the ex-slum woman and is a marvel to her friends and relations. Underprivileged people, speaking freely for the first time in the midst of their dreadful environment, made a powerful impact, very far removed from Grierson's heroic worker. Although the film was produced, directed and written by Elton and Anstey with John Taylor as cameraman, it has been widely recognised that Taylor, and Grierson's other sister Ruby, by their sympathetic handling of the people in setting it up contributed a great deal to the success of the interviews. Some have carried it so far as to denigrate the share contributed by the producer-directors, but in addition to the actual quality of the film the whole conception of it as location interviewing and as altruistic commercial sponsorship was of tremendous importance. Anstey in particular always took the social purpose of the movement very seriously and it is no coincidence that he was associated with this first significant extension of its function.

Their next film in 1935, *Dinner Hour* for the B.C.G.A., satisfied the gas industry's wish for some direct promotion as well, and showed something of the manufacture of gas and its use by a big bakery, a West End restaurant, a hospital kitchen and a staff canteen. Made with their usual clarity, it uses narration but has introductory and final sequences in which installation men have brief exchanges of conversation. However, with the Gas Light and Coke Company's *Enough to Eat*, directed and written by Anstey and shown in the autumn of 1936, the gas industry ventured further into the sponsorship of social studies and Anstey into a new and more verbal style. Known during its production as "the Nutrition Film", it was based on the work of Sir John Boyd Orr relating malnutrition to income and social class in Britain. Lacking the human and visual appeal of the appalling slum film, it is much more like a lecture; and although its direct interviews were a new departure they were mostly of experts rather than of ordinary people and it appears now, after thousands of such films, as a clear and worthy but slightly flat treatment of the subject. Nevertheless it was pioneering work both in style and in content. A long rolling title introduces us to the subject, and Julian Huxley's voice starts; we see him facing us across a desk as he tells us about undernourishment. He continues as we see what is going on in the field – scientists at work, experiments with rats, Sir John's work, diagrams about our food needs, all explained by Huxley and interspersed with interviews. Nothing dramatic or emotional disturbs its careful account.

It was an immediate success and much admired for its dispassionate and interesting treatment of a subject which, it must be repeated, was unfamiliar at the time. It was handled for commercial distribution by Kinograph, and Graham Greene was one who admired both the Gas Company for raising the subject and Anstey for the way he tackled it. "Using the camera as a reporter" seemed to be the modern phrase. *Film Art* was explicit in its praise: "Anstey has therefore concentrated the film into the sound track, and used the screen action as a background."[51] Nothing could be further from the heroic worker and the purely visual Russian style of the early films. It seemed to please everyone, those who distrusted the arty and the impressionist as well as those who were committed to social improvement. It firmly established the sponsorship of films unrelated to the commercial interests of the backer, it developed the direct interview, and confirmed the use of the sound-track to carry the bulk of the meaning.

Meanwhile Rotha was making his independent way in a similar direction with some difficulty. Still attached to Bruce Woolfe and G-BI after *Contact*, he found himself being used as the spearhead with which Bruce Woolfe tried to force his way into mainstream documentary. Rotha says that he made four other films at G-BI in 1934–5.[52] After *Roadwards*, made for the Daimler Car Company, he embarked on a film about the huge dry dock being built at Southampton to accommodate the *Queen Mary*, the project being wished on him by the company, some 5,000 feet having already been shot by Pocknall and others since the building of the ship began several years before. The resulting film was *Rising Tide*, a three-reeler finished in 1934 and officially subsidised by the Southern Railway. Transforming it into a real documentary with social significance, Rotha set to work on the theme that the employment and economic prosperity of this one part of Britain brought by the building of the dock had economic consequences extending far and wide, bringing renewed work to other industries. Taking cameraman Jimmy Rogers he shot sequences in northern areas of the paper, cotton, glass and steel industries as well as the graving-dock. The finished film was given a full review by Grierson in *Cinema Quarterly* in which he praised highly the visual qualities and "power of tempoed sequence", and claimed at last "These virtues may demonstrate a great talent".[53] He criticised it, however, on the grounds that Rotha had not demonstrated adequately how, for example, the Lancashire cotton industry would be set humming by the construction of a dock in Southampton. In this criticism he confirmed his permanent antipathy to Rotha's objective, which was to arouse awareness rather than to teach. The style he characterised as still that of the silent film. He also had some hard, if pertinent, remarks about the harm resulting from a director working with a producer with whom he was not in harmony. Rotha was only too aware of his unhappy position in this respect. He claims that the film cost £1,500 to make and was shown in the West End but that the G-B circuit cinemas showed a version, *Great Cargoes*, shortened to one reel and shown without credits.[54] In fact *Great Cargoes* was registered in November 1935 at 1,953 feet and did credit Rotha, but had an Emmett commentary added to it.

Rotha now found his feet at last with a film in which, although he was still attached to G-BI, he had a real documentary subject worthy of his ambitions. For Vickers Armstrong and the Orient Shipping Line he made the two-reel *Shipyard*, made over a period of many months in 1934-5 as the Orient liner no. 697, the *Orion*, was being built at Barrow-in-Furness. To his interest in the skills and craftsmanship of shipbuilding Rotha added something; the consciousness that when the task was finished and the ship gone the thousands of workers would once again face unemployment. This theme was deeply integrated in the film, in which the growing bulk of the ship is seen to dominate the town, and it is sad that Rotha was later to feel that its importance had not always been sufficiently recognised by a movement that set increasing store by the social significance of its films, but that still regarded him as too much the artist. Certainly the film got a warm reception from Basil Wright, who wrote that Rotha, "tied as he has been by influences beyond his immediate control", puts the shipbuilding over in terms of Barrow and its people. "Visually, the growing ship engrosses the screen. The sound is permeated with the clangour of the yard . . . by cunning punctuation (in terms chiefly of dissolve and soliloquy) the sociological method is stressed." Rotha's use of sound, "the shipyard's terrific row", is greatly improved, and "overlapped for continuity with considerable skill". Wright feels Rotha "is now finally in control of his medium".

But where Rotha pushes himself well up on the directorial roster is in his final sequence – a smooth and impressive treatment of the launch (the camera restraint is most gratifying), followed by a really moving anti-climax as the workers move uncertainly away from the empty stocks. The pathetic indecision of the worker in the final fadeout is masterly.[55]

In the next issue of *Cinema Quarterly* Grierson made the film the occasion for one of his theoretical examinations of what they were all doing. Calling it "Two Paths to Poetry", he contrasted the slogans of the information school, "observe and analyse", "know and build", "out of research poetry comes", to Rotha's broad canvas. While appreciating again "the splendour of his camerawork. . . . Force and fervour of tempo'd description" and noting the added use of sound and the sociological implication that would have been plainer "if he had freedom" – whilst appreciating all this, Grierson could not resist suggesting that lingering impressionism led to a sketchiness which failed to convince us of the reality of the ship and its construction.[56]

Be that as it may, the film is one which has not lost its power over the years. From the flat seascape at the beginning, through the introduction of the men with their ages and their trades as plater, corker, driller, their craggy faces and their whippets on a Sunday morning, we see the work progress as a huge edifice towering over the town and its life. Behind it all lies a vision of the cruise life. "Women walkin' about, dressed in silk dresses and gents in natty suits, don't suppose they'll think of the bloke that did the blinkin' rivet . . . ," muses one of the men. "The life of the town goes on. Every mouth being fed, everybody being clothed by the work of the men in the yard" – as we see the busy and thriving shops. Finally after the climax of the launch the cheering dies down, the ship floats quietly out of its position in the town and the men turn away. Beautifully shot and constructed, the film does exactly what Rotha wanted it to do, not what Grierson would have wanted it to do. It did not send the audience away with a clear idea of how the building of a liner was organised and carried out, but it did send them away with a new awareness of the size and meaning of the undertaking.

From now on, Rotha was to move back into the mainstream. We have seen elsewhere that the Central Electricity Board was having elementary films of the old industrial type made to popularise the spread of electricity, especially in rural areas, through Bruce Woolfe and G-BI. Rotha's next film, in some ways one of his most characteristic, was sponsored by Hugh Quigley of the Central Electricity Board.[57] This was *The Face of Britain* in 1935, and the theme was the planning of a better Britain using power from the national electricity grid. Perhaps the true subject matter was the England that Rotha had got to know as he travelled back and forth over the many months he spent making the shipping films. Rotha himself devotes comparatively little attention to *The Face of Britain* and describes it as over-ambitious. Yet with all its faults the film is theatrically convincing and moving, bursting with passionate meaning, forming a complete contrast to both the dry information style and the delicate perfectionist style. It was well received by both trade and art critics, won an award in Brussels and was a definite step forward in Rotha's progress. It starts with a rural idyll, "The Heritage of the Past", showing in some exquisite images how the pattern of past agricultural society made an economic structure which was beautiful to look at and live in : old methods of harvesting, working horses, trees swaying gently. The casual commentary is delivered by the Liberal journalist A. J. Cummings. This pastorale fades out and the Smoke Age takes over, all dark photography, discordant music and the harsh noises of industry, a changed pace of cutting, trees sweeping in the wind, the sky dark and menacing and clouds tearing across the ground in black shadow. Smoky townscapes and slag heaps show an industrial landscape in which coal, the centre of power, ruined the environment for the people who lived in it. The two final sequences, water-power and electricity, show how a new age is possible, without the ugliness of the Smoke Age. These necessary parts are essential to the message, but they contain less of the drama and impressionism and are less exciting than the rest of the film. The sectional structure, the idyllic rural prologue and the impressionist style were all becoming Rotha characteristics.

Early in 1936 he made, for the Ministry of Transport, again through G-BI, "the Road Safety Film" *Death on the Road*.[58] We have seen that road safety was a big issue in this year and other films were also being made, each with its little interview with the

Minister Leslie Hore-Belisha. The Exhibitors' Association urged its members to show Rotha's contribution, although at 1,500 feet some of them thought it too long. It was in the form of an anecdote, "beginning with the gaiety of a roadhouse, which enables him to present a neatly-cut jazz-band sequence, and follows through, with dramatic suspense, the tragedy of death as a result of carelessness";[59] and Rotha says it "was cut very fast like a gangster film".[60]

Meanwhile there was formed an independent company to produce sponsored films worthy of the documentary movement but made to be shown in the cinemas on a commercial basis. Sponsored films advertising a product were already numerous, but very inferior to those evolved by the documentary mainstream during the last few years, and distributed by paying the exhibitors to show them. But during 1935 a moribund company was acquired and the Strand Film Unit was formed, to make documentary films which would compete with commercial shorts. It was formed by young Donald Taylor, who had earlier been at the G.P.O. Unit but was more commercially inclined than the others and later became a feature director, and Ralph Keene, earlier a painter and picture dealer, who had originally been with Rotha when he persuaded Beddington to sponsor *Contact*. Backing was obtained chiefly from the South African, C. L. Heseltine. Two early films in 1935 were a history of bathing, *Taking the Plunge*, and *Citizens of the Future* made in collaboration with G-BI and the National Union of Teachers as a survey of state education. Both were made by Taylor with George Noble as cameraman. In addition a number of T.I.D.A. films were made. The early work of Donald Taylor and Marion Grierson has been mentioned already, and the films *For All Eternity*, *The Key to Scotland*, *Heart of an Empire* and *Beside the Seaside* were legacies from this which were put out in 1935 as Strand films. The two Grierson projects for the Ministry of Labour also came out as Strand films in 1936. Edgar Anstey's film about retraining and instruction camps and centres, *On the Way to Work*, was one of these; the other, *Work Waits for You*, was a non-theatrical film explaining job prospects for young people outside the depressed areas, and was directed by Alex Shaw. Strand also made "Mr Therm" films for the gas industry.[61]

Paul Rotha joined Strand early as Director of Productions,

bringing with him three contracts for films, which were in production during 1936. All three were distributed theatrically by A.B.F.D., and marked his transformation, like Grierson and so many others, into a producer. At the same time Ralph Keene, Ruby Grierson and a new young director from Cambridge University, Donald Alexander, with cameraman Paul Burnford, made four very cheap, simple London travelogue films which received quota registration and were used by M-G-M, *Rooftops of London*, *Statue Parade*, *London Wakes Up* and *Parks and Palaces*.[62]

An extramural activity in early 1936 was the making of what is usually called "the Peace Film", although its actual title was *Peace of Britain* and it was nominally produced not by Strand but by Freenat Films. In March 1936 national rearmament plans spurred a group of politically minded people at Strand, including Rotha, to make a very short three-minute film asking the public to appeal to their M.P.s to stand up for collective security and resist the arms race. Music was provided by Benjamin Britten. Work was voluntary and the film cost only £500,[63] and was to be distributed free. Despite delaying tactics by the film censors, who at first claimed that it contained War Office footage, which in fact it did not, it was very widely shown. *Sight and Sound* estimated that it was seen at 570 cinemas, reaching 4,300,000 people.[64] The whole thing, given publicity by the censorship delay, was discussed a great deal in the press and was welcomed by many people. Simultaneously using large loom titles, voices and images, with very rapid cutting, it repeatedly emphasised "there is no defence against air attack" and criticised as a fallacy the theory that arming would stop war. There were sensible short comments from ordinary people, using the new interview technique, and the film pressed home the message that the spectator could take responsible action and write to his M.P. to demand "Peace by Reason". It was short and forceful, although strictly speaking not a documentary and not a Strand film. We do not know how many letters to M.P.s were written as a result of it. This was a direct call to action and moreover, unlike "Post Early for Christmas", to political action. It was a practical application of that education for democracy which Grierson was always talking about, but one suspects altogether too real and too urgent for the master's unqualified approval.

Before Strand's Ministry of Labour films came out the first of Rotha's contracts, *Cover to Cover* made for the National Book Council, appeared in the autumn of 1936. Directed by Shaw and shot by George Noble, it was about writing as a form of communication and had studio interviews with literary celebrities T. S. Eliot, A. P. Herbert, Somerset Maugham, Rebecca West and John Masefield and also with Julian Huxley. The commentary in verse was by Winifred Holmes. This "poetic narration",[65] otherwise described as romantic narration or prose with a cadence to fit the scenes and cutting, had been attempted by poor Creighton in his early film *Southern April*, and was to be used later by Mary Field for G-BI's *They Made the Land* in 1938.[66] Graham Greene welcomed it,[67] the literary *Life and Letters Today* hated it.[68] A non-theatrical film on the same subject, *Chapter and Verse*, was directed by Stanley Hawes and handled by G-BE.

Next *The Way to the Sea* was made for the Southern Railway about the need for railway electrification. The director was J. B. Holmes, husband of Winifred Holmes and recently making his reputation with such G-BI films as *The Mine* and *Mediaeval Village*, and Rotha was the producer. Good camerawork by George Noble and good cutting were held by some to be marred by the construction of the film in three distinct sections, which continued to be a Rotha habit. A historical survey of Portsmouth and the road to London with a rather declamatory commentary, a staid and informative middle section on the position of the railway in 1935 and the need to electrify it, and a final imaginative and impressionist piece on how the way to the sea represents holidays and fun are somewhat perfunctorily combined. The last sequence, with its updated phantom ride past imagined domestic interiors, its beaches, the Isle of Wight and the spectacular Navy Week events, with music by Benjamin Britten and an "end-commentary" by W. H. Auden, seems to be from a quite different film.

But with *Today We Live* in 1937, producing with Hawes as his associate, Rotha came into his own. The style is warm, personal and involved, with a richness of observation and feeling and a persuasive expression of social ideals. Made for the National Council for Social Service with money from the Carnegie Fund United Kingdom Trust, it shows how assisted self-help brings new life to two communities which are enabled to form community centres. The first sequence showing the idyllic countryside stresses that the village used to be the unit of society, but the lovely images are ended by an explosion of music and smoke, the coming of power, and the coming also of an urban society with endless-houses and slums; the 1914 war was the end of an era. This is followed by a sequence in which industry and unemployment are intercut and lead to a melancholy picture of life for many in Britain in the thirties' aftermath of the Depression. Rotha calls this "a prologue in one reel in *March of Time* style" with a commentary, rather heavily delivered by Howard Marshall, written by Stuart Legg. True that the message is largely verbal, but the accompanying visuals are strongly reminiscent of the beginning of last year's *The Face of Britain.* The rest of the film is in two parts, one directed by Ruby Grierson about how the villagers of South Cerney, Gloucestershire, under the leadership of a determined lady ex-teacher and with a lot of hard work from the community get their village hall, with funds from the N.C.S.S., with a final happy scene of the village ladies in their hall doing PT in tweeds and stockinged feet; and one by the militant left-wing Ralph Bond about how the unemployed of Pentre in the Rhondda got their occupational centre with funds from the same source and a similar amount of hard work on their own part. It was the first Rotha film to take the microphone out for direct location work. The people of the two communities and the officials of the N.C.S.S. took part in the film, not in interviews but in reconstructed dramatisation of their affairs, but the style is so much more subtle and "unseen observer" in character that to identify it with the *March of Time* form of reconstructed incident would be misleading. A remarkable and much quoted passage in which unemployed miners, sad, bored cloth-capped figures, pick over the smoking slag heaps for usable scraps of fuel was contributed by Donald Alexander, who had already made a short 16 mm. silent film about conditions in the Rhondda when he was still at Cambridge in 1935. In 1937 he was to make a Strand film about farming co-operatives of the unemployed in distressed areas in Wales, called *Eastern Valley.* This was produced for Strand by Hawes. From the description by Graham Greene it sounds as if it has the Rotha concern for the environment, although Greene mistakenly ascribes this to Basil Wright and not to Rotha: "Life as it once was before industry scarred and mutilated the valley; life as it is; life as it should be."[69] And once more, among the slag heaps and fag packets of a semi-rural slum, the directly recorded interview was used.

Today and Tomorrow was a non-theatrical film on the same subject as *Today We Live*, directed by Ruby Grierson with an introduction by Viscount Bledisloe, a description of the work of the N.C.S.S. in depressed areas, villages turned into housing estates, and the provision of children's holiday camps. An unemployed miner, a lorry-driver and a blacksmith are all "brought to the camera and the microphone"[70] in the new fashion, and the film ends with an appeal for money by the Duke of Kent. Different in structure and style from the other, it is on the same subject of the modern need for community centres and the help available from the Carnegie Trust. Less dramatised and more like a lecture than the other one, it too was highly commended for its direct interviewing.

The delightful *Give the Kids a Break* made by Ruby Grierson also showed children in camp, and was made for the Necessitous Children's Holiday Camp Fund. Superb shots of the children of the Glasgow slums, wonderful images of shocking conditions, are introduced by a letter-writing exercise in school, "How I would like to spend my holiday"; then a committee, then camps being set up and the scenes of camp life, with a few titles but very little commentary. Apart from a rather idealised scene of the released city children picking flowers in the sunny meadows, the film is outstandingly spontaneous and unsentimental, with three gorgeous performances from children entertaining their fellows, especially a little boy who stands and sings "Misty Islands of the Highlands" in a loud clear voice undeterred by his large handed-down shorts which require a mighty hitch every now and then. Once again a final appeal for funds is the reason for the film, but in it Ruby Grierson had a chance to use to the full her unusual gift for capturing the natural behaviour of ordinary people.

Back at the G.P.O., for a short while until Grierson left it in June 1937 there were a number of films produced, or at least initiated, under his régime which appeared in the G.P.O. catalogue printed in September 1937. These were being produced variously by Grierson himself, Cavalcanti and Basil Wright, all of them except Grierson also directing, along with Harry Watt, Evelyn Spice and William Coldstream. Among the newer recruits Norman McLaren, Pat Jackson and Ralph Elton were given a chance. Cameramen included the G.P.O.'s own young men, previously G.P.O. messengers, Chick Fowle and Jonah Jones, as well as S. Onions; sound recording was credited to George Diamond and E. K. Webster, but Cavalcanti's influence was still very important. The unit continued to be enterprising in its choice of musicians, with more from Britten and Walter Leigh, the arrival of E. H. Meyer, and scores for two Swiss films by the French composer Maurice Jaubert. In addition to all this, the remarkable work of Len Lye with Jack Ellit was taken under the G.P.O. banner.

Len Lye, a half-Chinese New Zealander, was one of the most original and creative people working in the cinema at the time, although his work was so specialised that his name was hardly known outside a small circle. Having worked at manual occupations such as farming in New Zealand, carpentry in Australia and as a stoker on the way over to England "to keep his mind free", he had started drawing direct on to film with *Tusalava* in 1927–9. Jack Ellit, whom he had met in Sydney, and who also did the music for Francis Bruguière's experimental *Light Rhythms* in 1930, began his collaboration with Lye on this first film, and although his work went under such names as "sound editing" or "musical accompaniment" sound was in fact such an integral part of the films that his contribution was of key importance. Ellit was an innovator, and as conscious of the experimental nature of what they were doing as Lye was. He wrote "On Sound" in *Life and Letters Today* in favour of "new and imaginative sound forms", not necessarily musical but leading to a new sound aesthetic; he wished people to abandon "tight-laced musical values" and try the new electro-acoustic sound.[71] Painting directly on to celluloid film, Lye in 1935 made the 110-foot *A Colour Box* as an independent venture. To the music of a beguine, an abstract visual composition in colour of wiggling lines, hatching, blobs jellying about, whirling shapes and stencil punches, based on the soft greeny-blues of Dufaycolor, it makes a gay and light-hearted, eye- and breath-catching little film.

In the same year Lye and Ellit had made *Kaleidoscope* for Churchman's cigarettes, also to a beguine, and both films immediately attracted the favourable attention of artistic and critical circles. Quick as usual, Grierson acquired *A Colour Box* for the G.P.O. and the words "G.P.O. – CHEAPER PARCEL POST", with the prices, were superimposed towards the end of the film. It was trade shown as a G.P.O. film in January 1937.

Meanwhile in 1936 they made an advertising film for Shell-Mex and B.P., *The Birth of the Robot*, which also credits "colour directed and produced by Humphrey Jennings". It uses animated models filmed in rich jewel-like Gasparcolor, with elaborate lighting by the Austrian cameraman Alex Strasser, and accompanied by part of "The Planets" by Holst. It makes use of a mechanical figure already used by Shell as their "sign of Lubrication". A once-upon-a time beginning shows Old Father Time making the planets go round by turning an ancient machine like a mangle. We see a motorist in a sandstorm, his car runs out of oil, he dies, Venus weeps and her tears turn to oil. The robot is born. The world-turning is mechanised. The film ends with a famous image of the robot's shadow looming over the globe.

This film, somewhat longer than the others at 630 feet, was shown at the Film Society in April 1936 and confirmed Len Lye's reputation. Like Humphrey Jennings, he was associated with the important Surrealist Exhibition held in London that year, and besides writing avant-garde poems in *Life and Letters Today* he wrote about his work in terms which show him to have been as theoretical as he was original. Writing in the spring of 1936 about possible relationships of colour to voice, he envisages "voice-and-colour film" and outlines possible experiments:

> . . . a type of sensory ballet, consisting of words, pictorial shapes and sound knit into a film continuity in such a way that any one of these elements could become dominant in turn, in the rendering of the sense definitions in it . . . it is certain that a good colour accompaniment can enhance the reception of any word arrangement presented as speech.[72]

As an artist and sculptor, writer and film-maker, he was an all-rounder like Jennings, and it is interesting that these two extremely intellectual people should have made some of the most delightful and appealing films, easy for ordinary people to understand and enjoy.

By now Grierson had taken Len Lye and Jack Ellit under his wing and the next film, *Rainbow Dance*, was given the full resources of the Unit with a production credit to Basil Wright and Cavalcanti, and Jonah Jones on the camera. Only 357 feet, it was perhaps the most explosive and brilliant of all the films and a great success when it was shown in late 1936. Once more to Caribbean music, it begins with a colour-changing rainbow for the credits, and then a live-action City Man, complete with umbrella, seen in positive or negative silhouette in the animated rain; the sun comes out and he dances in the sunshine, leaving successive images of himself on screen as echoes, as a hiker, as a tennis-player and in various holiday occupations; we see symbolic representations of fish, boats, a tennis court surrealistically sporting a Belisha beacon; and towards the end of the film a voice says "The Post Office Savings Bank puts a pot of gold at the end of the rainbow".

Turning back from puppets to the direct manipulation of a two-dimensional image, but in a far more ambitious and elaborate way than in *A Colour Box*, Lye wrote several times in explanation of the technicalities of this film. Its purpose was to use the three layers of dye – pink, yellow and blue – of the Gasparcolor film, and by attempting to get away from literary values use them in colour-flow composition as a stimulus to sensation. The things photographed were all painted in black, white or grey, and a black-and-white camera was used with no colour filters. To quote Vesselo :

The three colour-separation records are produced, not by photo-graphing with filters from a coloured original, but by arranging the separate records deliberately in varying black-and-white densities, determined entirely according to the colour which they will assume in combination in the final print.[73]

And Lye wrote :

This method of colour control meant that our colour would be clean and not suffer from any opacity of photographic colour light. In other words, an artist separated the colours instead of leaving it to the colour filters. So that all colours for the objects were pure colours achieved without the necessity of reproducing the colours of different pigmentation by the colour dyes of the film stock.[74]

Colour was brought under the artist's direct control and the whole design was conceived and composed in terms of the Gasparcolor dyes. Further, the coloured components were in places "deliberately combined out of synchronisation, so that one image of one colour is accompanied by others of different colours going through the motions the first has performed or is about to perform".[75] The moving images, especially the ballet movements of dancer Rupert Doone, leave echoes of themselves as the dancer moves away. In the *World Film News* article Lye tabulates his "aspects of colour treatment" thus : (1) three-dimensional colour-flow between the colour of moving objects and their background emphasise the relation between the two; (2) the use of unnatural colour to emphasise the fantasy element; (3) moving object remaining in one-dimensional plane but use of colour changes of spatial depths of intensity to indicate movements in depth; (4) moving objects leaving successive images of themselves in graduated colour, as echoes; (5) abstract colour sensations synchronised with music; (6) "sour" colour to offset bright "saturation" of colour.[76]

Individual artistic experiment is necessarily rare in the cinema. We see how Grierson's way of welcoming any talent, however unlikely, could lead to results which were unhappy in the case of Flaherty and rather eccentric in the case of Moholy-Nagy, far-sighted in the case of Norman McLaren and Richard Massingham and controversial in the case of Cavalcanti. But in the case of Len Lye and Ellit he is seen at his best, throwing his usual seriousness to the winds and supporting one of the few experimental and exciting techniques in the cinema.

Lye's next animated film, again with the carefully edited syn-chronisation by Ellit to Caribbean music, was *Trade Tattoo*. This time in Technicolor, it carried on the combination of animation with lab-treated live film. Beginning with disorientating effects of film slipping in the gate and ragged cuts, it went on without using voices, and rammed home the message to post early in the day with beautifully shifting graphics and simple written tags, with an emphasis on rhythm :

The rhythm of work-a-day Britain
The furnaces are fired
Cargoes are loaded
By the power of correspondence
The rhythm of trade is maintained by the mails
Keep in rhythm by posting early
You must post early to keep in rhythm.

Lye made several more films[77] such as *Full Fathom Five*, which according to *Life and Letters Today* included the speech from *The Tempest* spoken by John Gielgud, *Conga*,[78] and later *Swinging the Lambeth Walk*. Made in Dufaycolor for T.I.D.A. in 1939, the last seems to be a purely experimental film with no justifying tag, although presumably this popular song from a successful current show was believed by T.I.D.A. to have a public relations value for Britain. In 330 gorgeous and joyful feet it uses the optical printer and colour matts to give visual accompaniment to the well-known tune of the title, played not in the stage and film convention of big dance bands but in the manner of Django Reinhardt and the Quintette du Hot Club de France. In soft brown and greens, cream and maroons, bars, fans and geometrical shapes, lines waving or plucking, soft blobs and stars all undulate and flash in synchronisation with the music, and the film ends with a representation of a hand with thumb uplifted in the traditional "Oi !"

But back to more serious matters. Certainly the most renowned film of these years was *Nightmail*, which was registered in March 1936. It was theatrically distributed and was a deserved success, arousing much comment among critics and intellectuals and acquiring a lasting reputation as one of the finest achievements of the Grierson days. Much has been written about it. It shows the special postal express train from Euston to Glasgow, collecting and delivering mail through the night and sorting it on the way, and perhaps the two most famous sequences are the dramatic one in which a heavy mail pouch is taken aboard from where it hangs on a post, by way of a net extended with split-second timing from the rushing train, and the final sequence as the train nears its destination, up Beattock and down into Scotland : the hills and dales are pale in the dawn, a dog runs, rabbits, telephone lines, faster and faster and more lively and then down into Glasgow. All this latter section is accompanied by verse written by W. H. Auden to match the already edited film. Music was by Britten, who like Auden had worked on the earlier sound experiment *Coalface*.[79] The words, it seems, were spoken by Stuart Legg and Grierson himself. There was comparatively little commentary. A sequence in the railway carriage where the letters were sorted was actually reconstructed in the studio and shot as sound film. It seems they could not afford a rocker unit to simulate the motion of the train and Harry Watt has spoken with pride of how they suggested it ingeniously with swaying string and the like, and achieved "absolute verisimilitude",[80] although in fact Vesselo in *Sight and Sound* at the time made special reference to unsatisfactory measures taken to simulate the train's vibration. Let it also be confessed that in this patronising review Vesselo was especially doubtful about the "jog trot rhythms recited towards the end". Seen today the film is fast, interesting and still an exhilarating experience, and this is at least partly due to the use of sound, mostly recorded on location and laid over. Throughout the film the feeling of the train tearing through the silent sleeping countryside is emphasised by unobtrusive but evocative noises, the signalman phoning "Can you take the postal special?", a shriek and rush of sound past the solitary passenger waiting at a station, the rattle on the criss-crossing rails, the shouts and short exchanges between rail and postal workers all over the country. It rises to a climax after the stop at Crewe, with the run down into Scotland and the verse commentary :

> This is the night mail crossing the border,
> Bringing the cheque and the postal order,
> Letters for the rich, letters for the poor,
> The shop at the corner and the girl next door. . . .

The film was an achievement of the whole unit, well conceived in the first place although the final verse passage which added so much to it was an afterthought, beautifully shot and directed with warmth, observation and interest in the people, as well as considerable technical verve and experiment in the actual filming. It was brilliantly put together, especially in the overall use of a sound-track of absolutely crucial importance to the total effect. Alas, the subsequent difference of opinion as to who did what indicate once more the absurdity of trying to fit the teamwork of this Unit into the conventional credits of producer, director and so on. Versions differed. At least on one copy of the film, apparently the first, 'it read strangely : "Produced by Basil Wright and Harry Watt, Sound direction Cavalcanti, Auden and Britten." Harry Watt, young and ambitious and given a chance at last, certainly directed almost all of it and today no one seems to deny that the interest in people which he was to show so clearly in his later films was already present, and affected the way in which he shot it. In his book he clearly states that he wrote a full treatment, having been given only a rough outline.[81] Basil Wright is equally clear, in the nicest possible way, that he had written a shooting script which was given to Watt and that he, Basil Wright, became producer under Grierson and Cavalcanti and "the film as it was finished (up to the Auden–Britten section, which was an afterthought, anyhow) more or less followed the shape of the script I'd written".[82] Watt admits he was not keen on the idea of the contribution by Auden, which was suggested by Grierson, Cavalcanti and Wright, but agreed later that in this he had been mistaken. It seems likely that a row Basil Wright remembers as having taken place over the verse section was in fact more due to, or at least aggravated by, Watt's angry disappointment when he discovered he had not been given an outright credit for direction. Whatever the truth, it would seem fair to say that it was written in the first place by Basil Wright, with subsequent interpretation by Harry Watt and with Grierson exercising his usual overall influence, that it was almost entirely directed by Watt with the assistance of young Pat Jackson, that it was shot by Jonah Jones and Chick Fowle and that the vital editing by Basil Wright and R. Q. McNaughton was of course inextricably bound up with the "sound supervision" of Cavalcanti. It is sad that such an achievement should have caused such sour reverberations. Watt goes so far as to say that he never forgave Grierson for the denial of a clear credit for direction, and that the only reason he did not leave the Unit was that there was nowhere else to go.[83] The splendid isolation of Rotha was not for him, it seems.

Anyway, he fared better with his next film, *The Saving of Bill Blewitt*. It was a plain assignment to make a film to popularise National Savings Stamps and the Post Office Savings Bank, an apparently routine subject, but this time he wrote it all himself. And with this script he consciously and deliberately steered documentary in a new direction, towards the story or anecdotal film. Shot at the Cornwall fishing-village of Mousehole and played by local people, it tells a simple story about two fishermen and how they lose their fishing boat when it drags its anchor; they have to take paid work, Jo on a drifter and Bill in a quarry. Bill Blewitt played himself, but Jo Jago, brother-in-law to cameraman George Noble, was a member of the Unit and later became a cameraman himself. Both save from their pitifully small earnings, Jo in the Post Office and Bill in the National Savings Association. After two years they have a down payment of £50 and are able to buy a boat and go back to sea as their own masters. Watt explains how Cavalcanti was of great assistance to him as associate producer, partly no doubt in the new exercise of getting genuine performances out of people, but most of all in the whole new concept of fiction production, in which continuity was no longer governed by actuality. The story is built up quietly in fragments making few demands on his amateur players. Music, the natural sounds of the wind, sea, gulls and the local accents and idiom combine with camerawork by Jonah Jones and S. Onions of the sea and ever-changing light in the creation of a sense of atmosphere. There is no commentary until half-way through this three-reel film and then but little. Instead, there is considerable characterisation of the people, particularly of Bill, who blunders by accident into the Savings Association on his way to the pub and is too embarrassed to get out. It was Watt's last film before Grierson left the unit. From now on Watt, with Cavalcanti behind him, was in favour of fictional anecdotes to dramatise the message of the film, and ultimately, of course, he went into the realist or documentary feature film. Original, beautifully made, it again had Pat Jackson as assistant and music by Benjamin Britten.[84]

His next film *Big Money* was also in the September 1937 catalogue as available after October, presumably produced by Cavalcanti soon after Grierson's departure. Edited and co-directed

13 Night workers at
Crewe station
(*Nightmail*, 1936).

14 J. B. Priestley says
"Nowadays . . . we
live in two worlds"
(*We Live in Two
Worlds*, 1937).

15 An environment
without beauty
(*Today we Live*,
1936).

by Pat Jackson, with a modernist score by Brian Easdale, it was about the finances of the G.P.O. It moves at a spanking pace and the shots of Post Office counters, the City, the Ministries, shipping, airways and sorting offices are imaginative, brightly and freshly photographed by Jones and Fowle; but the commentary, which starts at once and is almost continuous, carries the whole message. Watt's desire to suggest personality appears only late in the film and it would seem that this was a routine assignment.

As for Cavalcanti, with John Taylor as cameraman he went to Switzerland in 1936 and as a result the G.P.O., with the co-operation of Pro Telephon, Zürich, made a series of Swiss films which were all reviewed together in the summer of 1937. Cavalcanti's *Message from Geneva* was a short film about how "our observer" at the League of Nations can give a B.B.C. broadcast by way of the Post Office land-lines; it is a workmanlike film affording scope for a subtle and assured sound-track, with nations talking across the countrysides. *Line to Tschierva Hut*, a single-reel directed, written and edited by Cavalcanti with music by Jaubert, and according to the titles on the film produced by Grierson, was also made in 1936 and is reputed to be Cavalcanti's favourite of the set, a nice, smooth, good-to-look-at film, short and to the point, an honest phone film with no particular social significance but beautifully made and with Cavalcanti's mastery of sound at its most mature. It concerns the installation of a telephone line in a mountaineering hut near Pontresina. At the beginning a subscriber tries to contact the hut and discovers from the telephonists that it is not on the phone. After this there is no speech, but a casual commentary alternating with natural sound and Swiss-motif music. The installation of the strengthened telephone poles and lines in this difficult but superb Alpine terrain ends when we see the hut keeper answering his new phone. A longer and much more showy, even pretentious, film was *We Live in Two Worlds*. It would appear that this was edited from surplus footage from the Swiss trip, written and narrated at Grierson's request by the popular novelist and general pontificator J. B. Priestley. Cavalcanti is credited as director, however, having shot additional footage of bluff Jack as well as once again providing a brilliant sound-track which is extremely intricate. Sub-titled "A Film Talk with J. B. Priestley", it starts with him in a plump armchair, puffing at his pipe and saying "Nowadays, we live in two worlds". His theme is that one world is that of national barriers, which divide us, and the other is the real world which is one, and becoming ever more closely connected by methods of communication. With this ingenious excuse they could use the Swiss material to show how communications aid unity in a small area of differing nationalities, a sort of super travel film with music by Jaubert and using all the resources of cutting, mixes and camera mobility as well as sound flexibility to give it style. Then with a glad cry of "Why, they're taking a telephone line up the mountain" we get material used in *Line to Tschierva Hut*. Towards the end Priestley's voice repeats some of his more telling phrases and these are taken up, repeated and amplified in an echoing double voice. Back to the spinning globe with which he began his talk, and his voice becomes sepulchral as the deep dark sky fills the screen. Two other more routine single-reel films, *Four Barriers* and *Men of the Alps*, appear credited on the film as produced by Harry Watt, and edited variously by the youngsters Pat Jackson, Maurice Harvey or Ralph Elton and with no director, apparently editing jobs of yet more off-cuts, and not mentioned in Watt's autobiography. The first was an account of Swiss economics showing how they had overcome their four barriers of lack of raw materials, the mountains, political and economic nationalism; the second was simply a background film about Swiss history and geography. They must have had less to do with the Post Office than any other film the Unit ever made.

Evelyn Spice had two films. *Calendar of the Year* was a somewhat rapid and cursory collection of such landmarks of the year in Britain as sporting events, entertainment and leisure activities, seaside holidays and Christmas festivities, the import of which was that they relied on the network of communication by post, telegraph and phone. A year in the United Kingdom was thus crammed into 1,500 feet with music by Britten, post-synchronised natural sound and commentary; but perhaps more of Rotha's style of impressionism and less of Grierson's information would have made a more interesting film. This was shown before Grierson left. More enjoyable was her *A Job in a Million*, made just about the time of Grierson's departure, although he is on the film as producer. Here music was by Brian Easdale, and editing by young Norman McLaren. A sympathetic and warm director, she is seen to advantage in this small film of the selection, training and general schooling of a Post Office messenger. It is noticeable that the two women directors, Evelyn Spice and Ruby Grierson, were particularly good at getting natural performances out of their subjects. The humble and anxious position of the 14-year-old boys, the brisk kind posh ladies of the Vocational Guidance with their emphasis on how lucky the undersized nipper John Truman is to have been selected, the pep talk about what a great service the boys belong to and how they are responsible for its good name, all imply values long gone, and make this very much more like a piece of social history than a mere film about training.

Young William Coldstream followed *The King's Stamp* of 1935 with a very different production in 1936, *The Fairy of the Phone*. This was a humorous little film produced by Basil Wright, in which formal instructions to the public are conveyed playfully by means of fantasy. "Obsolete directories should be discarded" say the instructions, and a heap of fat volumes rises and floats out of the window. Twelve pretty girl switchboard-operators in frilly white collars sing sweetly at their switchboards :

> Just telephone,
> And we will put you through.

The fairy, actress Charlotte Leigh, appears and disappears as she guides us through the rules, and dainty fairy music alternates with atmospheric in a score by Walter Leigh. It is the sort of film people either find charming and imaginative or despise as facetious, and Rotha dismisses it as meretricious.[85] It was certainly unusual for the documentary movement. Coldstream's next, produced by Cavalcanti and co-directed by Legg, was very different. It seems to have been initiated before Grierson left but was not shown until after October 1937. *Roadways* was nominally about the G.P.O. stores, but from its opening sequence of lorries loading, weighing up and starting off, with a sound-track of instructions, loading figures and atmospheric industrial music, it turns into a general picture of life on the roads. Ambulances, bikes, picnics, traffic of all kinds, with the structure of traffic control and the new concrete by-passes, it gives an incidental look at life in mid-thirties Britain which is far more evocative than the deliberate picture in *Calendar of the Year*. The music, which made an important contribution to the film with its dissonances and odd rhythms, was by Ernest Meyer, who had recently arrived from Germany and had a special interest in the combination of music and sound effects.

Finally, apart from the usual minor and anonymous items, Norman McLaren joined the Unit under the aegis of Grierson. At this period of his career he was a junior member of the team and made two small films which did not appear until well after Grierson had left the Unit, *Book Bargains* and *News for the Navy*, which are discussed later.

The middle years of 1934 to 1937 were a time when directions began to change, but the documentary boys were still very conscious of themselves as a group. The word "documentary" began to seem inadequate and imprecise, and efforts were made to give the word "realist" greater currency. The need to organise, to keep the movement together despite a growing diversification, led to the formation of a body called Associated Realist Film Producers, which was registered in December 1935 with £100 capital by Elton, Anstey, Donald Taylor and Paul Rotha.[86] Others associated with it included Marion Grierson, J. B. Holmes, Basil Wright and, surprisingly, Andrew Buchanan. Grierson and musician Walter Leigh figured as "consultants" along with such popular pundits of the day as the scientists J. B. S. Haldane, mathematician Lancelot Hogben, naturalist Julian Huxley, designer McKnight Kauffer and architect Basil Ward.[87] A.R.F.P. was intended to consolidate and promote the documentary movement, and provide a consultancy service to put bodies wishing to sponsor a film in touch with film makers. Such bodies might be official, as it had been established that the G.P.O. Film Unit was not the natural channel for official films. But after the success of Rotha's *Shipyard* and the Elton–Anstey *Housing Problems*, it was realised that even greater scope, and certainly greater freedom to criticise the *status quo*, might be obtained from commercial sponsorship. It is interesting to speculate that had the Select Committee's report not confined the G.P.O. Film Unit to Post Office subjects it might have been fully occupied with official films and left the development of the commercial field to others such as Rotha.

Both Grierson and Rotha were indefatigable writers and talkers on behalf of the movement, but so were many other members of it, and indeed one of the activities of A.R.F.P. was to supply lecturers. The earliest serious film magazine in this country had been the Pool publication *Close Up* edited by Kenneth Macpherson, along with his wealthy wife Bryher, Oswell Blakeston and the London correspondent Robert Herring, who became film critic for the newspaper *The Manchester Guardian*. But this rather precious magazine died at the end of 1933. In the autumn of 1932 the two-year-old Edinburgh Film Guild, with its moving spirits Forsyth Hardy and Norman Wilson, started *Cinema Quarterly*, which ran until the summer of 1935 and, with its foreign correspondents and reviews and articles, many of them by members of the documentary movement, for a while had almost a monopoly of serious writing about films. *Film Art*, founded in 1933 by B. V. Braun and Irene Nicholson and published irregularly for a few years from Chelsea, was comparatively unimportant. Naturally as documentaries began to appear it was in *Cinema Quarterly* that they were most sure of receiving attention, and it is here, also, that some rather fratricidal reviews of each other's work appeared, with Grierson rapping knuckles like a true dominie. *Sight and Sound*, the British Film Institute journal, pre-dated *Cinema Quarterly* by only a few months and in fact was taken over by the B.F.I. slightly later. But it was staid and conventional in comparison, and long remained more interested in educational films than in documentary. Outside the film world, from December 1934 *Life and Letters*, a literary magazine started in 1928 and edited by Desmond MacCarthy and later Hamish Miles, with some very distinguished literary contributors, started regular but anonymous film reviews and articles which took a viewpoint more like that of the deceased *Close Up*, that is, the attitude of a highbrow but sympathetic outsider rather than that of one involved in production. In 1933 this was bought by the Brendin Press and was thereafter edited by Robert Herring and Petrie Townshend, being called *Life and Letters Today* from September 1935, and many of the old Pool writers on film reappeared in it. Like the writers of *Cinema Quarterly* and *Film Art* they devoted considerable attention to documentaries, but their attitude was very different. On the whole they disliked the Grierson high fliers and preferred the style of Gaumont-British Instructional, with the exception of Len Lye and Humphrey Jennings, who were both very much at home in the world of modern art and were greatly admired by Herring. With the assistance of Basil Wright's wealthy family, money was found by the Grierson group to breathe new life into *Cinema Quarterly*. A larger and much more social and political monthly, *World Film News*, consequently appeared in April 1936. It was less literary and arty and more like a political weekly, with coverage of current events in the film industry and cartoons by the young cartoonist Vicky. In a way it was like a very intelligent trade paper. Nominal editors changed but the spirit of Grierson was everywhere, and his young film-makers might at any moment be required to research, report or write for it. Films and the film industry as a whole were its subject, but it gave a good deal of its attention to documentary, as well as to the film societies. An austere advertising policy and a certain amount of administrative chaos lay behind its collapse in November 1938, but before it died it had an offshoot of which members of the movement have since been exaggeratedly proud. This was the appearance in early 1937 of a book called *Money Behind the Screen*, researched by Stuart Legg and written by a young Communist art historian, sociologist and writer called J. D. Klingender.[88] This consisted of a mass of information, more or less uncollated and uninterpreted, concerning shareholdings and directorships in the film industry. The information was not confidential and it must have been clear to any but the most naïve that a business as large as the film industry must get its capital from somewhere, and that the pattern of directorships would reflect its origin. However, the book drew apparently scandalised attention to the interlocking nature of much of the industry and its links with big business and was regarded as an exposé. There had recently been a most unhealthy expansion of the feature industry, financed by unsound financial manœuvres involving banks and insurance underwriters. Large sums of money were invested in production without adequate safeguards, and in the nature of things this was bound to lead to a crisis when the films concerned failed to make money or, in some cases, even to be made at all. The collapse duly occurred, and has been held by enthusiasts to have been precipitated by the Klingender and Legg book.

From now on, changes were to take place in the style of the documentary films produced by the mainstream of the movement.

In the earliest days this style had been influenced by the silent Russian films, both because Grierson had cut his teeth on them and because the compilation work and the absence of sound facilities at the E.M.B. Film Unit put a premium on silent film techniques. The early attempts at post-synchronisation with other firms' equipment and the passing visit of Flaherty did nothing to change this basic approach. The extremely serious Grierson saw Flaherty as the father of documentary, already of an earlier generation, but deplored his interest in the remote and primitive, preferring what he saw as the Russian attitude of public education. The father-figure was in fact rejected by the movement at this time. The South African David Schrire's attack on what he saw as idyllic or evasive documentary in 1934, describing it as a positive hindrance to the growth of documentary, called up only a half-hearted defence by Grierson. He simply said that one must not be "disrespectful of a great artist and a great teacher".[89] Yet in a way his own preoccupation with the dignity of the working man was as emotional and romantic as Flaherty's interest in the primitive.

Because the move to the G.P.O. and Blackheath, with its acquisition of sound, had coincided with the arrival of Cavalcanti there had been a ferment of experiment and the development of a very advanced counterpoint sound-track. At the same time the Unit had flirted with fantasy. But from the time of Harry Watt's success with Bill Blewitt onwards, the possibility of an alternative, more narrative approach to documentary was to play an important part in the movement.

From the beginning, when *One Family* had shown a tour of the Empire by centring on one little boy's adventurous trip and *Drifters* on the other hand had been impersonal, individual films had differed in the degree to which they stressed particular protagonists. Wright's *O'er Hill and Dale* of 1932, for example, had shown the shepherd Martin in his lonely work in the hills and in bringing the stray lamb back to his home where he and his wife warmed it in the stove, a personal treatment which lingers in the memory. It would, however, be impossible to call either this or *One Family* a story or anecdote in any but the widest sense. Outside the mainstream an amateur film of 1932, *Black Diamonds*, had tried to hang a description of the dangers of coal mining and a plea for better conditions on a rudimentary story theme, and in 1933 Dand's "dramatic reconstruction" *Men Against Death*, another independent film, set against the background of Welsh slate quarrying, had done the same and had been favourably noticed by Grierson. In both cases, a desire to tell the world what life was really like in two dangerous occupations, combined with the lack of adequate resources, had led to production being carried on as far as possible in real settings, but the films were moral tales rather than documentaries. But stories now began to creep into mainstream documentary as well, by way of fictional anecdotes concerning identifiable people who were acted, whether by professional actors or simply by the kind of people the story was about. In *Cinema Quarterly* in the summer of 1933 Grierson had referred to J. N. Davidson's *Hen Woman* as the E.M.B.'s only story documentary.[90] Davidson had apparently been sacked[91] and the film never finished. But three G.P.O. story films appeared in 1934. Two of them, not unexpectedly, were connected with Cavalcanti's influence. But one was credited to the steady Elton, not normally given to flights of fancy. His treatment of the subject of the Post Office Savings Bank *John Atkins Saves Up* was described as a romantic comedy and had actors as well as a commentary. Cavalcanti's *The Glorious Sixth of June* and *Pett and Pott*, as we have seen, were whimsical concoctions complete with elementary plots and denouements. In 1936 Rotha's *Death on the Road*, also, was described as a drama. But Harry Watt's Savings Bank film about Bill Blewitt was much more elaborate. It was immensely successful, and finally made it clear that stories were a viable alternative to the information film as a way of getting a message across. He, Cavalcanti himself and Pat Jackson were all to prove increasingly interested in the use of human interest to involve the audience and make their point rather than plain exposition. This later led easily into the documentary drama, or a story set against a background of apparent realism.

Meanwhile a different, and opposed, development was taking place. While the experimental films made deliberately to get the hang of sound had been fun, most members of the group had extremely serious aims and did not go along with Cavalcanti towards drama and human involvement with such enthusiasm as Harry Watt did. Some even felt that Cavalcanti was not wholeheartedly in sympathy with the aims of the documentary movement.

When these more earnest members of the movement mastered sound they used it for quite a different purpose. It was their ambition to show the working man as he really was, and once the facility existed they were bound to let him speak as well. Recording the casual and apparently spontaneous speech of the subject of the film in action or interviewing him on location in his own surroundings were two possibilities developed in this country by Elton and Anstey. *Cable Ship*, a group film of 1933 which owed a lot to Stuart Legg, had already used the voices of two repair men to explain what they were doing on the screen, as post-synchronised voice-over commentary, before the unit had its own sound facilities at all. "That's me on the left," one of them remarks, recording in the studio afterwards. But the key film was *Workers and Jobs*, made by Elton for the Ministry of Labour. Elton was still with the G.P.O. but the film was made separately and shot by the Korda cameraman Osmond Borrodaile, apparently about 1934–5; it was shown at the Film Society in March 1935. As we have seen, Elton used the unemployed and officials of the Poplar Labour Exchange to show the work of the exchanges in action, not by silent shooting and a commentary as had been done so often before, but by taking the microphone out on location. Thus, although the film was not considered an important one, it was a forerunner of *Housing Problems*, which carried the technique very much further.

Workers and Jobs and *Housing Problems*, as we have seen, must have been conceived if not completely made before *The March of Time* could have had any influence on Elton or Anstey. But when *The March of Time* did come, with its tremendous publicity and backing, its new style of screen journalism reporting on controversial problems, it was credited with rather more influence than it had. Writing after seeing *Housing Problems* late in 1935, Robert Herring referred to it as "following the *March of Time* method".[92] If by this he meant the location sound recording of ordinary people putting their point of view, this was not in fact very characteristic of *The March of Time*. Elton and Anstey included it because they now had the technical facilities and because it suited their own purpose, rather than because of American influence. Nor was the appearance, from now on, of a stream of important investigative documentaries of social problems simply to be ascribed to American leadership. Social purpose had been an integral part of the movement from the beginning. Rotha's social comment in *Shipyard* was the true forerunner of the reflective British approach, and it was the adoption of enlightened commercial sponsorship by the gas industry at this time, with its liberal interpretation of prestige publicity, that made the production of these films possible rather than the *March of Time*'s example, which was more political than social.

The real change in the British documentary movement brought by *The March of Time* was the abandonment of the vestiges of the early visual editing for an entirely literary style, the editing of shots accompanied neither by their recorded sound nor by sound counterpoint but made to fit a commentary bearing the burden of the message. Much of the documentary movement was greatly influenced by this, but not all. Not everybody liked the new technique. Harry Watt, for example, who made items for *The March of Time* himself, worked out his own style in the opposite direction.

(iii)　Maturity

The movement had now been going long enough, and was big enough, to be showing divergent tendencies. In June 1937 Grierson left the G.P.O. Film Unit and, together with Elton, Legg and his administrative assistant J. F. R. Golightly, set up a new body called Film Centre.[93]

It is tempting to dramatise the split as a difference of opinion between Grierson, with his growing preference for the non-theatrical market and the film lecture, and Cavalcanti, who because of his belief that a film should always be interesting and entertaining enough to get into the cinemas was glad to encourage the narrative or dramatic documentary. The picture of the fun- and art-loving Latin face to face with the Scottish missionary and teacher may not be entirely a fiction. Donald Taylor of Strand, frankly commercial, in his letter to *Kine Weekly* in May 1937 wrote that an acceptable documentary might run three to six weeks in London, and get from 400 to 1,200 subsequent theatrical bookings, providing

exhibitors with an alternative to a bad second feature and a way
of varying and adjusting cinema programmes.[94] And certainly in
the next few years with the arrival of the shorts quota in 1938 many
moved in the direction of a commercialism quite antipathetic to
Grierson. While expanding the non-theatrical market, Grierson
films were increasingly shown in the cinemas as well, but from now
on the difference in style between the gravely polemical and the
tempting entertainment which improved its viewer by stealth
became more marked.

Rotha describes Grierson's reasons for leaving the G.P.O. as
"clouded".[95] It seems unlikely that there was an open row, but the
aims and inclinations and presumably the temperaments of Grierson
and Cavalcanti were so different that in the end they would have
had to go different ways. One might perhaps expect the autocrat
to oust the artist rather than the other way around. But in fact
the obligation to stick to Post Office subjects was too confining for
Grierson, and he must have been searching for a way to circumvent
it. It was not as if they were the only producers in the field. There
were always plenty of industrial competitors for the new contracts
from official and big commercial sponsors. The first body formed
to promote the movement as a separate entity and prevent it from
being stifled in the Post Office while interesting contracts went to
commercial film-makers had of course been Associated Realist Film
Producers in 1935. Although it had not produced films itself, it had
been prepared to lend directors.

Things moved quickly. There, in 1936, had Grierson been,
limited by the rules to Post Office subjects, whilst the Strand company had already started and Rotha had contacts of his own. It
must have been clear to Grierson that there was enormous scope
in the field of commercial sponsorship. The start of the new Realist
Film Unit seemed to have been closely connected with this.
Grierson's original intention was for Cavalcanti, Basil Wright and
John Taylor to start a new unit late in 1936, to undertake commercial assignments. Doubtless Realist would have been in the
market for contracts but under Grierson's influence, perhaps through
A.R.F.P., in a way that Strand and Rotha were not. In the end,
however, Cavalcanti stayed at the G.P.O. and in 1937 Grierson left
it, not to run Realist but to form a new organisation to mastermind

the whole expansion. Thus he formed Film Centre, in the same building in Soho Square as A.R.F.P. but dominated by him in a way that would have been impossible with the earlier and more democratic body, which gradually withered away. At the same time Realist was formed, also in the same building, by Basil Wright and later John Taylor. This left Cavalcanti, with J. B. Holmes as director of productions, in charge at the G.P.O. Film Centre was to act as professional adviser on all matters relating to films and as consultants, advising sponsors, arranging and supervising production and distribution, as well as undertaking reports and opening up the field in other ways. It took over the gas industry and Shell business from A.R.F.P. The latter was dissolved as a limited company, being re-formed as a loose society meant simply to co-ordinate the movement.[96] In reality it was left more or less high and dry, although it did continue in existence for a few more years as a public relations body with meetings and a panel of lecturers, no longer necessarily connected with the movement, and with a professed aim of watching over the interests of the group. Although Rotha, Basil Wright, Harry Watt and Arthur Elton remained members, others like Shaw, Evelyn Spice, Marion Grierson, Stuart Legg and John Taylor left it.[97]

Taylor joined Realist at the end of 1937 after making *Dawn of Iran* for Strand. From Film Centre, Grierson kept Realist supplied with valuable assignments and was a power behind the new unit, which used studios in Marylebone. Its output was comparatively small but included some very important films and, although Basil Wright, like Rotha a director at heart, did much of the producing, he was also able to direct two notable films, *Children at School* and *The Face of Scotland*, whilst Taylor made *The Smoke Menace*. Cinematography was mainly by A. E. Jeakins.

Grierson flung himself into the work and a number of the more important documentaries of the next few years were arranged through Film Centre, including several for the gas industry and a series about Scotland. The Films of Scotland Committee was formed in 1937 by the Scottish Development Council. A programme of promotional films financed by government and industry were made for the Committee by Realist, Strand, G-BI and Pathé, planned and co-ordinated by Film Centre. Grierson and Basil Wright also wrote a report on *The Possibilities of the Production and Distribution of Films by the International Labour Organisation, Geneva*, for that body in 1937[98] and an eloquent account by Grierson of what they suggested was published in *Adult Education*.[99] Briefly, the idea was to circulate amongst member countries films of the best developments in industrial welfare from each of them. Grierson wrote and lectured as tirelessly as ever, developing the non-theatrical market and acting as Film Adviser to the Imperial Relations Trust, the International Wool Secretariat, Shell and The Times Publishing Company.[100]

Meanwhile the new company of Strand was always busy. On the strength of a £5,000 contract from Imperial Airways, a unit left England late in 1936 on a 35,000-mile journey and returned in March 1937 with some 50,000 feet of film. The chief production made from this was *The Future's in the Air*, but *Air Outpost* was also made on the way back and some lesser air films appeared later. In addition, on the way home two other films were made for other sponsors through Film Centre, *Five Faces* for the Federated Malay States and *Dawn of Iran* for Anglo-Iranian Oil. *Watch and Ward in the Air* was made for Imperial Airways at home. All five main films were distributed theatrically. According to a reference in *Film Art* the company was also responsible for some scientific work for the Air Ministry.[101]

The main film, *The Future's in the Air*, which appeared towards the end of 1937, was produced by Rotha and directed by Shaw with photography by George Noble. It was made to celebrate the inauguration of the Empire Air Mail and had a commentary written by Graham Greene. Thus with music by William Alwyn, his first for films, it was an illustrious and auspicious production. The stillness of the first sequence, waiting in the outback of Australia, titled "January 1937", shows an isolated air-strip in the glaring heat, desultory and silent except for the cricket commentary on the radio; a title "Four days later" and, with "Waltzing Matilda" on the accordion, through the same heat and emptiness we hear at last the drone of the plane; it lands, and a chap strolls over to the shed with the letters. On we go with the plane, over mountains and rivers. It is not until here that the commentary begins. Superb overhead shots of sea and air take us on a journey eastwards from

Southampton, Alwyn's lyrical, soaring, lifting and rippling music weaving with the commentary; at each further stage towards the East with its bazaars and temples the music becomes more exotic. The brilliant light of the Gulf, the craggy Afghans, coolie women at work on Karachi building sites, majestic Ankor Vat all add up to a travelogue by the best people with the best of reasons, the best of facilities, and wipe out the disappointments and frustrations attending the production of *Contact*.

Air Outpost was directed by John Taylor, who also photographed it, and Ralph Keene, and again had music by Alwyn. It was ostensibly about a stop at Sharjah, an airport and city on the Persian Gulf. The countryside was a gift and the young cameraman-director was fascinated by it, taking the opportunity to make a lovely, small, quiet film with very little commentary.

On the way home from Australia after *The Future's in the Air,* Shaw stopped in Malaya and made *Five Faces* for the Federated Malay States, on the theme of the five different races and cultures living together in harmony in this area. According to Graham Greene it made imaginative use of existing ruins and old prints,[102] and Rotha also speaks of it with approval.[103] Meanwhile Taylor, who was in the Middle East, made a film for the Anglo-Iranian Oil Company arranged through Arthur Elton at Film Centre, which he directed, shot and edited in what Rotha again calls *The March of Time* style.[104] Music with a suggestion of the Persian was by Walter Leigh. Called on the film *Dawn of Iran . . . Dawn in the East . . . The Story of Modern Iran,*[105] it begins with the crowds waiting in February 1937 for the Shah to open the first railway in Iran, and then tells by means of the commentary something of the history of the country and how it had been modernised since the early twenties by Reza Khan. As a cameraman Taylor again made full use of his opportunities, and from the mosques and minarets, the dramatic black clouds and flaming flares of the oil, the steel and concrete, and celebratory marching youth, Abadan with its fantastic industrial installations and tankers it is a film that is photographed handsomely but without personal involvement. His aloofness and preference for a heavy commentary was in accord with his dedication to the information ideal. One of the most famous and haunting sequences is that in the desert, when the words of Darius accompany shots of the broken columns and bas-reliefs of Persepolis lying in the dusty sand.

Ralph Keene, who had been unit manager on *The Future's in the Air*, also made an Imperial Airways film in 1937 called *Watch and Ward in the Air*, an efficient if not sparkling film about the training of pilots for the flying boat service, ever in touch with Control, the weather man, and the sea captains below them. Another film made somewhat later for Imperial Airways was a compilation on the history of flying called *Aerial Milestones*, interesting if amateur, put together by air experts rather than by film makers. And finally, with all this aerial filming it was perhaps appropriate that Strand should be asked by Korda to rescue his ill-fated film *The Conquest of the Air*. This was done as what Rotha calls a "make-do-and-mend" job by Donald Taylor and Shaw, but the result was not to Korda's satisfaction and was not used.

Meanwhile Rotha produced *Here Is the Land* for the Land Settlement Association in 1937 before going to America in September. This film, also arranged for Strand by Film Centre, was directed by Stanley Hawes and is an interesting two-reeler explaining a national scheme for rehousing unemployed families from depressed areas on rural smallholdings. After an opening sequence on how coal had revolutionised the rural scene and left whole communities unemployed, the bulk of the film shows how a group of men are taught how to farm and their new houses are prepared. There is a joyful sequence at a little country railway station when their families are able to join them, followed by their first year's crops being collected, packed and marketed. With a quiet, intermittent commentary and a little music, the film is interesting for its very natural and unforced conversation from the hard-up families and their instructors as they go about their business. The film is in very different mood from the glossy *Dawn of Iran*. Made for non-theatrical showing, it was later given commercial distribution. It must have been made about the same time as, or just after, *Today We Live*. Rotha does not make much of it in his autobiography but there is a thread of similarity running through these two films and Rotha's own personal film *The Face of Britain*.

It may have been noticed that in each of these three Rotha films we have spoken of an introduction in which a quick résumé is given of a happier and more beautiful rural past, which gives way to the dark, noisy and ugly advent of some form of power, requiring a re-adjustment to bring man back into better harmony with his environment. The fullest and most beautiful of these pastorales is the early sequence in his own film *The Face of Britain*, but all three show a very early concern with a problem which was to grow in importance during later years. From his autobiography it can be seen that Rotha was familiar with the work of writers like Lewis Mumford and that his concern with the environment was not just fortuitous. In so much as it is was an underlying preoccupation it was to prove, perhaps, a more important concept than Grierson's dignified worker.

In September 1937 Rotha went to America to lecture and show documentary films in association with Museum of Modern Art Film Library, which had been formed early the previous year by Iris Barry. The Rockefeller Foundation, which had partly financed the film archive through its General Education Board, gave him a Research Award for five months. He left production in the hands of Stuart Legg, but before he returned he was asked to resign from Strand. He is reticent about the reason, but one can only surmise that there was some friction between him and Donald Taylor. He has suggested that the policy of the company was changing and that Legg was also about to leave, although in fact Legg became a member of the board in January 1938[106] and it was not until considerably later that he left. All the films made in 1938 were produced by Legg, and they included two excellent contributions to the Films of Scotland programme arranged by Film Centre. During the few months after Rotha's departure several other people did also leave, including J. B. Holmes and Ralph Keene. Shaw and Hawes stayed for a while and Evelyn Spice joined, replacing Holmes. The financial backing of Heseltine and A. J. Bott was withdrawn, with consequent difficulties. Legg departed in 1939, leaving the field clear for Donald Taylor with his more theatrical orientation.

The photographer W. B. Pollard made *Duchy of Cornwall* for the Great Western Railway and T.I.D.A. as a Strand film. The company's biggest success of 1938, however, was a series of six animal films made with the co-operation of the Zoological Society of London under the supervision of Julian Huxley, who acted as commentator and appeared in most of them. Put out early in 1938 under the general title *The Animal Kingdom*, they were produced by Legg with music by Alwyn and "sound editing" of some by Jack Ellit; photography was by Jago, Burnford, Noble, Onions and Harry Rignold. Rotha says the series was financed mainly by the Carnegie Trust.[107] With the new quota legislation approaching, which was expected to introduce a shorts quota, there was obviously going to be an opening for popular and entertaining shorts of good quality, and these films, which were distributed by the new company Technique Distributors, were designed to balance real scientific quality with popular appeal. Basically they were biology films, using zoo animals to explain evolutionary development from a single cell to man in size, complexity, feeling, intelligence and independence of environment. One of the best was *Monkey into Man*, directed by Stanley Hawes, with the assistance of the authority on primates, Dr Zuckerman; and Evelyn Spice's *Zoo Babies*, while using fully but without cuteness the endearing qualities of young creatures, showed seriously how the smaller the number of young produced by a species the more helpless they are, and the longer and more careful the rearing process; Alexander's *Mites and Monsters* discussed the factors which limit the physical size of the members of any particular species. Others, such as Spice's *Behind the Scenes* about the administration of the Regent's Park Zoo, Burnford's *Free to Roam* about Whipsnade and Ruby Grierson's *Zoo and You* showing the zoo from the animals' point of view, were lighter and more humorous but still admirably avoided the facetious and sentimental tone of the ordinary interest films. However, they were nearer to the G-BI type of film than to the mainstream documentary and demonstrated the growing divergence of aims between the leadership of Strand and the old Griersonians.

At the end of 1938 the company, under Donald Taylor, merged with a publicity film company at Merton Park Studios and its formal title became Strand Film Company and Strand Film Zoological Productions. There was a second series of animal films, also handled by Technique, which came out during the course of the year from December 1938 to the end of 1939, *Animal Legends*, *Fingers and Thumbs*, *Time of Your Life*, *Animals on Guard*,

Animal Geography and *The Gullible Gull*. In addition *Birth of the Year* was directed by Spice with her lyrical and happy approach, beautifully edited by Jack Ellit and using Dr Ludwig Koch's bird-song recordings as well as music by Alwyn. Despite the slightly heavy opening and closing narration about "Persephone, the Lost Spring Maiden", the film with its lovely images of misty water, rain and umbrellas, animals both big and small stirring, emerging and nesting, looking after their young, and a final shot of a small deer disappearing into a cavern combines the academic care of the G-BI films with a much greater delicacy of approach and an absence of the jocularity to which their attempts to interest the audience so often led.

By now Film Centre, securing the sponsors and handing out the contracts, dominated the field. Rotha, after leaving Strand, was invited by Grierson at the same time as Basil Wright to join its staff for a small guaranteed salary. Any possibility there may have seemed to be that Strand might set up an alternative centre of serious and important documentary activity had been destroyed by the personalities involved. But Grierson could not fail to recognise that Rotha, independent though he might be, was an important and sincere colleague and, though they did not work closely together, Rotha was thus tied in once more to the centre of the movement.

One of Strand's own films which was commercially popular was a very optimistic review of the Navy early in 1939 edited by Ellit from material of Commander Hunt's Educational and General Services, *The British Navy*. But they also continued to get some serious contracts through the good offices of Film Centre. *Speed the Plough*, about the mechanisation of farming, was directed by Hawes but produced by Elton from Film Centre. Also made early in 1939, it was supervised by Professor Scott Watson. The two films made for the Films of Scotland Programme through Film Centre were Donald Alexander's *Wealth of a Nation* and Alex Shaw's *The Children's Story*, both produced by Legg, first shown late in 1938 or at the beginning of 1939 and taken as quota by M-G-M. *The Children's Story*, shot by Jo Jago, was about the Scottish school system and how, since the First World War, Scotland had been thinking about leisure as well as lessons and had aimed to turn out not just scholars but good citizens. Shaw followed the new fashion, and despite excellent visuals the message was conveyed by the commentary. *Wealth of a Nation* was shot by Harry Rignold and Jo Jago with Harry Watt, for once acting as commentator, declaiming in hurrying, ringing, rich tones about "a planned country, and the common good", stressing the need for the Scottish Development Council to plan the economy and welfare services if heavy industry in Scotland was to recover from the Depression. Here, again, Donald Alexander was using the modern journalistic style.

Two final Strand films which appeared after the war began were both directed by Shaw, *Men of Africa* and *These Children Are Safe*. The first was written and produced from Film Centre by Basil Wright for the Colonial Office and is a clear, detailed statement of progress in such things as education, agriculture and medicine brought to the colonial empire, particularly in East Africa, by British administration. Justifying the British presence in Africa, it suggests that the objective had been a population to whom self-government could be safely granted. A thoroughly straightforward, lucid and interesting film, with commentary rather than interview but with the sound-track alive with tribal singing and drumming, it has moments of beauty. The paternal tone was still acceptable in 1939, and is perhaps summed up by a final sequence of long lines of women performing tribal dances, with bright shining faces but their bodies enveloped modestly in ground-length European-style dresses. *These Children Are Safe* shows the wartime evacuation of children with a quiet, cosy, kindly commentary by novelist John Hilton, putting a good face on things for T.I.D.A. Shaw, showing here the warmth and human feeling of which he was capable, made a gay, clear and persuasive film, humorously proud that the evacuation had gone as well as it had. But it is impossible not to read between the lines and here again, post-synchronised with a heavy commentary-burden as it is, one feels he would have been happier if less useful as a face-saver if he had been able to interview on the spot the unwilling hostesses, the resentful mothers and children, the un-welcome hordes of visiting relatives, the swamped country schools and harassed officials. Both these films are designed to make a good case for their official sponsors, a vindication in the one case of British Imperial rule and in the other of a difficult social operation

16 The battle against pollution begins (*The Smoke Menace*, 1937).

17 "I am Darius, King of Kings . . ." (*Dawn of Iran*, 1937).

18 A new life begins (*Here is the Land*, 1937).

which went far less happily than the film pretended. They are a long way both from the altruistic examination of a social problem paid for by a disinterested sponsor, of which the movement had been so proud a few short years before, and the long-forgotten education for democracy.

While Strand had tried everything, from earnest films for industrial sponsors to social documents, excellent short interest films and finally official whitewashing once war had started, the other unit, Realist, had pursued a different and more crusading course.

One of its first productions was Stuart Legg's *The League at Work* for the League of Nations Union. Then in 1937 John Taylor directed *The Smoke Menace*, made through Film Centre for the British Commercial Gas Association and first shown in October. As a Film Centre production it named Grierson and Basil Wright as joint producers, and the *Sight and Sound* review also credits Basil Wright as co-director,[108] but it has always been known as Taylor's film.

The Smoke Menace shows how burning raw coal as a source of energy causes waste and pollution. Good clear explanation, discreet implied encouragement for the use of gas, important social content together with excellent visuals are typical of the rather sober best of the documentary movement of the latter thirties, and it is *par excellence* one of the films in which the commentary bears the burden. The smoky skies and chimneys, the thousands of commuters arriving by rail, the people who use a lot of coal like the housewife, the baker, the potter; the "dirt trades" which exist to clean the tons of soot from our cities; J. B. S. Haldane, who wrote the commentary, addressing us on the need for Vitamin D, which depends on reaching us through sunlight, and a final encouraging promise of better housing and a cleaner life are knitted together with a mixture of titles, *March of Time* reportage and good editing. Probably because Taylor was originally a cameraman the film still looks good, and leaves powerful images of the smoky city skyline as a symbol of wasted energy and a polluted world.

At the same time a second Realist film for the British Commercial Gas Association, this time completely disinterested, was Basil Wright's *Children at School*. This was again shot by Jeakins and officially produced by Grierson from Film Centre. It is a survey of the best of our state education, contrasting the British desire to encourage each child as an individual to the regimented education of totalitarian countries, and leading to a plea for better buildings, better equipment and a better teacher–pupil ratio. This enables the film to show some of the worst of the schools as well as the best. It takes the form of sections on nursery, infant, primary and secondary schools, a horrifying sequence on inadequate schools, a "Ten Year Plan for Children" explained by a distinguished committee, and finally a staged discussion between some teachers whose most earnest endeavours have managed to achieve only a handful of new desks. The different parts are introduced by a desk interview with H. Wilson Harris, editor of the *Spectator*, who provides a commentary refreshingly unlike that of the usual plummy professional narrator and really sounds as if he is speaking because he has something to say. It will be seen that again the film is in the *March of Time* manner, and Wright himself has said that it was "made as a reportage film, although I did have some aesthetic sequences in it".[109] The division into sections might even be thought a little mechanical. The thesis, however, is clear, the justification for it is established and our sympathies are deeply engaged. And yet. . . . To speak of having some aesthetic sequences in it is surely very strange. It is as though Wright, and indeed this applies to Taylor as well, has been completely persuaded by Grierson's conversion to *The March of Time* reportage method and set out to make just such a film, but that his own artistic instincts are still in there, making a different sort of film at the same time. The sympathetic observation of the children, never sentimental, is remarkable and shows the quiet self-contained assurance characteristic of Wright. The children's voices singing, from nursery rhymes with the smallest ones and the more mature singing of older children, is certainly more than reportage. The use of detail and the sound-track to point the contrast of the worst and best seems to belong to another film, to be on a different level. The famous passage of the small girl coming down a dirty, cracked concrete corridor while from behind the closed classroom door come magical words from "The Golden Road to Samarkand" is presumably just an "aesthetic sequence"?

The co-production by Realist and Victor Saville Productions of *Modern Orphans of the Storm* for the National Joint Committee

for Spanish Relief was somewhat outside the documentary movement. It is also interesting that at this time Ralph Bond, an active
left-wing unionist who was to be made a vice-president of the
Association of Cine Technicians in 1939, was working at Realist
and made two films for bodies with working class support, *Passport
to Europe* for the Workers' Travel Association and *Advance Democracy* for four London Co-operative Societies. During the thirties
the luxury cruise was a popular holiday for those who could afford
it, but in the belief that travel promotes the brotherhood of man
the Workers' Travel Association was arranging foreign travel for
people with smaller incomes and different tastes, and the first of
these films shows large friendly groups of working people in more
homely foreign resorts and steamers. *Advance Democracy* was
directed and written by Bond and shot by the Unit's cameramen
Gerald Gibbs and A. E. Jeakins. It is a politically motivated film
and completely out of character for Realist, and indeed for the
whole documentary movement, and was distributed by the Communist body the Progressive Film Institute. Starting with contrasts
of rich and poor in London, it goes into an unconvincing scene in
which an actor playing a London worker, who earns £4 a week
as a craneman when he is lucky enough to get work, listens with
his wife to a broadcast talk by the Co-operative M.P. A. V.
Alexander on the history of the movement; into this are cut
re-enactments of incidents in its history. The man, persuaded by
this talk and by his wife's enthusiasm, joins the movement. They
march in the May Day procession in London in defence of the
unions, freedom, democracy and peace. The film ends with a
synthesis of marching songs arranged by Benjamin Britten. Despite
good outside filming, the oversimplified moral tale and the poorly
staged sequence make this film an odd contrast to other Realist
films. A third film by Bond was one arranged by Film Centre for
Scottish Oils, *Paraffin Young, Pioneer of Oil*. This was a clear
and competent account of how a nineteenth century inventor found
a way to get paraffin oil from shale, and founded a firm which
still existed as part of Scottish Oils. Using enacted sequences with
the air and lighting of a small studio, old prints, working models
of old equipment excellently lit, and shots of Glasgow and modern
industry, it is interesting but no more, a factual film lacking

imagination. It is, moreover, quite different from Bond's other two films, which contain real, dusty and clamorous filming in the streets, out of step with the calm reportage now so fashionable.

In the summer of 1938 Basil Wright left the running of Realist in the hands of John Taylor, and joined Film Centre with Grierson. In this year he made *The Face of Scotland* as part of Film Centre's package for the Films of Scotland Committee. The film was made as a Realist production, however. It was distributed by M-G-M in 1939.

This magnificent film, one of which any country should be proud to be the subject, seems to have been inexplicably overlooked by many writers, perhaps because it was so near the war, perhaps because the Scottish programme aroused little enthusiasm, mixed as it was with commercial producers. Photographed by Jeakins, and with music by Walter Leigh which is unobtrusively perfect for it, it has unwavering momentum and in its conception and imaginative handling it has something in common with the longer and more exotic *Song of Ceylon*. It starts with superb shots of the bleak and desolate border country with its long straight tracks, deserted hills and Roman Wall; a voice speaking in Latin is taken up and translated, a Roman commenting on how how uninhabited it was. "Not a soul came out to meet us." Wonderful shots of mountains, moors and lochs are accompanied by the wailing pipes; as they built roads they also built the Wall, for there was "one land they were not to conquer". The meagre life of a stern and hardy race, the small crofter communities limited in size by the infertility of the soil lead us on to the strict Calvinist religion and the stress on education for everyone; the many great men produced by this hard tradition and the early advent of its industrial revolution are shown; to the sound of a pipe band there are shots from the trenches in the First World War, and the shrine to its dead in Edinburgh Castle. "Her greatest asset is the character of her people." A vivid and even rather frightening look at Scots at a football match certainly shows much passion, grimness and determination. The film ends with a quotation from Holinshed. Perhaps this sort of image was not quite what the Films of Scotland Committee had in mind. But the picture of a strong people in a tough environment is effective and memorable, with a poetic quality which, it seems, was by now rather out of favour.

At Realist itself Taylor continued by directing and writing another Gas Council film arranged through Film Centre, *The Londoners*, on which Basil Wright and John Grierson are credited as producers. *The Londoners* was a long and ambitious film made to celebrate the fiftieth anniversary of the London County Council, and contrasted the insanitary and disorganised past of the city to the benefits of modern democratic local government. With Philip Leacock as assistant, an introductory section of the commentary in verse by Auden and music by Meyer, it was a major production and much admired. It seems, however, that over a reel was cut after its first registration. It contained a short political speech, with no concessions made to the film medium, by the politician Herbert Morrison, Labour leader of the L.C.C. But it was chiefly remarkable for the well-staged historical reconstructions with which it began, illustrating the distressing lack of hygiene or welfare in the past. The element of costume theatricals, which was creeping into a number of the films relying otherwise on the reportage style, made it very acceptable to the trade press. Sequences showing the modern organisation of the city, of more importance to the true documentarist, were less dramatic or personal.

Taylor, as a good Griersonian, then became a producer and was responsible for a film directed by Sidney Cole, *Roads Across Britain*. This presents another credit problem. Taylor's name is not on the film but he was in charge at Realist, and is credited with the film in some sources. Cole is on the film and in various other sources as director, his cameraman Arthur Graham like himself having been one of the P.F.I. unit which went to Spain to film the Civil War. But Rotha states: "Its direction was by Sidney Cole but some confusion arose and I was asked to take over."[110] The film, made for an oil company, was an account of the importance of roads and a plea for planned development as recommended by the report of the Highway Development Survey of 1937. Our dependence on roads both for commercial and private use, their neglect and inadequacy in Britain and questions of road safety are described in a commentary spoken partly by Legg and partly by the taxi-driver writer Herbert Hodge, and it is in fact another film in which the commentary carries the burden. It is punctuated by titles, used rather like chapter headings, and there is an effective score by

William Alwyn. The improvements recommended by the report – fly-overs, motorways, clover-leaf intersections and tunnels – are shown. An American section with an American commentator, acquired from an American producer, shows a "parkway" and leads to a final plea that we, also, should have a road plan. It is a document rather than a film, but it is put together as a good forceful argument with a definite socio-political aim. In fact, there seems to be more overt political content in Realist films than in most. It is interesting that Robert Herring in *Life and Letters Today* uses this film and *The Londoners* as examples of the dangers of sponsorship of films which, he claims, while appearing reasonable and fair, actually are by their very definition bound to be one-sided.

Cargo for Ardrossan was directed by Ruby Grierson for the Petroleum Films Bureau, showing the arrival of a tanker of oil, and its uses, at this installation south of the Clyde. It is another commentary-based film with illustrative shots and, like *The March of Time*, has sequences in which the people concerned re-enact typical conversations. Considering her gift for putting people at their ease and helping them to behave naturally this should have been a good assignment for Ruby Grierson, but the subject, technical and unsympathetic and with little emotional meaning, seems to have lacked interest for her and this, possibly her most ambitious film, was disappointing. Alan Rawsthorne, who was already doing some work for the Shell Film Unit, wrote the music. Ruby Grierson was to die at sea during the war when she was making a film about the evacuation of British children overseas, a subject which would have suited her much better.

It will be seen that Realist had quickly established itself as an important production unit with some outstanding films, which had the commentary-based style well developed, but which with a few exceptions were somewhat lacking in flair. All were now for theatrical distribution. An exception to the predictable and solemn, as ever, was Paul Rotha who was taken under the Grierson wing in 1938 with two Film Centre contracts made at Realist.

When Rotha returned from America, no longer a member of Strand, Grierson and Film Centre arranged for him to make a film for the gas industry at Realist in the summer of 1938. He was to be both producer and director, and had Rignold, Onions and

Jeakins to shoot it, music by William Alwyn, and Alistair Cooke as commentator. They had the use of the G-BI studio at Cleveland Street for a day and a night in which to film a theatrical "Victorian" introduction. With such facilities, after his vicissitudes, he might be expected to have been glad to take the task seriously. Instead we have here a film, *New Worlds for Old*, which presents us with certain problems.

It was a time when gas and electricity were vying with each other as to which was the best form of modern domestic and industrial power. We have seen how the electricity industry was making lack-lustre little public relations films, whilst the gas industry was sponsoring its remarkable series of social document films. The rivalry of the two forms of power is symbolised in this film by one splendid shot which remains in the memory, a very long shot of a huge gasometer with an equally enormous power station in the distance, and a train racing across the bottom of the screen in front of them, dwarfed by these two giants. Yet in his autobiography Rotha claims that he felt the respective merits of gas and electricity as contained in the recent P.E.P. report "would be impossible to dramatize in human terms" and even that "gas is not exactly easy to 'bring alive' ",[111] an amazing statement for a documentary film maker to make. Anyway he seems to have decided to make what he calls a "cod" film, or skit, and says that he was not very serious about it. Perhaps, returning from abroad, he may have been repelled by the seriousness with which the movement now took itself.

The film begins with an exceptionally long list of acknowledgements for "facilities", a skit on a certain type of film making, even if it also seems rather like biting the hand that fed him. Carefully lit shots of Tussaud's waxworks of Queen Victoria and other Victorians, with pictures and posters, lead into a series of what he calls *tableaux vivants* of Victorian gas-lit night life, including a can-can sequence, which were staged in front of two very long flats built in the G-BI studio and used with a travelling camera. This wilfully "impressionist" sequence, of which he makes much for some difficulties with the censors over the can-can, is in fact very short. Deceptively conventional stuff follows, with animated diagrams and industrial scenes to show how using coal directly is dirty and wasteful but that using it as coke, by-products and gas is preferable.

Shades of *The Smoke Menace* of the previous year? The confident voice of Alistair Cooke is interrupted by a cautious doubter in a voice-over duologue, recorded separately, which was intercut with great effectiveness. Rotha cast Grierson's assistant Golightly as the stupid foil. The comic trio of bowler-hatted scientists chanting in their labs seems slow and unfunny now. There follow three interviews, one in tortured English with restaurateuse Mme Prunier, one with the manageress of the D. H. Evans restaurant, and one with a cinema usherette who is happy working in an air-conditioned building. This seems a skit not so much on advertising films, as he would suggest in his book, as on *Dinner Hour*, to which it bears an uncomfortable resemblance. But alas, nothing dates like a skit or a private joke, and what remains years afterwards is an apparently rather bad film in static shots, long takes, with poorly interviewed people. There follows the routine sequence of bad old housing, shots of gas, and then modern, clean housing. A "Working Class Wife" with ineffably middle-class accent and Mrs Bumble the cook-general, a fat stage cook, are both fulsome in praise of gas for cooking. There is a sequence with a grotesquely cute and unnatural little girl. The final message is that gas cooking is so clean and efficient that it gives people leisure, and we see humble people knitting, sewing and gardening, in the dignity-of-ordinary-people format.

Rotha claims "chaotic success" for this film and that Richard Griffith wrote from America that Jean Lenaur " 'thinks *New Worlds* is just about the slickest documentary job he has ever seen. . . . Just about everyone says it's a wholly new departure, the most assured documentary to come over here from England' ".[112] Were they entering into the skittishness themselves? In the film Rotha cleverly mixed all the formulas, the new fad for costume reconstructions, interviews, the animated diagram, the rapid surveys of industrial processes, the obligatory contrast of bad old housing with new flats. All, it would appear, to make fun of the school of production that was taking him back into the fold. As a final unexplained postscript to the production, Frank Sainsbury, who had been Anstey's assistant on *Enough to Eat*, was credited on *New Worlds* as associate director, his name appearing on the film. Remembered by Rotha only as an editor, Sainsbury had himself made a film for the Gas Light and Coke Company in 1937, *Kensal House*, about a block of flats put up as part of a slum clearance. The film was designed to show how economical and efficient gas and coke were for domestic purposes. It is difficult to be sure, as the copy now available[113] appears to be a re-edited version made in 1946, but it seems a clear and interesting, unostentatious film with effective and sympathetic interviews with working class people and a distressing incidental glimpse of the conditions to which they were accustomed. Sadly, this modest and uninspired work has dated less than the irrepressible Rotha's joke.[114]

Anyway, realising that Rotha was definitely not a group-film man, Grierson and Film Centre preserved and got him another and even better chance to make a personal film. This was *The Fourth Estate*, a six-reel film which he was to produce and direct for and about *The Times* newspaper. Once more working through Realist, he had Rignold and Rogers as cameramen as well as Jeakins, music by Walter Leigh with the Sadlers Wells Theatre Orchestra, and it was to cost, according to him, the unusually high sum of £7,500. Thus no expense was to be spared. He even had the great Carl Mayer as scenario consultant, the film being the only British production ever to bear this credit. Surely this time all would go well.

He was given a free hand and took some months to make it, having shot 36,000 feet of negative before war broke out, and cutting it in the months thereafter. It contains the material for a message of some importance, that a democracy needs to know the facts and that for this it depends on a free press. But once again it would seem that Rotha was not truly in sympathy with his subject. Although he certainly believed in a free press, he seems to have seen *The Times* itself as the personification of privilege, the Establishment, the enemy. This complex man, from the account in his autobiography, would seem to have been antagonised by the idea that the England of *The Times* was the England "of the minority in numbers, but maximum in wealth and ownership"; and yet at the same time this very England of great houses and parklands, culture and privilege, appealed to him. The result was a film in sections, as usual with Rotha. A first part shows the paper, the presses roaring, the bundles of papers going by rail and van to the village newsagent, *The Times* in action with the circulation department, the crossword, the drama critic, letters, editorial and all. Next comes a section about what actually goes in the paper, which is presumably what he refers to as the "Heritage Sequence"; it is about an upper class world of Royalty, the Guards, the beauty of great estates, pretty villages and grand houses with only the merest mention of ordinary people and poverty, and with a commentary delivered in ringing patriotic tones. Then follows a section about the history of the paper, the only part to rely largely on commentary, as the camera wanders through luxurious rooms, past book-lined shelves and portraits of past editors. The final sequence is when the paper is at last put to bed, the presses race and the whole thing is drawn together with life and purpose.

According to his book Rotha allowed the film to be cut from six reels to five, and the "first casualty of shortening was the Heritage Sequence *in toto*",[115] a cut made apparently in January 1940. He refers to this sequence several times as a "cod" British Council sequence, as though it was a deliberate spoof of the Establishment world of *The Times*. Yet his attitude was not only tactless but ambivalent, as he clearly put a lot into it and it does, in fact, contain some beautiful and obviously affectionate filming. He says this sequence was mislaid during the war, but the copy of the film now in existence was apparently duped from his own personal copy and is six reels long again. The matter is obscure, perhaps deliberately so, but it seems likely that the dig in the ribs was not appreciated at the time. However, even when shortened, the film was quietly put away by its sponsors in the vaults and not publicly shown. Apart from two reviews of it in *Documentary News Letter* in June 1940 it remained only a legend for many years. The cut version, lacking the semi-mocking picture of the world of privilege, was meant to be a representative day in June 1939 during which the business of bringing out the paper was followed through, the activities in the building and reflections on its past were woven together in such a way as to build to a climax when a late item was included at last and the waiting presses finally went into action. The sponsors' excuse that this was rendered untimely by the arrival of war is only half-convincing, and what he refers to as "the arrows of satire in the film"[116] may have been a more likely cause for its suppression. Whatever was actually said or felt, *The Times* refused to let the film be shown until a public performance in 1970, when it emerged as a well-made, interesting film about a unique institution, including some leisurely and beautiful filming of upper class England in the thirties accompanied by a commentary which certainly seems uncharacteristically rhetorical for a mainstream documentary film, but hardly satirical. Strangely enough, after all these years the film was successful in a way that Rotha had not intended. It is a matter for regret that so much film-making talent and good intentions were devoted to subjects in which he did not really believe and with people whom he did not whole-heartedly like or respect. But despite the uneven course of his career at this time his importance as a major figure in the movement was undeniable.

Other companies continued to develop in their own particular way. As well as their important films made through Realist, the gas industry also had several less ambitious productions with Elton producing and J. B. Holmes directing, at the G-BI studios in 1937, a second Boulestin film on *How to Cook* and one called *Pots and Plans*. There was also, oddly enough, a rather more successful piece of fun than Paul Rotha's called *Happy in the Morning* and made by Cavalcanti and young Pat Jackson. Made in 1938 at Merton Park nominally by Publicity Films, this humble little film used the Merton Park staff and was rather outside the mainstream, but promoted gas appliances, especially the Ascot water heater, by an enjoyable little happiness fantasy. A serious broadcaster trying to tell us about the ideal kitchen, a housewife who switches over to Henry Hall's dance orchestra, his listeners include some people on their way to a circus, dancing elephants, a nightclub, guilty realisation that we are supposed to be making "the Ascot film", followed by a film-making sequence and a jolly song about how Mrs Brown used to get up early and light a fire but now all she has to do is turn on a tap, a happy chorus from Henry Hall and "Here's to the next time" with a close-up of an Ascot heater. It is unassuming film which neatly uses a disjointed associative technique to have a little fun.

The Shell Film Unit, also, continued to turn out its outstandingly clear, lucid explanations of different technical subjects, including

Oil from the Earth in 1938 made by D'Arcy Cartwright and *Transfer of Power* in 1939 directed by Geoffrey Bell. Both were produced by Elton and are perfect examples of his handling of technological matters, the latter especially being a brilliant explanation of the development of the gear-wheel.

Back at Blackheath was the rump of the G.P.O. Apart from a few good films and two remarkable ones it was to achieve comparatively little during the next couple of years, after which it merged into the war-time set-up at Crown Film Unit, whose achievement encompassed, of course, the work of the whole movement. Cavalcanti was now in sole charge, with J. B. Holmes as his director of production after leaving Strand. The key names were no longer there. Legg, Taylor, Basil Wright had left with Grierson; Anstey and Elton had gone long ago; and Evelyn Spice was soon to leave. The camera work continued to be in the hands of their own capable Jones, Fowle and Gamage, sound recording still very much in the Cavalcanti manner at first by Diamond and from 1938 by Ken Cameron, who was to prove one of the best sound recordists. And most of the editing was still by R. Q. McNaughton, who had been with the G.P.O. since 1934. The choice of composer continued to be unusual and adventurous, with contributions from Meyer, Rawsthorne and Britten, several by Brian Easdale and one each from the French composers Jacques Ibert and Darius Milhaud. Harry Watt was his chief director, with youngsters Pat Jackson, Maurice Harvey, Ralph Elton, Norman McLaren, Humphrey Jennings and even McNaughton being given a chance, not always successfully, and some larky stuff from Len Lye and outsiders Richard Massingham and Lotte Reiniger, a good if untypical and rather heavy film by John Monck, and two little films directed by Cavalcanti himself. Of all of them, only Harry Watt's *North Sea* and Jennings's *Spare Time* were outstanding. Both of these, however, were amongst the most important films of the decade.

The first film produced by Cavalcanti after the final departure of Grierson was Pat Jackson's first directorial assignment, the short film about postal deliveries in the windy flooded Fenland village of Horsey, *The Horsey Mail*. Featuring two real postmen with regional voices-over, it is an unpretentious but promising affair already showing that Jackson preferred people and narrative. A film about industrial health started by Watt in 1938 and meant to be called *Health in Industry* was handed to Jackson and finished as *Men in Danger* in 1939. Two reels, it is competent but conventional and is modelled on the commentary-based documentary without having its usually controversial content. A long rolling title tells us about the suffering caused by industrial accidents. A speech by Sir Henry Bashford, chief medical officer of the G.P.O., follows with scenes of factory and industrial processes, interrupted by a shock cut of a man slipping and screaming as he is hurt. We see guards, armour and visors with comments on "coal maners and their pithead baths – orf with thet graime!" As the Post Office had been the first large industrial undertaking, and was by now the largest, to take steps to ensure industrial health and safety, the Unit was able to make a film on a broader subject than usual, showing industry, the ceaseless movement of boring repetitive processes, and girl workers "allowed" to choose a song to sing as they pack biscuits. But the tone is unremittingly complacent, for this is justification of the sponsor, not investigation.

Meanwhile Harry Watt made his film about the finances of the Post Office, *Big Money*. Brightly and freshly photographed by Jones and Fowle, briskly edited and accompanied by modern atmospheric music by Easdale, it presents a commentary-based account of the mechanics of this vast public enterprise and its political and administrative background, kicking off with someone buying a $\frac{1}{2}d$. stamp at a sub-post office and ending, after Budget Day, with the man in the Ministry grumbling because the cost of his cup of tea has gone up to $1\frac{1}{2}d$. A few staged "spontaneous chat" sequences are embedded in illustrated commentary, but it moves smartly.

North Sea, however, was to prove not only an outstandingly good short film but a milestone in Watt's own development and in the development of the narrative documentary. Three reels, made at a cost of £2,000, it dramatised the ship-to-shore radio service by reconstructing a real incident in the lives of deep sea fishermen, played in the film by others of the same community. At last going along his own lines without the influence of Grierson, Watt made the film as a short dramatic feature about ordinary people. The results justified his approach triumphantly. A film that delighted and impressed documentarists as well as the public, the critics and the trade, it was distributed widely by A.B.F.D. on the circuits, and pointed the way to the feature documentaries of the war. It converted even Herring to documentary, the Grierson brand of which he had consistently attacked.[117] Backed to the full by Cavalcanti, with the usual team of Fowle, Jones, McNaughton,·Diamond and a marvellous sound-track with helpful music by Meyer, it was shot partly on location in Aberdeen and on a boat hired for a week up there, and with ship interiors shot back in the studio at Blackheath. It was played by real seamen, including our old friend Bill Blewitt from Cornwall. From the point of view of the more socially conscious documentarists who were now adopting the reportage method it lacked social content. Nevertheless few would deny that it was a fine film, and Harry Watt's own contribution, the very opposite of the commentary method. This fishing film with its quality of personal drama can even be seen as a symbolic rejection of Grierson and his *Drifters* and *Granton Trawler*.

We see the Aberdeen quays, silent except for an occasional ship's hooter or a shout, the misty, empty, mean streets; someone comes aboard the ship; seamen leave their houses and join up together; lovely shots of Aberdeen follow and the music steals in as the camera pulls out to the waves; the misty dockside, the ship's bows; to mournful hoots the men come on board, and more of them emerge from their homes, passing neighbours and saying goodbye to wives and girlfriends. Preparations on board, the odd remark, the clock strikes, the skipper and "All right! Let her go!" Ding! Ding! and the ship backs away with engine noises, hoots and great activity on deck; beautiful long shots of the receding harbour, the sight and screams of the gulls, noises of the ship, and the music lilts as we reach the waves and see our last of Aberdeen. After this lovely introductory sequence the music fades as we see the people back home at work and shopping, the men of the Wick radio hut keeping in touch with the ships. But the sea is getting up and as the men work oilskins are donned in the whistling wind. Wick is called up, and they brew tea in the cabin as a B.B.C. voice gives a gale warning. Fade out. Next morning there are heavy seas. Quick cutting of waves, the wheel turning, people running, shouting and a threatening, heaving seascape as they are struck. Shore asks if they need salvage tackle, but despite the smashing of more heavy seas they refuse. It is discovered that the pumps are choked but then, just as they are going to ask for salvage after all, the radio mast snaps and they are cut off. Across the misty sea and spray we see another ship but our hooting is carried off by the wind. Back at home, Wick tries to locate some ship that might be near us but for hours our seamen, grumbling a bit, work to heave coal overboard to lighten the ship. The office of the shipping company, a boat setting out to find her, the waiting women : back to sea, with waves crashing on to the deck and frozen hands in the wind. Fade to smoky Sabbath Aberdeen, with the sound of hymns and the minister's voice as people go to church, and ships remain still and silent on the waterfront. At sea the storm still rages, the men shout at each other through the wind as they try to fix the aerial. Silent waiting back at Wick. At last, with an inane burst of jazz, the aerial is fixed, and they send out a May Day call. Wick is delighted and gives them their bearings. The salvage boat is on its way, tea is brewed, the pumps are cleared, the men relax. The salvage tug is cancelled and the music swells as the ship rides the seas, returning at half speed. A quiet cigarette on deck. The radio officer in his comfortable office at Wick stretches, and says "Cheerio !" As we pan once more over the rooftops of Aberdeen, a voice says : "All round our coasts we have these radio stations to guard our ships".

Pat Jackson and Harry Watt were both, later, to channel their interest in people and the drama of everyday life into the feature film. Other young men working at the Unit were given an opportunity to prove themselves at this time. Maurice Harvey, who had been with the Unit since 1934 as cameraman and editor, directed two minor films, *North of the Border* and *The Copper Web*, the latter a typical phone film, and then graduated in 1939 to a more ambitious two-reeler produced by J. B. Holmes called *The Islanders*. The theme, possibly a little fancy for a G.P.O. film of this date, was that whereas before mankind a continental shelf had united land from Europe to America which was later divided into continents and many islands by the sea modern communications were new life-lines which united them again. A tiny community of Eriskay crofters, large bustling sophisticated Guernsey, the bird sanctuary island of Inner Farne and Great Britain itself are taken as examples of the islands made mysterious and inaccessible to each other by water. As an excuse for some nice filming by Rignold and Jones, sound by Cameron with some very tactful music by Darius Milhaud and commentary delivered richly by actor Jack Hawkins, it added up to a pleasant film, way out of line with contemporary trends but lacking the creative editing which had given interest to earlier films in this almost romantic vein.

Norman McLaren, also, was given a trial. In 1937 he made *Book Bargain*, a simple account of the making of the London Telephone Directory, which was fast and interesting and used the commentary to give the facts. *News for the Navy* next year had a narrative base, showing the progress of a letter from a sailor's sweetheart to his Bermuda posting, and using actors for the main parts. McLaren, however, was too much of an individualist to fit into conventional patterns. He was later to become one of the greatest workers in experimental abstract animation, and what seems to be his first animation film was now made at the G.P.O. as an advertisement for Empire Air Mail, *Love on the Wing*. It is worth mentioning that, although his time at the G.P.O. overlapped that of Len Lye, he has stated definitely that he never worked with him.[118] This brief and charming film with music by Ibert, not as dazzling as Lye's work, is quite different in style. In very pale Dufaycolor pastels, softly glowing backgrounds, it consists of hollow shapes outlined roughly in white which move and are transformed to represent a dramatic love affair being conducted by correspondence – the outline of an envelope changes to two mouths kissing, hearts, matchstick figures, a horse; two outline envelopes dance a sensuous dance together; it ends with the title "$\frac{1}{2}d$ for $\frac{1}{2}$ oz. – Empire Air Mail".

Ralph Elton, Arthur Elton's younger brother, made two run-of-the-mill phone films and one, *How the Telephone Works*, which used the sound-track, visual analogies, first class animated sequences and live action in a marvellously lucid explanation of a technical subject, worthy of his brother. He then made a two-reeler produced by Cavalcanti with commentary delivered by Herbert Hodge and music by Rawsthorne, *The City*, about the underground mail train from Paddington to the East End. Built because of city congestion, it opened up the whole question of the growth of London, but despite this important social issue little is ever heard of the film, possibly because it came on the market just after the outbreak of war. Even editor McNaughton was pressed into service, compiling *Community Calls* in 1939, and later directing a film about how the phone service enables press and radio to get and transmit instant information about sports events to the public, called *What's on Today*.

In his search for material Cavalcanti, of course, was not averse to humour. Lye made a live action film, *N or NW*, in 1937 which he directed, scripted and edited with his sound editor Jack Ellit, and although live action was unusual for him the film was as full as ever of imagination and experiment. Made to remind the public to address their letters correctly (the title refers to London postal districts), it intercuts a pair of sweethearts writing to each other after a quarrel. We look up at the writers and their letters as though from beneath glass tables. Their voices speak the words they write, telling of all the delay and despair caused by a faulty address; the whole film is set to three Fats Waller records, "Write Myself a Letter", "T'Aint No Use" and "Give Me a Break, Baby". It is not characteristic of Len Lye, but as a catchy public-advice film it could hardly be bettered. Another rather odd and even freakish little film was *God's Chillun*,[119] a compilation fitted to a sound-track consisting of a poem by Auden, music by Britten with a weird Caribbean slant, chanting, singing, quotations, drums, a woman singing and a West Indian voice explaining that unfortunately the land is in the hands of Europeans; they produce food with cheap labour whose standard of living is low, and education is needed to change this situation. The visuals include maps, old prints of the Caribbean, masks, ivory and gold objects, sugar-cane workers, buildings, faces, the moon – everything that comes to hand is flung together to re-create the place and retell the story. It is difficult to see what it has to do with the G.P.O. and the three editors, not known members of the Film Unit, seem to have created editing chaos.

Two outsiders who made G.P.O. films at this time were Richard Massingham and Lotte Reiniger. Massingham, introduced by Grierson after two experimental amateur films had demonstrated his interest in film technique, made three films for the G.P.O. produced by Cavalcanti, *The Daily Round* in 1937, *Mony a Pickle* in 1938 and *At the Third Stroke* in 1939. The first, on which Karl Urbahn continued his previous association as his cameraman and assistant, shows a humble country postman on his rounds and then a fantasy sequence in which he dreams of glory and revenge. Some nice scenery, members of the G.P.O. Film Unit taking parts and enjoying themselves, and some mild and facetious whimsy, it is hardly worthy of its two reels. Perhaps the most interesting thing about it is that Massingham was still using silent film techniques with non-synchronous sound, and every possible device is used to avoid showing people when they are talking; two people conversing as they walk towards the camera are even shown with their mouths just above the frame level. It also would seem to have very little justification as a Post Office film. *Mony a Pickle*, in which Massingham directed one of the two disjointed sequences to promote the Post Office Savings Bank in a light, humorous and fantastic vein, was more justifiable but very little more effective. Not a documentarist at heart, Massingham did not really fit the movement until he found his own special talent for putting over good advice with humour during the war.

Lotte Reiniger had started making animated silhouette films in Germany about 1930, using a style based on the baroque treatment of fairy subjects popular at the time. A film of Dr Dolittle made in Germany in 1928 was synchronised at Wembley studios in 1931, with music by Philip Braham. The first film she actually made in England was a one-reel *The King's Breakfast* from the children's poem by A. A. Milne. It was handled by A.B.F.D. in 1937, with music by Harold Fraser-Simson and musical direction by Ealing studio's Ernest Irving. Although the well-known E. H. Shepherd drawing of the King is used with the credits, the rest of the film is in the ornate style so suitable for German fairy stories and completely misses the cosy nursery world of A. A. Milne, a misunderstanding which is accentuated by the almost operatic singing of the children's poem by Olive Groves and George Baker.

For Cavalcanti she made two films, *The Tocher* in late 1937–8 and *H.P.O.* in 1939. The first, described as a film ballet, with themes by Rossini arranged by Benjamin Britten, concerns a fairy princess who is saved from marriage to a rich fat old man by the last-minute arrival of the hero with his Post Office savings book, representing the tocher or marriage portion. With her delicate figures, all the movement in their articulation except a little in thin wisps of cloud which drift and rise, for example, to uncover a fairy in a flower, the film is charming but, one would think, hardly likely to have much persuasive effect on an audience. Popularisation of the Savings Bank seems to have been the subject upon which the G.P.O. Film Unit had the greatest variety of film. More effective was *H.P.O.*, made late in 1938, her first film using cartoon and colour as well as silhouettes. Using Dufaycolor in very delicate blues and greens and faint peachy whites, the letters of "Greetings" appear as blobs on the pale blue, and the sketchy white outline of a cherub bearing "H.P.O." for Heavenly Post Office on his chest instead of "G.P.O." He appears and reappears delivering greetings telegrams to people on special occasions such as the arrival of a baby by stork, a child's party, a fox hunt, these being dramatised by *scenas* using her silhouettes, the black figures moving against the delicately coloured backgrounds. The final message appears in childish writing : "It's Heaven to receive a Greetings Telegram – Be an Angel and Send One. The Heavenly Post Office." With pleasant music by Easdale, it is an elegant trifle.

But all this was unimportant in comparison with Watt's *North Sea* and the work of the other major talent in the Unit, Humphrey Jennings. After his three early films made with still material Jennings had been busy with the Surrealist Exhibition in London and his involvement with Mass Observation. Jennings, a tall, thin young man who had known other members of the Unit when they were all up at Cambridge, where he was a brilliant undergraduate, was an all-rounder who painted, wrote and had many other interests. He helped to edit the first Surrealist bulletins and manifestoes produced in London and was one of those who arranged the famous exhibition at the New Burlington Galleries in June 1936, the first important international Surrealist exhibition. During 1937 he was associated with Tom Harrisson and Charles Madge in the foundation of Mass Observation[120] as well as taking Dufaycolor film about fashion featuring Society dress designer Norman Hartnell, including that used in *Design for Spring*.[121]

In 1938 he was back at the G.P.O. and directed *Penny Journey*, a short reel with the title "The story of a post card from Manchester to Graffham" over a page of penny stamps. With this small, gentle but compelling little film, he began to show what he could do. Over the Manchester skyline a quiet voice says "This is Manchester". A little boy with docilely plastered-down hair is writing a postcard to his aunt in Sussex and we follow it into the pillar-box for the 2.45 collection. Various Post Office procedures are followed, with an occasional quiet helpful remark. Then we see the pleasant Sussex countryside in the morning and a village, where the postmaster is opening up shop. The postman rises, cycles and walks to Aunty's farm and there she is. She reads it out. Photography is by Fowle and Pollard, although it seems likely that some of it is stock material of Post Office procedures. Nevertheless even as a very modest beginning this little film with its peaceful air of observation deserves notice.

In 1938 Jennings made a two-reeler called variously *Her Last Trip* or *S.S. Ionian*, an understated and remote glance at a trip in the Mediterranean made by a Merchant Navy ship.[122] *Speaking from America*, also in 1938, was a single-reel film by him shot by Pollard and Gamage explaining the radio-telephone system between the United States and Britain, a clear but routine film giving him no scope for development. But next came *Spare Time*, made before the New York World's Fair in 1939. It was directed and written by Jennings with Cavalcanti producing, Fowle as cameraman and the poet Laurie Lee as commentator, and was the first undeniable proof that Jennings was an exceptional film-maker.

We are told "This is a film about how people spend their spare time". Certainly not a Post Office subject, it is said to have been made primarily for Mass Observation, though there is no formal credit to this effect.[123] It covers the leisure pursuits of working people by grouping them in three sequences : the practice of a works brass band in the steel industry, the marching of a carnival band in the area of the Manchester cotton industry, and the singing of a coal miners' choir. These three main subjects are seen against the background of the bikes leaning on garden sheds, the pigeons, greyhounds, the houses and streets, the rubbish dumps, the dinner tables, the football and model boats, greenhouses, the Zoo, wrestling and amateur dramatics, the ballroom dancing and old people playing cards. Throughout, the emphasis is on the people, unexplained but individual. The camera dwells on them in all their diversity amid the litter of their personal preoccupations. In the sound-track, with the music of the three sections so deeply integrated into the film, he shows himself one of Cavalcanti's most intelligent successors. Like the earlier Orient Line films it is almost entirely without commentary, telling the whole thing by its selection of detail. But unlike them its selection is not oblique but direct, vigorous and fresh, face to face with its subjects with little need of words. Jennings, an almost alarmingly highbrow and well-connected person in the most rarefied of intellectual circles, showed a deep understanding and feeling for the ordinary men and women of England. Not so much poetic or warm as watchful and intelligent, he put his finger on what people did, said, thought and looked like; but he added to it that twist which makes one look at things with an awakened eye. The approach is intellectual, and in his cutting lay the rich associations of a highly literate mind. Clearly his final style, of which this film was only a beginning, was to combine the strands represented in his interests by both Mass Observation and Surrealism. At the end of the film a voice says "Spare time is a time when we can do things we like, can be most ourselves".

This most subtle of film-makers made some of the most easily watchable films which, however, were deeply layered with meaning. But he did not receive immediate admiration. Even at the end of Grierson's life he spoke of Jennings, in the Sussex tapes, in disparaging terms, referring to him as stilted, a minor poet, and "fearfully sorry for the working class". Nor was he headed in the same direction, of story or entertainment, as the breakaways Watt and Cavalcanti. The sequence which aroused most antagonism was the middle one, in which the Manchester Victorians' Carnival Band, youths and girls in thin cheap costumes, parade gravely in the grey, cold, windy recreation grounds, in a second class imitation of the American parade they had no doubt seen at the pictures. Even as late as the memorial programme held after Jennings's early death in 1950, Basil Wright was to write that this sequence was made "in terms of a cold disgust".[124] Seen later, it would seem that this disgust was read into the film by a school of film making which idealistically wished to see the common people as other than they were. It seems more likely that by using the same careful, unemotional observation of what was, in fact, a rather gloomy attempt at festivity Jennings simply tells the truth as he does in other more intrinsically warming subjects. It was not until his next film *Spring Offensive*, strictly speaking out of our period as it was made after the outbreak of war, that he was more fully appreciated. But here he had a subject which, inherently more sympathetic, allowed the same intelligent observation to appear more warm, more human. The film is about how War Agricultural Committees worked and how farming was mobilised for war. Two main strands, the evacuation of a little city boy to a farming family in East Anglia and how he learns about the country, and the work of that family in getting the farm back into shape to produce more food in wartime, are intertwined. With a script by feature film writer Hugh Gray and photography by Fowle and Eric Cross, commentary by farmer-writer A. G. Street and editing by Geoff Foot, and with music by Liszt arranged by Easdale and conducted by Muir Mathieson, it was obviously a much more important production. Outstandingly beautiful visuals of the countryside and a sympathetic treatment of the people made it, apparently, an easier film to like. In fact, however, the yardstick of warmth, or coldness seems irrelevant to Jennings's talent. Deeply felt by an honest and receptive intelligence, the subjects are treated with humanity but without sentiment, with understanding but without overt comment.

Cavalcanti himself produced a little compilation in French, edited by Robert Hamer, about the co-operation between the English and French armies. This was *La Cause Commune* of 1938 in which, incidentally, Oliver Bell of the British Film Institute acted a small part. Cavalcanti also made a short and delightful personal film produced, written and directed by himself called *Midsummer Day's Work*, which used the laying of an underground cable in the Chilterns to give a picture of midsummer in that part of England in June 1939. Scenes of Oxford and the countryside, children at P.T., life on the farms, holiday campers and, rather by the way, the G.P.O. men labouring in the hot sun make a pleasant film but suggest the growing inadequacy of the Post Office as a theme.

A more important production was that made by John Monck, who like Watt and Anstey had shot English sections for *The March of Time*. This was *Health for the Nation*,[125] which was made not

for the Post Office but for the Ministry of Health, with the collaboration of the B.B.C. Powerful yet at the same time conventional,
with an outstanding sound-track, this film did not break new ground
except in trying to make a social document film directly about its
sponsor. In examining housing conditions for the gas industry, Elton
and Anstey had been under no obligation to compliment their
sponsor. But in tackling health for the Ministry it was a foregone
conclusion that the resulting film was not going to criticise its work.
Thus despite some excellent filming with telling selection of detail
and a remarkable sound-track in the first two reels, which cover a
similar story of country-idyll-to-power-revolution with consequent
environmental disaster that we have seen in the Rotha films, leaning
fairly heavily on the commentary but still impressive, when the
film reaches the final sequence it changes to sweetness and light
with the commentary ramming home the hospitals, Green Belts,
school meals and National Health Insurance. It presents not so
much an investigation as a promotion. Yet the sound-track,
especially with the thump, thump, the clanking and hissing,
trundling, blasting and shrieking whistles and the terrible rending
noises of industry, some of the smoky industrial vistas, the dirty
kids and mean housing all suggest a talent which could have been
better employed than in simply making out a case for a backer.
There is one sad sequence of old age pensioners, sexes segregated,
and a firmly conducted sing-song for the old men with the aged
birthday boys compelled to stand, unsmiling but compliant, while
their ages are read out by a well-meaning clergyman. As an example
of how the State was looking after its members it sends another
of those little chills down the years.

This film was registered in May 1939 and was virtually the end
of pre-war production by the G.P.O. A shorter film prepared just
before the war under the title *If War Should Come*, to the com-
forting strains of Elgar, tells people to listen to the B.B.C., disregard
rumours, dig a pit for the A.R.P. shelter, not to hoard, to clear the
loft, and have buckets of water and sand on every landing. Its
title was swiftly changed to *Do It Now* when war broke out and it
was shown later in the year. But perhaps this account of the G.P.O.
should end with the film roughly put together and edited by
McNaughton out of observational material shot by members of the

19 Nowhere to play
(*Give the Kids a Break*, 1937).

20 Farming in the
thirties (*Around the Village Green*, 1937).

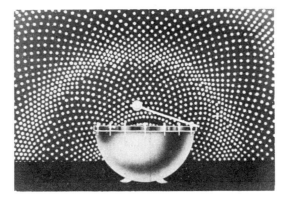

21 The use of
animation (*How the Telephone Works*, 1938).

Unit who found themselves in London, with nothing much to do, during the early days of the war. It was put out under the title *The First Days*. Sandbags, young soldiers training in the parks, Spitfires, the evacuation of children by rail, soldiers leaving and women left behind, the removal and packing of art treasures, the registration of foreigners, it conveys the feeling of life in London that September of 1939 and how the city braced itself for trouble. Comfortingly one-sided perhaps, with a sad-heroic and self-congratulatory commentary, it was a tonic for morale at the time, and successfully shown in the cinemas. The main body of the film is introduced by a prologue, with silent children at play; slowly the commentary and First World War tunes softly steal in, then that sunny Sunday of 3 September with Chamberlain's broadcast, the door of No. 10, the listening people. It ends with the assertion that while the nation turns over to war ordinary life is still going on, babies are still being born, people are still whistling at their work. The varied, imaginative and essential sound-track proves it, once more, a result of Cavalcanti's teaching.

(iv)   The End of the Decade

Thus the thirties came to an end. The young film makers and their works were more mature, and perhaps for that reason there was less excitement in the air. During the last two years the G.P.O. Film Unit had ceased to be in the forefront of the movement despite the talents of its producer Cavalcanti and its two chief directors, Watt and Jennings. Partly, of course, its early celebrity had been a reflection of the personality and the talent for publicity of Grierson himself. Watt had given the story documentary a big push forward, but a large number of the other G.P.O. films adopted *The March of Time* commentary-based style of the Grierson group, although lacking their real investigative qualities. In this they diverged from the rest of the British movement, the doyens of which were now deeply involved in the social significance of their work. At its sober social best, this was very effective. But the late G.P.O. films which had the same appearance of social enquiry, *Health for the Nation* and *Men in Danger*, were fundamentally false in giving an appearance of detachment when reporting on the work of their own sponsors, an impossible thing to achieve. Of course, shortly all documentary film makers would be engaged in direct promotion, for with other makers of short films they would be making official films designed to support national morale. But had there been no war it is hard to see how the G.P.O. could have continued on this course, of making apparently investigative films about the people who had commissioned them, without losing some of its reputation.

Even if there had been no war Grierson's thoughts were already elsewhere. As early as August 1938 he was known to be making plans for documentary production in Canada.[126] No longer the unchallenged leader, he may have felt it was time to move on and spread the movement elsewhere. The removal of his dominating influence, and therefore of Film Centre's also, by his departure to Canada would anyway have meant the end of the movement as a tightly knit group. The Imperial Relations Trust set up by the Government had on it Sir Stephen Tallents who, after leaving the G.P.O. in 1935, had been controller of public relations at the B.B.C. Overseas Service. When the Trust set up a film sub-committee, what could be more natural than that Film Centre, and Tallents's old friend Grierson, should be made their film adviser, and that when the question of the production of Canadian documentaries was raised Grierson should be invited to undertake it? The Canadian Government had long been interested in the use of films for promotion, as we know. Grierson duly departed to Canada, where he was to remain for some years.

One incident which might have had a happier outcome if Grierson's heart had still been here was the dispatch of films to the World's Fair in New York in April 1939. The British Council had been set up in November 1934 to establish closer cultural contact with other countries and to spread knowledge of British life and culture overseas. It considered the question of films but had neither funds, experience nor machinery for production. However, in 1936 a Joint Films Committee was set up under the chairmanship of the popular and witty historian Philip Guedalla. With only £400 in 1936, £1,000 in 1937 and £2,600 in 1938 it was not in a position to sponsor production but its terms of reference made it, as a public relations body, the appropriate organisation to arrange films to represent Britain at the World's Fair. Members of the

Committee, among them Oliver Bell for the B.F.I., A. F. Primrose for T.I.D.A., A. G. Highet for the Post Office, and representatives of the Foreign Office and the Department of Overseas Trade, made their choice. Such a body was sure to select films to show Britain in a good light rather than to win prizes as films. There was disquiet, and on 7 September 1938 *The Times* correspondence columns carried a letter from Donald Taylor complaining that while other countries were organising their films there was no plan here which involved the film makers themselves; he instanced the Films of Scotland Committee as an example of what could be done to produce special films, and asked for action. Nothing happened. Nearly three months later, a letter from Sir David Milne-Watson of the Gas Light and Coke Company, who was no doubt mindful of the excellent exposés of social problems sponsored by his own industry, wrote to *The Times*[127] pointing out that other countries would be more impressed by our ability to make films which told the truth about ourselves than by attempts to present a favourable picture, and the following day[128] yet another letter, from the Director-General of the English-Speaking Union, A. F. Whyte, also asked for action. On the same day, however, a letter from Guedalla was also printed in *The Times*, a traditional smooth diplomatic letter making light of the whole question and claiming that there was no shortage of the type of film they wanted, films which should be "a pleasure to look at and advantageous to Britain". The Committee did, in fact, choose some of the most famous documentaries including *Song of Ceylon* and *Shipyard*. But needless to say it excluded those like *Enough to Eat* and *Housing Problems* and relied on the T.I.D.A. type of travelogues of beautiful Britain. A few days after Guedalla's letter *The Times* carried a letter attacking him and signed by Rotha, Wright, Elton and Flaherty, as well as the original consultants of the old A.R.F.P., Haldane, Hogben, Huxley and Kauffer. This claimed that his "views are quoted to be that pictures should be shown which are 'a pleasure to look at and advantageous to Britain . . . and that doesn't mean pictures of glue-factories by night, photographed the wrong way up, with crude Russian music' " Guedalla's original *Times* letter had not used these latter words, which imply a philistine attitude to films which the signatories must have believed was held by the Committee.

There was sympathy for their views in the press, and as a result of behind-the-scenes activity two sets of entries were shown, the official selection in the British Pavilion, and films sent by Film Centre on behalf of the film makers themselves and which were shown at another pavilion. The absence of timely leadership from Grierson over this matter, or of a Film Centre plan to produce a special programme similar to the Films of Scotland, was noticeable.

War broke out and the Ministry of Information was set up. But Sir Edward Grigg, Parliamentary Secretary to the Minister, replied to Geoffrey Mander's Question in the House of Commons that government policy was to encourage, but not to subsidise, the production of documentaries[129] and it was some time before the talents of the documentary movement were mobilised. Here again, things might have been different if Grierson's energies and strategy had still been in the thick of things in this country. Just after the outbreak of war *Kine Weekly*, confirming his appointment as the Canadian Government Film Commissioner, insinuated that his talents might have been better employed in war propaganda over here.[130] It does, indeed, seem inappropriate that the great propagandist for democracy should have spent the war making films in Canada. It is characteristic of his aloofness from international affairs that he should have made his plans to move at a time when many concerned with the survival of democracy already felt that such a war was inevitable. To be fair, however, it must be added that according to friends Grierson himself was unhappy about the situation and was only persuaded to remain in Canada by their argument that he could best contribute to the war effort by continuing his work there. The skill of the members of the movement which he had founded was in itself a contribution back here.

For a movement it certainly was. Admittedly, the technological basis of anything develops step by step, each development making the next one possible; and what is possible is done. If not Grierson, then someone else. But how things are done depends also on the individuals who do them. The technical basis of film making developed, and as it did so many people were using it for the same purposes and in the same ways at the same time. A study of the whole field of films made outside the feature industry reveals that realism, social purpose, sponsorship, even disinterested or enlightened sponsorship, were not peculiar to mainstream documentaries, any more than direct speech recording of ordinary people, compilation, lecture commentaries and all the other techniques. And the talent to use these things in the same or similar ways to the E.M.B. and G.P.O. Film Units was there, ready for Grierson to harness. The educated and intelligent young were preparing to use film for serious purposes, and if anybody can be said to have deliberately started employing them thus it was Bruce Woolfe in the twenties, not Grierson in the thirties. Maybe these particular young people might not have been the ones, or maybe those who successfully imprinted themselves on the course of film history might have done so in slightly different ways, but some such developments would certainly have taken place simply because film technique now made them possible. Indeed, there were similar developments in other parts of the world.

But as a matter of historical fact in Britain it was John Grierson, with his talent for spotting opportunities, who did it. And because of his personal qualities of dominance and leadership he gave his young adherents a feeling of separateness and mission that made it a movement.

As a movement, it should not be too sharply defined. They were simply an identifiable group of more or less like-minded people working together in a certain field, in a roughly similar way, although with many and growing differences. Their work in fact overlapped other fields – instructional, travel, educational, news and entertainment films. But they were a group because they considered themselves to be a group, indeed an élite, membership of which was virtually by invitation only. Marion Grierson's films were really travelogues, but she was a member; Massingham and Len Lye, especially the latter, were making films of a totally different type, yet were taken up by the group almost as honorary members; and the Lotte Reiniger films, like the early attempt to use the Moholy-Nagy film, must be included as attempts by the Unit to use these talents for their own cause. Many of the G-BI films had more social content than these, yet Bruce Woolfe and Mary Field were excluded from the charmed circle with something like ferocity. Andrew Buchanan, who himself claimed, and was claimed by Oliver Bell and others, to be a documentary film-maker, was simply not acceptable as one of the boys. The films made with Julian Huxley could be regarded as educational, and no more documentary than those he made for G-BI on heredity. The excellent zoo films made with Huxley by Donald Taylor were both educational and entertaining and, as a step in Taylor's move into the entertainment industry, marked him as a fallen angel to the solemn minded and received only grudging attention from them. Arthur Elton, despite the importance of his early break-through in direct reportage and social significance, became associated with exquisitely lucid and perfectly photographed technical films which it would stretch the definition of documentary to include, but he was firmly one of the boys and his position in the movement is unquestioned. Rotha's position was also unique. Too independent to work satisfactorily close to Grierson, his obvious creative talent and his vehement commitment to similar social purposes and realistic styles as the others gave him a position of his own, right at the heart of the movement. These were the people, lively, talented and extremely articulate, many of them educated at public schools and a surprisingly large number at Cambridge, a few of them wealthy. Taking their work seriously, they wrote and lectured about it and talked endlessly amongst themselves, especially at the famous gatherings after work at a Soho pub, encouraged by Grierson who, while he was the centre of this coterie, exercised his power with zest.

It is impossible to ignore the complex character and motives of this unusual man, because of the extent to which they twisted the course of events. He was the great prophet of documentary, always summing up, exhorting, chiding, and he wrote and talked so much himself that one can find quotations for almost any view, and views on almost anything. But at the Perth Congress of the Educational Institute of Scotland in 1938 he seems to have summed up his position as well as anywhere when he said that he sought to use film "to tease out and articulate the new relationships of man and his work and make a connection narrative of them", believing in education not just as information but as "an explosive aid to interest and enthusiasm".[131] The Puritan drive and moral tone were there. With a basic wish to assert the dignity of the working man, and a conviction that ordinary people must be taught how society functions so that democracy could have real meaning, his work had the austere·purpose of serving society and he was frequently to remind the young members of his group of this. As a teacher rather than an artist, he became a producer himself and encouraged the best of his directors to do the same, and thus spread the word. According to Rotha, Grierson did not look upon documentary as an art.[132] At the time he covered himself with this sort of statement:

But only one thing gives the producer importance: the fact that he makes directors and, through directors, makes art.[133]

Art does not happen like that. It is not taken by assault. It is a better rule to say that art comes as a by-product of the more pedestrian task.[134]

But he was a creative producer, which seems to have meant that he took an interest in each film and that his comments and criticism unleashed the imagination of those who worked for him rather than that he took an active part in film making. Cavalcanti was also a creative producer, but as an artist and technician himself the quality of the contribution was necessarily different. And since Grierson was primarily a social teacher, when *The March of Time* commentary-based style came along he embraced it enthusiastically for its social value, unhampered by doubts about its relevance to cinematic art or visual style. His own imaginative flair was in the wider field of ideas rather than in the specific one of artistic creation. The two films he made himself are a doubtful basis for a reputation as an artist; one of them was original in conception only, its style being a faithful reproduction of Russian editing, and the second had a large element of doubt attached to its actual production. Where he excelled was in fixing, in making contacts, in getting money and facilities for others to make films and then encouraging talented people to experiment and develop, like a Calvinist public relations man, or a Puritan Diaghileff. The restrictions on the type of film to be made, accepted in the course of finding sponsorship, naturally affected the direction of the movement. But a movement it remained, in which certain forms and techniques were practised and "teased out". But did it fulfil his dream of educating people for citizenship? We have looked at the films, and few of them can claim to do this. Many years later Roger Graef, the producer of a series of television films made behind the scenes of certain social institutions, wrote of Grierson's "heroic realism". By comparison his own low-key realism, "observational cinema" silently watching, for example, a board of directors reaching a decision in discussions extending over a period of months, gives a far greater degree of understanding.[135] But in the thirties technical facilities did not exist which would enable a film maker to become an inconspicuous witness. Grierson was an opportunist who used what was available at the time and was quick to switch without regret from the new development, direct location recording of speech, to the commentary-based film as the best for his own instructive aims. There is no record that he was particularly anxious to get sound facilities of his own in the early thirties despite the obvious value of a commentary, and it was to be some years before he realised the much greater potential, for his purposes, of television. He was, in the end, a paradox. He would sack a man and yet continue to put work his way, split and abandon an organisation and yet continue to dominate the people connected with it, publicly and judiciously criticise a film made under his own guidance, and set out under Imperialist auspices to educate the public for democracy. He took his leave, moreover, precisely at the moment when that democracy was threatened by fascism.

What did the movement achieve, and what did these two to three hundred short films add up to, after all? They were economically but well made, always well photographed, and their content was more intelligently thought out than that of most commercial shorts. They had a very wide span of subject, type and style. Beginning amateurishly with silent films obviously based on the editing techniques of the Soviet film, which struck Grierson as a good medium of education, they changed as the film makers' skill increased. Not, for the most part, having much relevance to the education for citizenship of which he spoke, in the hands of one or two of the film makers even these early films showed artistry and imagination. With the acquisition of their own sound equipment and the arrival of Cavalcanti with his professional insistence on careful scripting, photography and editing as well as his adventurous lead in the use of sound, the films changed. Many of them drew attention to the real facts of society, especially amongst its poorer members, and systematically showed, for the first time, factual film of the working class and lower middle class, although the limitation of a part of the movement to Post Office subjects made it difficult for them to fulfil the broader ideal of social service. After a period of highly experimental sound production two main strands emerged, and diverged : the grave, socially orientated commentary-based social investigation; and the less didactic, more emotionally involving semi-story film conveying its message indirectly. On the whole the movement was not remarkable for its sense of fun. It ranged from pious dullness, plodding little films about telephone cables, for example, at one extreme to the fascinating, but more intellectually demanding, examinations of social conditions at the other. Amusement was introduced, sometimes to an almost embarrassing extent, by some of the whimsical films influenced by Cavalcanti in the middle of the period. The delicate lyrical strain was trodden somewhat heavily underfoot, and one can only wonder what small masterpieces were lost to us by Grierson's obsessive insistence on turning directors into producers, and be glad that he didn't work the same transformation on the magical talent of Len Lye. The two sides, representing respectively Grierson and Cavalcanti, were to be involved in a rather futile disagreement later as to whose influence was the more important. Clearly the movement existed, as a movement, only because of Grierson. The influence of his personality and views was overwhelming in the early years and, after the appearance of *The March of Time*, it carried a large part of the movement with him into a more verbal form of expression. But it is equally clear from our detailed examination of the films that Cavalcanti encouraged higher professional standards and new directions of his own, which gathered together those more interested in the individual. This later contributed directly to a mild semi-realist style of modest studio feature film at Ealing, for which British films received much praise. He was the artistic and stylish yeast, not sharing the boys' solemnity and not prepared to accept a difference in kind between filming reality and filming fiction, between non-theatrical teaching and films which would entertain as they informed.

Stuart Legg said, many years later in a B.B.C. television programme on the movement, that about 90 per cent of the films were negligible, 10 per cent remarkable. Harry Watt wrote ". . . and our films were generally pretty poor efforts, ballyhooed out of all proportion by Grierson's tireless writing and lecturing",[136] and later called them "a bit niminy-piminy", quoting also Flaherty's very unflattering opinion of them. The film industry resented them as potential competition while despising them as stuffy and arty, and it would be rash to believe that the cinema public would have been pleased to see more than a very small minority of them. There was a highbrow camp which deplored them, viewing them as the *Life and Letters Today* reviewer saw *Cover to Cover* – "All the documentary doings are here – pompous declamation, chanting of choruses . . . and whirring of machinery . . ."[137] – and preferred the G-BI educational films, recording gratitude to Bruce Woolfe: ". . . the only English cinema that counts is instructional".[138] But on the whole the films were welcomed by the intelligentsia, by film societies and by the film critics of the serious papers, especially those of the political left. They were in the forefront of intellectual movements, with connections with modern composers and writers, with Mass Observation, Surrealism, Maholy-Nagy and such leaders of public opinion as Priestly, Huxley, J. B. S. Haldane and others. Among people who cared about film as an art, too, they had tremendous prestige, and proof of this was given in the number of awards they won at exhibitions and festivals, although it is salutary to realise that G-BI also received its share of awards at the same events. The niche the movement carved for itself in the history of the film is considerable. Yet, all in all, Legg's estimate is more or less fair. His dismissal of 90 per cent as negligible is perhaps less than generous in view of the generally good standard of production and interest maintained with few facilities and often unpromising subjects. But it would probably be true to estimate that not more than twenty to thirty of these short films could be called remarkable.

The movement itself, however, was remarkable even if most of the films were not. But a final word on its practical influence on the British film is necessary in view of the temptation to draw the sweeping conclusion that it introduced a realist strain into the British feature film, and that it was a training-ground which led to a

flowering of the British film industry. It has been seen as leading
not only to the wartime documentary feature, but also to post-war
films and even, in the eyes of some,[139] to Free Cinema in the fifties
and later the controversial dramatic documentaries of B.B.C.
television.

The only well-known realistic feature films of the thirties in
Britain other than Flaherty's *Man of Aran* made for Michael Balcon
in 1934 were Norman Walker's *Turn of the Tide*, which was being
scripted in the early months of 1935, and Michael Powell's *The
Edge of the World*, for which plans were being made in June 1936.
Walker's film was tailor-made to please J. A. Rank, the Methodist
millionaire who had recently gone into film production only, in the
first place, because he saw the film as an instrument for moral
teaching. As for Powell, his book on the production of his film
makes it clear that he owed nothing at all to the idea of documentary. If his search for an original setting owed anything to
anybody, it is more likely to be *Man of Aran* than anything else.
But Balcon, who had borne with Flaherty in a way Grierson would
never have done and which Korda in his turn was unable to do,
produced at Ealing early in 1939 a film advertised as "Real people
– Real problems – a human document".[140] This was *There Ain't
No Justice*, a film about a working class boy who becomes a boxer,
and it was a forerunner of the "Ealing school". Realistic but not
sordidly so, modestly priced but not cheap and nasty, recognisably
about ordinary British people but in a reassuringly cosy way, it
was in marked contrast to other studio films. The associate producer
was Sergei Nolbandov, who was later in charge of Rank's version of
The March of Time called *This Modern Age*, and was himself
interested in the semi-documentary approach. *Ships with Wings*,
Undercover and *Convoy* were more or less realistic feature films
made at Ealing by Nolbandov during the war. Ealing was also
responsible for Thorold Dickinson's excellent *The Next of Kin* and
Charles Frend's *San Demetrio, London*. Cavalcanti, and later
Watt, neither of them true Griersonians, joined Ealing during the
war. Frend's *The Big Blockade* and *The Foreman Went to France*
were produced by Cavalcanti and *Went the Day Well?* was directed
by him personally, whilst Watt made *Nine Men*. Ealing also made
plenty of films with no claim to realism but the presence of these

two, both during the war and after it, when the typical Ealing film kept the semi-realistic approach alive for several years, is the only evidence that the documentary movement contributed anything to the feature film. Balcon, however, had certainly observed the possibilities of documentary drama and the advantages of a familiar British setting, and his own appreciation that this type of film making was well suited to the times was of key importance. The two big Australian films made by Watt for Ealing at this time had, in fact, been anticipated by similar big-scale location filming by Geoffrey Barkas in the thirties and even the twenties, although Watt had derived his own training for such films in the documentary years. Had Jennings not been killed in 1950 he might have made feature films of note. Even as it was, with his tragically small output, his films were much more to the taste of later break-away film makers like Free Cinema than the work of either the Grierson or the Cavalcanti groups, but he was a single individual and an outsider to both.

Wartime feature films which were successful at the time and which the war generation would remember with pride or affectionate nostalgia show little sign of realism. Askey, Formby, Will Hay and Old Mother Riley were dear old standbys from the music-hall. Pascal's *Major Barbara* and Olivier's *Henry V* were not realistic. The Powell and Pressburger films *49th Parallel, One of Our Aircraft Is Missing, The Life and Death of Colonel Blimp* and *I Know Where I'm Going,* and the David Lean films *In Which We Serve, This Happy Breed, Blithe Spirit* and *Brief Encounter* are happy memories, but even those about the war were studio productions and need only to be seen alongside a standard thirties documentary to show how great the difference was. If they seemed more real to British audiences it was because at last British film-makers had a reason, and enough courage, to make films about British situations instead of the imitation Hollywood films they had previously favoured. Leslie Howard is remembered for *The First of the Few, The Gentle Sex* and *The Lamp Still Burns,* studio films which showed a creditable desire to find subjects of significance in real life and film them in a credible imitation of reality, but they were still essentially studio films. On the other hand Carol Reed's *Kipps, Night Train to Munich* and *The Young Mr Pitt,* made before he went into the Army Film Unit, were frankly studio-made entertainment films. Anthony Asquith, after an erratic twelve years in the industry, had hit a theatrical seam of gold with *French Without Tears*, and his films, which included *Freedom Radio*, *Quiet Wedding, Cottage to Let, Uncensored, We Dive at Dawn, The Demi-Paradise* and *Fanny by Gaslight* and some shorts, culminating in one of the quintessential theatrical war films, *The Way to the Stars*, never moved far from the theatre. And long before the war was over the big novelette films which swept all before them had made their appearance with Gainsborough's *The Man in Grey* in 1943, *Madonna of the Seven Moons* in 1944, *Waterloo Road* and *The Wicked Lady* in 1945, as well as the Wilcox-Neagle luxury dream-world of *I Live in Grosvenor Square* in 1945.

The true beneficiaries of the movement were Crown Film Unit and the film units of the armed services. Not only documentary film makers but the personnel of all short and feature film production contributed to a very large body of official films mostly short but some longer, both to inform and encourage the people of Britain in their war effort and to make a good impression in neutral countries. The documentary people, with their experience of location filming and of combining reality with some form of message or story, had an advantage over the others. Thus it is not surprising that, of the longer films, apart from Roy Boulting's *Desert Victory* in 1943 and the Carol Reed–Frank Capra film of 1945, *The True Glory*, and also Carol Reed's commercial war film *The Way Ahead* made for Two Cities in 1944, the most important were made by the documentary school's old boys. It is Watt's *Target for Tonight* of 1941, J. B. Holmes's *Coastal Command* of 1942, Jennings's *Fires Were Started* of 1943, Rotha's *World of Plenty* of 1943, Pat Jackson's *Western Approaches* of 1944 and Jennings's *Diary for Timothy* of 1945 which are on this roll of honour.

This was propaganda, very high quality propaganda but propaganda none the less. Grierson, of course, had always meant to make propaganda films. But in the early thirties the word had been capable of a definition by now somewhat out of date :

In documentary there is this difference. The producer does not always serve purely commercial interests; unless, that is to say, you take the Marxian point of view, on which all service of the *status quo* is purely commercial. He can give himself the liberal . satisfaction of serving such interests as education and national propaganda : which, on any sensible definition, is itself a species of education. Or the producer may act on behalf of a business concern, large enough in its operations and its outlook, to turn publicity into education, and propaganda into a work of development.[141]

He had thought of propaganda as a neutral form of public education. But there were indeed those who took a Marxian point of view, as he called it, and felt that any such film was bound to be pleading a cause. In an article of 1936 called "Propaganda in the Films" Arthur Calder-Marshall maintained that all films were propaganda, and whereas commercial films were propaganda for capitalism Grierson's type of film was simply an advertisement for his own firm, the Government.[142] Definitions of documentary, of realism, of propaganda changed as the decade wore on. Writing in 1934 David Schrire sought to define documentary not by the fact that it employed "natural materials" but by the purpose for which it used them. His own belief was that "if the cinema is to mean anything it must serve a purpose beyond itself", and he carried on, as if he had proved this, to say :

. . . documentary pictures may be defined as the imaginative delineation through the medium of films employing natural material of current social struggle and conflict . . . it is not man's relationship with nature and the forces of production in our modern world which is the true subject of documentary. . . . Production today is adequate for our needs. The struggle is in a different sphere. . . . It is the relationship of man with his fellow man within the existing economic structure of society. . . .[143]

And so, step by step, he proved to his own satisfaction that the "proper" subject for documentary was inequality in the distribution of wealth, which is what he was primarily interested in himself, and as we have seen excluded Flaherty as a positive hindrance to the growth of documentary. In a way Grierson was rather like

Schrire, except that he was interested in the education of the citizen rather than in economic inequality. But both tested the excellence of films and the purpose of documentary against their own preferences, indeed obsessions. Rotha, who was like Schrire in his desire to right wrongs, was always anxious to plead a cause: witness his preoccupation with the environment in some pre-war films, and with food production and starvation in his war and post-war films; witness, also, the frustration which turned to a sort of bitter frivolity when the assignments upon which he worked did not permit him to deal with the issues for which he cared so deeply.

During the thirties the large-scale and untruthful manipulation of the means of communication by the totalitarian states to influence public opinion in a desired direction brought the word "propaganda" into disrepute, although the public education aspect of the Soviet films which Grierson had so much admired in the beginning had in fact been an early form of the same thing. But it was the usual situation, with everyone feeling that the propagation of his own views was simply neutral information, whilst the other fellow's views were "propaganda". Towards the end of the thirties the tendency to combine special pleading for sponsors with apparent objectivity had crept into some documentaries. When war broke out the movement as a whole easily made the transition to national propaganda, always with the sincere proviso that "our" propaganda was a helpful presentation of facets of truth, whereas "theirs" was unscrupulous lying.

If the movement had begun in order to strengthen documentary, in the end it did so in an unexpected way. Many interesting and informative films had been made, a number of them examining the quality of life in Britain. But, as usual, apparent agreement under an umbrella aim had included many different motives, including investigative journalism, public persuasion, a search for social change, and artistic creativity. When war broke out there was no time to look back. But what they had done was to forge an exceptional tool for national prapaganda in its most modern sense. For this, the country may well be grateful to Grierson. But it was not quite what he had in mind.

4

Reality and the Documentary Film

In the early thirties the film had seemed the ideal tool for education. In our second chapter we heard Ottley joyfully proclaim: "The Cinematograph is free from bias. . . . The record is a record of truth, since neither lens nor microphone can invent." But the decade was to suggest that he was wrong in every way. From the moment the film maker selected one subject rather than another, one angle on it rather than another angle, bias or subjectivity was present. And the film's capacity to invent and deceive was to prove almost without parallel.

In this book we have surveyed the didactic film in its two manifestations, the educational film and the documentary. It was accepted as a matter of common sense too obvious for discussion that there was a difference in kind between the film of instruction, which was to be objective and neutral and without conscious intention to impose a point of view, and propaganda. The latter was also a form of teaching, but one which sought to produce a particular belief or attitude. Indoctrination was, in the end, persuasion rather than information.

People found it hard to come to terms with the purely educational film in this country and comparatively little progress was made in the schools. The emphasis was much more on documentary, and after a while the documentarists themselves devoted considerable thought to questions of definition. This they always sought in terms of realism, fact and truth. The commercial makers of interest films, observing that their rivals' films always had a sponsor, referred to them as "propaganda films" from the start. But the documentarists preferred to think of themselves as a superior sort of educator. John Grierson's springboard had been education for democracy, as he described it. But he was always a great one for backing both ends against the middle, as we have seen in his pronouncements on whether documentary was an art or not: denying it all his life, he still managed to throw up a smokescreen of claims whereby documentary film-makers, it appeared, were artists after all. And with similar and characteristic ambiguity he initially chose to describe the function of the admired Soviet films as social teaching, a "sort of education", and at the same time as "the art of public persuasion". The battle for minds was gathering momentum everywhere during the thirties, and Grierson was a mind-manipulator of great enthusiasm. During this decade, however, the word "propaganda" became associated with dishonesty. By 1939 it no longer meant simply presenting a case, but presenting a case without regard for facts. To some extent where propaganda ends and lying begins is a question of semantics, or simply of where one is standing. However, as the fully fledged Griersonian documentary of 1939 was a serious work presenting a case on some social issue, the relation of the documentary film to truth, whether it is called realism, actuality, the factual film or anything else, is of some importance.

The whole thing, we have repeatedly been told, started with that original Lumière show of 1895. The train was filmed as it entered the station, and the people as they got off the train and walked along the platform: this was factual film, actuality. The little boy who crept up behind the gardener and checked the water in his hose, releasing it as the gardener bent over its nozzle to see what was the matter, was the beginning of arranged, or fiction, film. There they were, encapsulated in the very first picture show. It seemed so pat. But was it? How do we know that the Lumière brothers had not hired a job lot of likely-looking people to get on the train just outside the station, ride in and disembark, pretending to be travellers? How do we know the cameraman didn't just happen to be in the garden when a little boy was playing a perfectly genuine trick on the gardener? We certainly cannot tell from looking at the film. By the time the Méliès films and the Films d'Art were being made they were so obviously tricks and fancy dress that there was no doubt about their artificiality. But films of "reality" were always less easy to assess. Many early actualities, of which the fake Boer War news items are a well-known example, were simply more realistic in their appearance than the current staged films; and this was not difficult to achieve at that stage. By the time the documentary movement was in full swing, what was loosely known as the factual film was already a highly sophisticated structure, a great deal of interpretation being implicit in the original selection and editing, and frequently including a mixture of bits and pieces taken at other places and other times as well as the use of "justifiable" reconstruction. It was a highly subjective look at the world.

But because of the very unreal look of the stagey films of the time a distinction between fact and fiction seemed easy to make and became entrenched in current thinking, obscuring the fact that what the viewer saw was simply the screen. What the viewer thought he saw on that screen was what the film-maker wanted him to think he could see. This is not quite the same as seeing reality. Short of accidental and random operation of the camera, even the most basic shot (shall we say a long static take of the Empire State Building?) has been selected and the camera set up. The reality we see is always a chosen and arranged reality, which it is impossible for the film-maker to present without some standpoint of his own, however simple. The question is whether we always understand what we are seeing.

"The camera cannot lie," they used to say. But as was shown by Pudovkin's famous example of intercutting shots of different things into the same shot of a woman's face, whereupon she seemed to be expressing different emotions, the film can lie even if the camera cannot. The film can make us think that we see something quite different from what was filmed. And, of course, the more complex the selection and editing, the more it is an interpreted reality that we see.

In the case of Grierson, since his real aim was to teach, why did he get tangled up with the question of actuality? The moral tale was already a traditional form of social teaching, but Grierson disdained the idea of a story. A reaction was certainly due against

the falsity and foolishness of much current studio work, especially in
its treatment of ordinary working people, and under the influence
of the Russians and pioneers like Flaherty he led his followers out
into the ordinary world, seeking ordinary people. They were not
the first films to be made outside the studio. Far from it; and as we
see in the companion volume to this book the *genre* already had its
techniques. But the documentarists felt that they, at least, were
going to portray "real people" in their own surroundings. Begging
the question of what is an unreal person, it seems that what they
meant was working class people. It is all too clear that the upper
classes of the Establishment, which were the subject of Rotha's
Times film, did not seem real enough to be worth filming, although
their depiction in the commercial cinema was equally false and
absurd. Put crudely, whilst old father Flaherty watched the noble
savage, Grierson's boys watched the noble worker.

Incident and narrative were apparently felt to be a little suspect
under these circumstances, because they were arranged or contrived.
But Nanook had speared his seals in a certain way because it suited
Flaherty to film it that way, and the undersea shots of fish in
Drifters, however convincing in their green-blue tint, were perforce
shot in a tank. However real the streets and the hills, the buildings
and the factories, and however genuine the G.P.O. staff, the
porters and the welfare workers, most of the incidents in the phone
films, the shepherd in the mountains, the B.B.C., the films were
planned and set up and played for the camera. It was not a magic
eye observing life as it took place. Real fakery was present too, as
it had always been. The sequences inside the railway carriage in
Nightmail were shot in a carriage reconstructed in the studio. In
North Sea Harry Watt based his film on a true incident in a gale
off Aberdeen. It had really happened, but he reconstructed it. The
boat he hired was not the same boat, the men he hired were
seamen but not the seamen of the incident, nor even did they all
come from Aberdeen. Again, scenes inside the cabin were shot back
home at the studio. It was not a big feature studio, with glamorous
make-up and all the rest of the paraphernalia, but it was a studio
all the same. Even an intelligent viewer who realised he could not
possibly be looking at the original storm was likely to believe in the
authenticity of the surroundings. So what price reality?

22 The golden road to Samarkand? (*Children at School*, 1938).

23 Real drama played through again (*North Sea*, 1938).

24 "Mr. Money the postman walks nine miles to her cottage" (*Penny Journey*, 1938).

But the documentary movement sailed on with this slightly ambiguous connection with reality attached to it, seeking from time to time to define it. The original "creative treatment of reality" used by Grierson to describe Flaherty's work was expanded by Rotha in the second edition of *Documentary Film* in 1939 to "the use of the film medium to interpret creatively and in social terms the life of the people as it exists in reality". Any realistic dramatist with a social theme could say as much. With less finesse Bruce Woolfe, in an article in *Cinema Quarterly*,[1] put in a plea for a "measure of judicious fiction". The documentary boys were not at one with Bruce Woolfe. But in so far as they were prepared to reconstruct actual or typical events, even in their original surroundings, and to mix amateur actors with the people who were originally involved, they were manipulating reality to a considerable extent. And once they were prepared to reconstruct the surroundings as well, and mix even semi-professional actors, they were only doing to a different degree what the despised studios were doing. Realistic dramatisation was still dramatisation.

In the middle thirties there were two important changes which blurred the apparently safe distinction between fact and fiction. One was the coming of *The March of Time*, and the other was the increasing use of narrative in documentary films.

The March of Time was largely based on the unabashed use of reconstruction, not always very convincing reconstruction either. To the Luce group of companies, as journalists, the words and the message were the thing, not reality or visual qualities. Erik Barnouw quotes Henry Luce describing *The March of Time* as "fakery in allegiance to truth"[2] and of course it is a commonplace that there are many roads to truth. Years later, in an interview with Haskell Wexler, who had in *Medium Cool* (1969) used scenes of real violence in America as the background for dramatisation, Renée Epstein wrote :

For Wexler, words were not strong enough. The people's faces were not expressive enough. He needed artifice to come closer to reality.

"That evaluation is correct," he says. "I mean that a re-enactment taking on elements more real than the actual statements is an accurate description."[3]

and also :

"It is naïve to think that film-makers cannot create powerful reality images. I feel confident enough to defy anyone, after they have seen *Medium Cool*, to discriminate between an actual happening and a rehearsed scene."[4]

Our documentarists, with their experience of shooting on location and with amateurs, were better able than most to reproduce or fake when necessary and produce something indistinguishable from the real thing. Harry Watt, making British items for *The March of Time*, was not allowed to film the girls sorting football pool coupons so he used shots of similar sorting procedures in the Post Office. In an item he made for them on the tithe war of the thirties he reconstructed the whole of a raid on a farm, and claims with characteristic bravura : "I suppose it was the first time a dramatic reconstruction of a contemporary event had been done in a British documentary."[5] Incident imperceptibly developed into narrative. What struck the contemporary film theorist Rudolf Arnheim was not so much the introduction of narrative into documentary as the introduction of documentary into the narrative film, or an element of factual film into the studio-made story. Writing about *The March of Time* in *Sight and Sound* in 1939, and strongly supporting the view that the cinema was best where "It's work has been based on the natural expressiveness of the real fact . . . the whole effort of which has been dedicated completely to perfect more and more the faithfulness of imitation",[6] he observed a new tendency :

It began when the newsreel, in search of a method which should allow to give a more complete survey of the present-day events, added reconstructed scenes to the actual documents of reality. Personages of contemporary history were represented by actors, real events were remade in the studio. Of course, such a method involves serious dangers. As it pretends to give authentic truth fiction becomes falsification.[7]

He believed that the success of this new format had immediately influenced narrative films. Citing *The Lion Has Wings* as a milestone in this new type of feature film, he says:

> In comparison with the immediate strength of this type of film, all the other films of the usual kind appear suddenly pale and old-fashioned. They seem artificial without being art, whereas the R.A.F. film shows how the mere sticking to the facts produces, I would say, automatically more dignity and a keener human interest.[8]

The film itself, incidentally, Korda's propaganda-offering assembled hastily at the outbreak of war, is an uneasy mixture of newsreels, reconstructions and grotesquely stilted dramatisation which does not bear later examination in these enthusiastic terms. But whether Arnheim was right in thinking it was *The March of Time* that introduced the greater realism that eventually appeared in studio stories, or whether it was our own documentary movement and the success of its wartime dramatic documentaries, or whether indeed it had more to do with the improved technology that finally made inconspicuous and location shooting so much easier, he was right in seeing that a new question of veracity had been posed: "It must be fully realized that – from the point of view of moral responsibility – a very delicate situation arises as soon as instead of using reality as an element of fiction we begin to use fiction as an element of reality."[9] Whichever way round you look at it, once you admit the legitimacy of faking in what purports to be reality the power to deceive is unlimited.

But for the teacher both *The March of Time*'s use of commentary to convey the message and its reconstruction of situations were admirable tools. Grierson and his closest followers took to the new style with alacrity and both of its elements, albeit with much greater subtlety than in the American films, were also adopted by Rotha with great success in *Today We Live*. It is noticeable, by the way, that with these changed tactics the appearance of frankly staged historical reconstructions were also introduced into a number of documentary films. *Enough to Eat* was effectively the first of the movement's films that could be described as illustrated lectures, in which the message was verbal and could have been delivered without the visuals, however helpful these were.

At the same time another part of the movement was reasserting the narrative element in documentary. It was almost as if both factions, which now went their different ways, had been liberated by the new and more flexible attitude to reality. Like the others, this group also had a film which can be regarded as a turning-point. *The Saving of Bill Blewitt* was the first serious and conscious attempt to convey the message indirectly, by means of a story complete in itself.

Years later Grierson's successor in the business of educating for democracy, however, was to revert once more to the search for pure reality. Writing in 1976 in *The Sunday Times* of the television films of Roger Graef, Peter Lennon explained:

And Roger Graef's more complicated approach in *Decision: Steel* (Granada) attempted by means of impersonal and impartial recording to reveal the process by which decisions are reached. This, he hopes, will provide the kind of information which will equip the viewer better to understand, and if necessary challenge, decisions which affect his life. . . . His objective is television of record, which will not merely provide material for one show, but form a basis of accurate information, by which viewers will be better equipped to assess, and if necessary challenge, how our national institutions are run.[10]

Here the need for reconstruction and arrangement is apparently removed, the new lightweight hand-held and inconspicuous equipment allowing us at last, it seems, to record things as they happen. Two things intervene, however, showing it once more to be an unrealised dream. For one thing an enormous amount of film must be shot, and so much selection and editing is necessary that the result, far from being impersonal and impartial, is very subjective indeed. Secondly there is the heightened problem of intrusion. It has always been true, in any apparent reportage, that the act of filming becomes a factor in what is filmed. As the 1914 Tommies filed past the cameraman he was not filming them as they were normally, but as they were that day, with him present, some of them grinning at the camera, some annoyed and looking grimly away. Latter-day theory has been that technology has now produced such inconspicuous equipment that if a small film making team is around long enough their subjects get used to them and forget they are being filmed. The theory is hardly believable. Surely the only people immune from this intrusion factor are those who are filmed unaware or bugged. The Graef films are immensely valuable, and nearer to the ideal of educating the citizen about how a complex society functions than anything Grierson could have imagined with the technology of 1929. But they bring us no nearer to objective reality.

Something similar, at the same time, happened in later years to the dramatisation of reality. Various forms of so-called minimal cinema, armed with the lightweight equipment and trusting to the belief that the film-maker could refrain from being a factor in the filming, or at least reduce his intrusion to a minimum, sought in the late fifties and the sixties to capture real life through improvisation and the minimum of direction, narrative and editing. Thus reaction against the falseness of arrangement and manipulation, once again, had caused later generations to seek a closer approach to reality.

In the thirties there were not, as it happens, very many examples of the narrative documentary, which was to develop more fully during the war. But, just as Graef's observational cinema in the information field and the various forms of minimal cinema in the dramatic field later sought to re-establish reality once more, the very realistic narrative was also to surface again in a more advanced form. That strand in the documentary movement which can best be described as a story of some social significance treated in such a realistic way that it appears to be happening before our eyes re-appeared many years later in a form of television drama which became the centre of considerable controversy. Peter Watkins's B.B.C. television programme of 1964, *Culloden*, presented no problems as it was easily understood that no cameraman could have been present at the battle in 1745. It was acceptable as a pretended documentary. But a series of realistic plays, of which Ken Loach's 1966 *Cathy Come Home* may be taken as a key example, were not so lucky. Using techniques and modes developed for documentary, and associated in the minds of a huge and unquestioning audience with something dimly understood to be "true", they brought the question of narrative, realism and documentary once more to the fore. The legitimate use of modern equipment and methods to achieve what the dramatist has always sought, the suspension of disbelief, had surprising results. Doing what the realistic playwright had always done, dramatising what he held to be important truths in society, he used means so much more effective than those available to earlier dramatists of similar inclinations that they caused some confusion, even resentment. It was as though much of the mass television audience had really believed they were seeing the events as they occurred. Had they reflected, they must have realised the camera was unlikely to be there on the station platform as Cathy's children were taken from her, and that the people showed a strange indifference to the fact that they were being watched by a whole camera crew. But the more naïve felt they had been fooled, and even developed an impatient scepticism about the "truth" of documentary which they had previously accepted unthinkingly.

A delicate point, indeed. Arnheim's anxiety about moral responsibility lingers on. But in the end the documentary movement of the thirties embraced many different types of film, embodying many different degrees of illusion, and this welcome diversity has continued. If talented film makers of varying beliefs and interests are not to be hamstrung by preconceptions of categories, and of what is valid and what is not valid, the answer seems to lie in more discriminating audiences. Such delicate points would not arise with a public better educated in the nature of what they are watching, and with a better understanding of the relation between reality and film.

Appendix

The British Film Institute

In November 1929 an unofficial conference of well over a hundred people, drawn from educational, scientific and social organisations and government departments, was called together largely on the initiative of the British Institute of Adult Education and the Association of Scientific Workers. The Secretary of the former, a man of some importance in the early history of the British Film Institute, was J. W. Brown, who was described by R. S. Lambert as tall and imposing, an engineer, and a picturesque person of working class origin who had studied at Ruskin College and had a "gift of the gab" which he exercised in a' *tête-à-tête* mumble.[1] He organised two Exhibitions of Mechanical Aids to Learning and was to found a magazine, *Sight and Sound*, in the spring of 1932. The conference was drawn from a very wide circle and included representatives of the B.B.C. and the film society movement, but the emphasis was overwhelmingly on education.

As a result of this conference an unofficial Commission on Educational and Cultural Films was set up in December, to conduct a survey "into the service which the cinematograph may render to education and social progress". Its terms of reference were those originally visualised by the convenors of the conference :

"(1) To consider suggestions for improving and extending the use of films (motion pictures and similar visual and auditory devices) for educational and cultural purposes, including use as documentary records.

(2) To consider methods for raising the standard of public appreciation of films, by criticism and advice addressed to the

general public, by discussion among persons engaged in educational or cultural pursuits, and by experimental production of films in collaboration with professional producers.

(3) To consider whether it is desirable and practicable to establish a permanent central organisation with general objects as above, and among its particular functions, the following. . . ."

These functions may be very briefly summarised as advice on the production, selection, distribution and use of films.

Chairman of the Commission until he died in the spring of 1933 was Sir Benjamin Gott, former Secretary for Education in Middlesex; the Joint Secretaries were Brown and the Secretary for Education in the City of Oxford, A. C. Cameron. Of the forty or so participants and additional witnesses, most were in education, libraries, museums or government. Bruce Woolfe of British Instructional Films and Miss Margery Locket from his Educational Department, Neville Kearney of the Federation of British Industries Film Group and St John Ervine, drama critic of *The Observer*, were the only ones who might care about the film as such, and possibly the editor of the B.B.C.'s publication *The Listener*, R. S. Lambert, who was a friend of Brown. Many members of the Commission were already committed to the idea of an institute or some such permanent body. However, despite the impressive array of organisations, it was later said that most members of the Commission had not in fact been officially appointed to represent them.

The work of the Commission took several years, the bulk of it being done by Brown and Cameron. In June 1930 they obtained a two year grant from the Carnegie Trust, which was later extended and was to be their main source of support. In November 1930 a second conference of the organisations originally involved was held. News filtered out from time to time, and by July 1931 Cameron began to write the report. Meetings were held with the trade under Gott, with Cameron outlining various possibilities such as help for experimental and documentary films, certificates for good quality educational films, advice to government on registration, the cataloguing of educational films, experiments and advice on equipment for schools, and liaison with the film trade.

A year passed, during which there was guarded friendliness from the trade. A Parliamentary Film Committee deputation to the Home Secretary, Sir Herbert Samuel, in March 1932 suggested the creation of a National Film Institute. In May a proposal which was to have far-reaching consequences came from the novelist John Buchan, who was an M.P. and a director of British Instructional Films although not himself a member of the Commission. In a House of Commons debate on the Sunday Opening of cinemas he suggested that a National Film Institute might be financed by a percentage of the charity contribution which was to be levied on the box office takings of cinemas opening on Sundays. The Under-Secretary of State for the Home Office, Oliver Stanley, welcomed this idea, which was repeated by Buchan with much publicity at a big luncheon a few days later. Events were to show that it was this casual piece of opportunism, whereby a tax on the trade was made the basis of the Institute's finances, that gave the trade a strangle-hold on the resulting body.

The report, *The Film in National Life*, was published in June 1932 and was a valuable summary of the position of the film both as information and entertainment at that time, and of the possible functions and forms of an institute. It was written by Alan Cameron, a broadminded educationist and a public servant of the old school, married to the novelist Elizabeth Bowen; he was to play an honour-able part in the British Film Institute's affairs until he died in 1952. One of the most important recommendations of the report was for a "positive agency" to encourage good films and "exercise a con-structive critical influence over the whole field of cinematography". It emphasised the need to "educate an informed public" as the best way of promoting a demand for better films. Having examined various types of body, it finally favoured one which would be financed in part by public funds, and incorporated under Royal Charter. This was all the report had to say about financial arrange-ments. It suggested a board of seven governors appointed for five years on a renewable basis by the Government, and that this board should set up an advisory council bringing together trade and educational interests and government agencies. It envisaged certain functions for the Institute : to act as a national clearing house for information about the film; to influence public opinion in the direction of wanting and demanding good films, a function later described as film appreciation and defined by the Institute as "the building up of interest in the film instead of looking upon the cinema theatre merely as a convenient means of passing two or three idle hours".[3] The Institute should give advice on educational films; act as liaison between the trade, educational and cultural bodies: advise government departments; undertake research into the uses of the film; maintain a national repository of films of permanent value; catalogue educational films; and certify or endorse educational, cultural or scientific films if the Government should want it to do so.

Four days later Samuel suggested in Parliamentary Committee that it should be financed through the Privy Council. In doing so he used the fatal phrase "films of educational and cultural purposes". This apparently innocuous expression was to distort, and in time obscure, the fact that one of the chief preoccupations of the Commission had been to improve the quality of the ordinary commercial entertainment film as shown in the cinemas. The trade was quick to seize on the idea that there was something called a cultural film which was different from their own product. As long as the Institute confined its attentions to that, all was well.

At the end of June in a further Commons debate Stanley proposed the use of a Cinematograph Fund administered by the Privy Council "for the purpose of encouraging the use and development of the cinematograph as a means of entertainment and instruction". Immediately, the trade bared its teeth. *Kine Weekly* took a nasty tone over the proposal to use 5 per cent of the Sunday Opening contribution for "some nebulous body", a "grand-motherly attempt to 'improve' the film industry", and was righteously indignant that those in real need of charity would thus be deprived, "filching 5% of the hospitals' dole" as they sobbed with crocodile tears.[4] In the Lords, Lord Hailsham avoided commitment as the Institute was not yet in being, but commendably kept his sights on the real aim "of the improvement of films and of the character of cinema entertainments".

In August 1932 a significant exchange of letters in *The Times*, alas, shows the Commission selling the pass in exchange for the support of the trade. Simon Rowson's letter in the correspondence columns of 4 August astutely ignores the idea of raising the cultural tone of the commercial film, but speaks of a big increase in the "cultural film", treating it as a separate category but with a certain ambiguous connection with the educational film; he even refers to the "new films", pointing out that "this new demand" will not encroach on attendances in the cinemas, but by arousing interest among people who now shun the film may actually create new patrons. The trade is ready to meet this new demand, according to him. In his view the Institute should be controlled by the trade, and he asks for a representative advisory committee to be set up. Brown and Cameron as Joint Secretaries to the Commission replied in *The Times* of 9 August. Pointing out that the proposals had so far received no support from the trade, they encouraged it to offer its technical skill and experience, but affirmed that the Institute "must be in a position of indisputable disinterestedness". As we shall see, this was a vain hope. Already bending backwards to get the trade on their side, they fell in the trap and repeated the treacherous phrase "cultural films". Rowson's reply was confident. Money and expertise were to come from the trade, and an "amateur" body was unsuitable. He writes again of the "anticipated new demand for cultural films", and seems to envisage a special committee planning them, with the professionals making them.

During the next six months or so the Commission was busy rousing support and getting organised. Lambert addressed public meetings up and down the country and the Commission held conferences, invited interested bodies to discussions, consulted with the Government and individual M.P.s and took part in the 21st Annual Conference of Educational Associations. But, more than anything else, they tried to convert the renters' and exhibitors' associations, the K.R.S. and the C.E.A. It was primarily Rowson's achievement that in return for its support the trade was able to infiltrate the new body and neutralise it, turning it from a powerful enemy which would revolutionise the tawdry side of commercial production into an ineffective, well-meaning educational body largely under the trade's own influence.

Early in 1933 the new Home Secretary Sir John Gilmour made a provisional regulation under the Sunday Entertainments Act for 5 per cent of the total collected by the local authorities from the cinemas as charity contribution to be sent to the Privy Council and administered as a fund. In February a deputation called upon the Under-Secretary for the Home Office for approval of the constitution of the new body. Out of the nine members of this deputation no less than six represented the trade, along with Buchan, Gott and Lambert. Already by March 1933 it was widely known that the trade's choice for governors would be C. M. Woolf representing the Federation of British Industries Film Group, Sam Eckman of M-G-M representing the K.R.S. and Tom Ormiston the C.E.A. Ormiston was believed to have opposed the very existence of the Institute, and both Woolf and Eckman were shrewd, hard-headed businessmen who were very successful with films as they then were, and hardly likely to be interested in changing them. As it happened Eckman, being American, was ineligible and was replaced by F. W. Baker, a veteran dealer in some of the worst British films ever made, whose special talent for survival lay in cutting his cloth to fit the quota market. Not as hard and ruthless as Eckman, he probably had even lower standards of quality in films than the M-G-M manager.

Under this leadership, agreement was finally reached. The Commission finished its work, and closed its office in August, applying to the Board of Trade in company with the F.B.I., the K.R.S. and the C.E.A. for the registration of the British Film Institute. The Governing Council was duly appointed, and included Woolf, Ormiston and Baker with Sir Charles Cleland of the Glasgow Educational authority, Cameron, Lambert, John Buchan, John Lawson, M.P., and Lady Levita. The Institute was in existence at last.

The Articles of Association as it was incorporated on 30 September 1933 state that the "object for which the Institute is established is: To encourage the use and development of the cinematograph as a means of entertainment and instruction and, so far as the same shall not be inconsistent with that object, for the following ancillary objects . . ." and there follows a list of aims, many of which concern "films of educational and cultural value". Members, paying £1 10s a year, are mentioned. A later version of the articles is slightly different: "The object for which the Institute is established is: to encourage the development of the art of the film, to promote its use as a record of contemporary life and manners and to foster public appreciation and study of it from these points of view."

The Privy Council did not hurry to make its first grant. And, if proof were needed of where the real power lay, it was the industry which made two grants of £500 each, from the C.E.A. and the K.R.S., to keep it going. It was housed in an office provided by the trade, with an Acting Secretary, R. V. Crow, who as recently as 1931–2 had been President of the C.E.A. J. W. Brown was made General Manager rather than Cameron mainly, according to R. S. Lambert, because he was on better terms with the trade. His magazine about the use of films and the gramophone in education, *Sight and Sound*, which was now in its second year, was taken over by the Institute. It had been run by an editorial board on which sat Cameron, Lambert, Brown, and the left wing Paul Rotha and Raymond Postgate. At first it specialised in educational and technical information, especially about substandard film. It welcomed the Institute in the issue of winter 1933/4, after which its character began to change, the plain printed cover giving way to a more glamorous entertainment film still in spring 1934, by which time the editors had become anonymous. From January 1934 a *Monthly Film Bulletin* for members was also published, giving résumés, production details and an evaluation of new films. Although in the summer of 1934 *Sight and Sound* announced a new section, *The Cinema in School*, and it continued to include educational and religious news, the tone gradually changed and critical articles by Rotha, Alistair Cooke, Arthur Vesselo and later Alan Page began to assume greater importance. The Duke of Sutherland was made Chairman of the Institute late in 1933 and a system of committees dealing with finance, publications, information, entertainment, education and technical matters was set up. Plans for an international exhibition of educational films, for a summer school and for branches in the provinces were announced. In November 1933 a pamphlet was issued called *The British Film Institute: Its Aims and Objects.*

Not everyone was satisfied with what was going on. We have seen in the chapter on the educational film how Sir James Marchant and Sir Oswald Stoll had been in favour of some sort of Royal Institute within the trade or a Film University, and how the Central

Information Bureau for Educational Films had been formed and even brought out a large catalogue of educational films and apparatus before the B.F.I. was registered. Its most bitter critic, however, was journalist Walter Ashley, who published an onslaught called *The Cinema and the Public* in January 1934. This booklet, addressed to Stanley Baldwin as Lord President of the Council, originally appeared in a dust-wrapper marked "B.F.I. EXPOSED", but this jacket was withdrawn by the publisher. The booklet was said to have been published at the expense of Sir James Marchant, and was distributed to M.P.s and others.[5]

Ashley claimed that the governing body had not, as proposed, been chosen by the State. Cameron, Lambert and Cleland had been appointed by a commission which was now defunct, and those representing the public interest, Buchan, Lawson and Lady Levita, who were to retire annually, could be removed by a general meeting and their successors would be appointed by members of the B.F.I. Most important of all, he maintained that the three trade bodies had chosen one member each who could not be removed except by their own appointing bodies, and that the three men selected were wily and experienced negotiators with a knowledge of the film world which gave them the advantage in any discussion. There was, he concluded, little doubt that they would have it all their own way. The Articles of Association as finally agreed were very much to the trade's liking, with a number of important exclusions laid down. The Institute was not to interfere in trade matters or censorship, for example, a proviso which would silence it on questions of public concern. Worst of all, there were no provisions to ensure the financial independence which would have guaranteed the "position of indisputable disinterestedness" so bravely claimed by Brown and Cameron. This was to have been established by the public appointment of the governing body, but apparently had been forgotten. According to Ashley, the organisations invited to the original conference were in no way responsible for the report, so it is small wonder that they took no steps to prevent its complete evisceration while the Institute was being set up: "Direct enquiry of forty of those mentioned at the end of the report including some of the most influential, revealed that only *seven* of these forty were officially represented on the Commission, and that only *two* of them had approved its report."[6] The later history of the B.F.I. showed that the neutrality of the trade had indeed been dearly bought, but little notice seems to have been taken of Ashley at the time. The charity contribution method of finance, finally, was to prove totally inadequate and led to a pressing need to raise income from membership. This in time was to bring problems of its own. For, although the idea of having members had been inserted into the proposals as an additional source of revenue and moral support, the intention had always been for the Institute to serve society in general rather than fee-paying members. There was, therefore, no reason why the governing body, which dealt with matters of national concern and was financed mainly by public money, should include representatives of the small number of people who paid a subscription for the publications and other privileges offered by the Institute in return. This, however, was later to be demanded.

Work began in earnest in 1934. The Privy Council made a grant of £5,000 for the first year and £6,000 for the second.[7] A number of local branches were formed as Film Institute Societies, and a Scottish Film Council was founded. Panels of experts were formed for education, entertainment, international relations, the Dominions, India and the colonies, medical, social service, scientific research, amateur cinematography and documentary, in order to view and report on films and encourage their production. A plan to assess and certify non-fiction films on their instructional or cultural value came to nothing owing to the opposition of the trade, who claimed that it was a form of censorship and as such outside the Institute's powers. Nevertheless the Education Panel managed to form committees in science, geography, history and the arts, language and literature which listed and classified existing educational films and considered new ones. The Entertainment Panel was meant to encourage better films. The *Monthly Film Bulletin* came as near as such a body could to grading films and expressing a view on their cultural or instructional value. The Documentary Panel was of comparatively little importance since the documentary movement was already firmly organised around Grierson. But a steady stream of leaflets and select lists of various types of film began to be published, and a summer school was an annual event from 1935 onwards. Basil Wright, Grierson, Stuart Legg and J. B. Holmes from the documentary movement, L. J. Hibbert of the Polytechnic, Brian Salt of G-BI, Thomas Baird of the British Commercial Gas Association, Mary Field and Andrew Buchanan, technical experts H. D. Waley of the B.F.I. and R. H. Cricks of the British Kinematograph Society, and educationalists from Julian Huxley to G. J. Cons, J. A. Lauwerys, F. A. Hoare and H. R. Hewer of Imperial College were among the speakers during the next few years.

Meanwhile, however, the Technical Panel had become involved in the first of the B.F.I.'s many troubles, the row over the standardisation of substandard film and equipment already described in the chapter on educational films. The difficulties experienced in trying to effect a duty-free passage of educational films in association with the Italian Institute of Educational Cinematography has also been discussed.

While this was going on there were the first signs of scandal to come. R. S. Lambert, who was editor of the B.B.C.'s weekly paper *The Listener* and one of the original proponents of the B.F.I., now sat on its board of governors. According to his own account,[8] in the autumn of 1934 some remarks of his had offended certain members of the trade. The renter W. R. Fuller, a prominent member of the K.R.S., complained to the B.B.C. Lambert's immediate superior, the Controller of Public Relations Gladstone Murray, spoke to Lambert about the wisdom of remaining on the board of the B.F.I. if it meant the name of the B.B.C. becoming involved in public controversy. Lambert's colleagues at the B.F.I., John Buchan, and the husband of his other colleague Lady Levita spoke up for him and the matter was dropped. He thanked Sir Cecil Levita, for many years a vigorous defender of the cinema on the London County Council, who seems to have felt afterwards that by speaking on Lambert's behalf he had accepted some responsibility for his conduct.

Extremely important, although little was made of it at the time, was the birth of the National Film Library.[9] An archive was not a new idea. The official films from the war of 1914–18 were deposited in the Imperial War Museum in 1919 and, because of the technical problems which arose, were put in the care of H.M.S.O. under a Government Cinematograph Adviser in 1924. The Faculty of Cinema Art in 1927 had hoped for a museum. The 1926 British

Empire Film Institute under Aubrey Rees, set up as an information centre, had been given Ponting's Polar films and by August 1929 it was reported that they were starting a National Film Museum of films representative of English or Empire life, and that *Atlantic*, B.I.P.'s early sound film based on the sinking of the *Titanic*, was to be presented to them. Later, the Empire Film Association superseded the British Empire Film Institute. But the preservation of films for various reasons other than patriotism was also beginning to arouse interest, and even the trade saw that some prestige publicity might be gained from this. It was also realised that films which were chosen for preservation would in time deteriorate if not given special treatment. In October 1931 the Chief Chemist, Sir Robert Robertson, reported on government lab work on deterioration in officially preserved films, saying that the celluloid base was in good condition despite a little discolouration, but that some damage and discolouration of the silver image was already beginning to appear.

The official aims of the B.F.I. had included the maintenance of a national repository of films of permanent value. After films had finished their original circulation, most were either junked for reclamation of the silver deposit or left to deteriorate in some forgotten corner. But with neither a statutory right to demand copies nor funds to buy them, with a trade deeply suspicious in case old firms should circulate in competition with new, with no criteria of permanent value or technical knowledge about preservation, the problem was vast. Nevertheless, when the Empire Marketing Board was being disbanded and the new G.P.O. Film Unit set up, the B.F.I. sent a deputation to the Postmaster-General to request that the large E.M.B. film library should be handed to it for preservation. The request was refused, but late in 1933 the Institute asked the British Kinematograph Society for advice on permanent preservation and the B.K.S. produced an important paper on it, their recommendations being published in *Sight and Sound* in the summer of 1934.[10] In July 1935 the National Film Library was formed, and put in the charge of a young man who had joined the Institute the year before as Information Officer, Ernest Lindgren. About a hundred reels had already been collected. In his pamphlet Ashley had been pessimistic about the establishment of an archive, saying it was a task the B.F.I. was quite unfitted to perform, as it "would require the resources of some permanent museum, and is quite beyond those of a small semi-private body of doubtful permanence and with limited accommodation and staff". However, with youth and high hopes, and the B.K.S. paper to guide him, Lindgren set out with objectives later listed in the National Film Library Catalogue of 1938 :

1. To preserve for posterity copies of all films, fictional and non-fictional, outstanding either for their technical excellence or for their importance in the history of the cinema, and copies of all films valuable as documents of scientific or historical importance.

The Institute was fortunate in having as its first Curator one of the few members of its staff who knew and cared about the film, a tactful and likeable man whose deceptively mild and correct manner concealed a tenacity which overcame the lack of either money or real support from trade, public or education circles. With meticulous care he set about building solid foundations for a pioneer archive of worldwide reputation.

In other departments things were not going quite so well. There were discussions with the Board of Education in 1935 which led to a proposal to found a separate company, Educational and General Supplies, as a subsidiary of the Institute, which would give schools the benefit of bulk purchase of equipment. Brown was to be director of this company although still working as General Manager of the Institute, an arrangement which the trade regarded as unfair competition. In the search for financial backing for this company Dr Benjamin Gregory, editor of the *Methodist Times* and an associate of J. Arthur Rank in the field of religious films, came to the fore and became a governor of the Institute in place of John Buchan. After early enthusiasm, Lambert drifted apart from Gregory and Brown, whom he was later to describe as a bad administrator, and there also developed a coolness between him and Lady Levita, who was sympathetic to Brown. Lambert by now had become friends with the popular celebrity and self-styled ghost-hunter Harry Price, who had also entered the scene during the search for funds for the new National Film Library and had in fact been made Chairman of the Library Committee. It would seem from Lambert's account that Brown was as lukewarm towards Price as Lambert was towards Gregory.

The indefatigable Lambert went on a jaunt to the Isle of Man with his new friend in July 1935 to investigate some odd happenings involving the Irving family, who claimed to be haunted by a talking mongoose called Gef. In a spirit of light-hearted journalism rather than of serious research they produced a book called *The Haunting of Cashen's Gap* in 1936 which they described in the introduction as "an essay in the Veracious but Unaccountable". Throughout the book they carefully avoided saying they believed the story, but were equally careful to report it as though with an open mind. Even relating how a hair of the supposed mongoose was sent to Julian Huxley, and by him to F. Martin Duncan who photomicrographed it and pronounced it to be a dog's hair, the book still managed to remain equivocal.

This undignified behaviour was too much for the aged Sir Cecil Levita and he again spoke to Gladstone Murray, mentioning inconsistencies and even hysteria, saying that Lambert was under Price's influence and no longer fit to be a governor of the Institute.[11]

According to the account later given in the courts, Sir Cecil had felt that Lambert was no longer suitable for his position as he appeared actually to believe in both Gef and the evil eye, and that it was his own duty to mention this to Murray in view of his previous championship of Lambert. Murray was, in fact, no longer Lambert's boss. Instead of referring the matter to the appropriate person inside the B.B.C. he discussed it with Lambert himself. Lambert, unfortunately, was not the man to take this in good part, feeling that it harmed his standing at the B.B.C. and that Sir Cecil was out to remove him from the B.F.I. board. After various moves a slander writ was issued in March. By this time the bizarre Case of the Talking Mongoose was a popular joke, bringing ridicule on everyone connected with it. Lambert won the lawsuit, being awarded £7,500 damages plus costs, but as it was delayed until November 1936 discussions over the B.B.C. Charter, due for renewal in 1937, were also delayed on the grounds that the issue concerned staff relations at the Broadcasting House. Sir Stafford Cripps mentioned the case in Parliament as an example of the autocratic treatment of staff at the B.B.C. and a Special Board of Inquiry into the

B.B.C. was set up by Stanley Baldwin in November 1936, leading to a White Paper in December and the promise of a staff association. The Charter was duly renewed. Lambert remained with *The Listener* until January 1939.

After these high jinks and clashes of personality a certain amount of reorganisation seemed advisable, and during 1936 the team who were to guide the B.F.I. for the next ten years or so were assembled. At the third annual general meeting in October 1936 Lady Levita, Dr Gregory and J. S. Lawson were replaced on the board by Eleanor Plumer, Professor W. Lyon Blease and Sir William Brass, to represent the public interest. Brown departed and William Farr was made Acting General Manager in his place from January 1937 until he was replaced in May by Oliver Bell, who had been involved in League of Nations work and as a member of the Commission on Cultural and Educational Films. Bell, a large, genial man with a Conservative, public school and Oxford background, a J.P., with an interest in the educational aspect of film rather than the artistic, was perhaps a rather surprising choice for Director, as the post later became. He was, however, the traditional Englishman who took naturally to a career in public service of any sort. After Farr left in November 1937 Bell was joined as Assistant by Robin Dickinson, who proved a loyal lieutenant of similar background and beliefs. By temperament they were unlikely to get on well with members of the documentary movement who at that time were at the forefront in any serious consideration of the film, and although the necessary contacts and co-operation were maintained some hostility did exist between the "documentary boys" and the B.F.I. Olwen Vaughan, who had joined the Institute in 1935 as Secretary, was on the other hand passionately committed to the art of the film and was in contact with many of the best contemporary film-makers. Together with Lindgren, she supplied the enthusiasm and knowledge about films, he in a scholarly way and she in a sociable one. The Technical Officer was H. D. Waley, brother of the Chinese scholar Arthur Waley.[12]

Thus reorganised, the B.F.I. proceeded with more circumspection. It did not ratify its sponsorship of Educational and General Supplies, which went its own way. It held a conference in November on the subject of special entertainment films and film shows for children, under the title of Films for Children, which was under the chairmanship of Alan Cameron, who at the time was Secretary to the Central Council for School Broadcasting as well as holding his educational post in Oxford. Film lists and pamphlets, the provision of lecturers, the work of the Information Department and panels and committees, and the publication of the periodicals continued. In 1938 Bell and Simon Rowson, still a one-man statistical service for the film industry, considered the setting up of a Statistical Bureau. Nothing came of the idea but it illustrated the tendency to confine the B.F.I. to information functions rather than cultural leadership. Membership grew, as did provincial Film Institute Societies. Figures given in the annual reports for full members, including both individual and corporate members, and for associate members holding their membership through Film Institute Societies, show the growth :

	June *1935*	*June* *1936*	*June* *1937*	*June* *1938*	*June* *1939*
(*a*) Full members	400	597	769	921	1,091
(*b*) Associate members	1,370	1,370	2,050	2,190	2,500

The fee for membership was not high, however, and even with the Institute's share of the Cinematograph Fund, which amounted in 1938 to £10,350 out of £11,359, there was never enough money to do all the things they wanted to do.

As for the National Film Library, it gave its first show in March 1936 at the Regent Street Polytechnic. Films were now being given to it, including *Things to Come* and the Pavlova film *The Immortal Swan, The Private Life of Henry VIII, Evergreen, Man of Aran, The Ghost Goes West* and *Turn of the Tide,* and by May 1936 it was said to possess 800 reels. In the autumn the first edition of a catalogue of films in the archive, numbering 322, was published with a separate list of 49 which had been reprinted and were available on loan. In April 1938 an illustrated second edition came out, much bigger and containing 106 films in the Loan Section, although all of these, with the exception of a handful of early films, were interest and education films. According to *Kine Weekly*[13] the archive now had a million feet of film. In the same year a compilation film, *Drawings that Walk and Talk*, was made by Marie Seton and K. H. Frank for the Library, tracing the development of animated cartoon films. With the help of the B.K.S. work on preservation, a Library Committee and a Selection Committee, indefatigable borrowing and begging gathered the nucleus of a collection which depended entirely on voluntary donation. The enormous cost of preservation and lending was as yet not fully realised, but the Library's constant refrain was already the lack of money. In the absence of legal authority, also, the Archive made its selection but received only a small proportion of the films it asked for, and those usually in badly worn prints. The film industry was indifferent at best, and hostile at worst. Films were often donated out of vanity rather than charity, and the archive received a haphazard collection, from Harry Price's items of psychical interest to all Adrian Brunel's own silent films, and no less than two hundred depressingly unimportant silent films from Sir Oswald Stoll, who was never one to do things by halves. In 1938 an International Federation of Film Archives, F.I.A.F., with central offices in Paris, was formed by the Cinémathèque Française, the National Film Library, the Museum of Modern Art Film Library in America and the Reichsfilmarchiv in Germany, its first President being John Abbott of America and its Vice-President Frank Hensel of Germany and Treasurer Olwyn Vaughan. The first conference was held in New York in 1939. The many possible reasons for preservation were beginning to be understood and the whole thing had moved a long way from the original naïve idea of a museum of masterpieces. The Institute published in September 1939 a historical catalogue compiled by Arthur Vesselo, an enthusiast and critic who worked closely with Lindgren. This listed some 750 films made before 1934 and still available for study from over fifty sources in Britain, including the Institute itself. The author writes of his attempt to include anything "truly representative of a country, period or style". He calls it a selected list, but even he can surely have had little conception of the vast reserves of films as yet untraced, the almost limitless number of reasons for preservation, and the enormous expense of preserving, reprinting and making films available which lay ahead. Still treated as a mere department of the Institute, the archive had an importance which was hardly realised yet except by its own small staff.

As is so often the case, because the motives of those originally concerned with the setting up of the British Film Institute were not identical and the resulting terms of reference were confused. During the thirties it was casting around for its proper role. Little stress had been laid on its function as an archive. Such guidance as there was lay in the phrase used in the Articles, "to encourage the development of the art of the film, to promote its use as a record of contemporary life and manners and to foster public appreciation and study of it from these points of view". What the ambiguous instruction to promote its use as a record of contemporary life and manners really means has always been a problem. But film appreciation was making headway at this time in all Western countries, and here the Institute did play a part, while the National Film Library was beginning to amass the material basis for future film studies. But most of the interests represented on the original commission had been educational and much of the Institute's work was concerned with the educational film, especially under Oliver Bell, although as we have seen in the chapter on school films the absence of strong practical measures to encourage and train teachers in the use of film in the classroom meant that even here its efforts met with only partial success. The leadership of the Institute was personally quite unsuited to take any positive action towards improving the artistic or even technical standards of the commercial film, and as its very existence depended on the goodwill of the film trade the attitude of the latter was important. In America, the various sections of the industry had got together in 1927 to found the American Academy of Motion Picture Arts and Sciences, which by training, co-operative research and the fostering of a sense of professional pride had been an important influence in the maintenance of a high standard of production. But the trade bodies in this country saw no need for self-improvement. Instead, they managed to confine the Institute to a sort of educational half-world, where it was tolerated with everything from vague goodwill through indifference to contempt as long as it did nothing to interfere with the commercial film.

Notes

CHAPTER 2 THE EDUCATIONAL FILM

1 W. H. George, *The Cinema in School*, p. 70.
2 D. Charles Ottley, *The Cinema in Education*, pp. 23–4.
3 *A National Encyclopaedia of Educational Films* (ed. William Lally), p. 11.
4 ibid. pp. 23–4.
5 The University of Leeds, Leeds Educational Authority, Bingley Training College, Bingley and Bradford Branches of the Workers' Educational Association and the Educational Authorities of Bedfordshire, Bradford, Tottenham, London, Wolverhampton and the East and West Ridings of Yorkshire.
6 See Appendix for an account of the Commission and of the foundation of the British Film Institute.
7 *Sight and Sound*, no. 8, winter 1933/4.
8 *Cinema Quarterly*, autumn 1934, pp. 12–14.
9 *Arctic, Rice, Seaports* and *Canals*.
10 *Sight and Sound*, no. 22, summer 1937, p. 97.
11 See Appendix.
12 Catalogue of the Second Exhibition of Mechanical Aids to Learning, Sept 1931.
13 *Sight and Sound*, No. 4, winter 1932/3, p. 106.
14 *Kine Weekly*, 3 Oct 1929, p. 31.
15 According to *Close Up*, vol. VIII, no. 2, June 1931, *Cambridge* was made by Noxon, editor of the Cambridge review *Experiment* and founder of the Film Society at Cambridge, for British Instructional and Wardour Films, and was helped by Stuart Legg.
16 *Sight and Sound*, no. 2, summer 1932.
17 *Cinema Quarterly*, vol. 2, no. 1, autumn 1933, p. 64, calls this *Roadways*, also referring to J. B. Holmes's *Where the Road Begins* as *Hillman-Humber*.
18 *Cinema Quarterly*, vol. 2, no. 2, winter 1933/4, p. 96.
19 *Sight and Sound*, no. 22, summer 1937, p. 89.
20 According to P.E.P. p. 111. *Kine Weekly*, 20 July 1939, p. 13, states that between its beginning in 1934 and July 1939 they had made 400 shorts; the discrepancy is presumably due to *Kine Weekly* counting theatrical and school versions as different films. According to *Sight and Sound*, vol. 7, no. 25, spring 1938, Mary Field and Bruce Woolfe had been filming for 15 years and made about 200 films.
21 *Sight and Sound*, no. 18, summer 1936.
22 *Film Art*, no. 9, autumn 1936, pp. 18–20.
23 Ceylon, Cyprus, Kenya, Federated Malay States, Mauritius, Nigeria, Trinidad, Uganda.
24 L. A. Notcutt and G. C. Latham (eds.), *The African and the Cinema*, p. 10.
25 ibid. p. 205.

CHAPTER 3 THE DOCUMENTARY MOVEMENT

(i) *Early Stages*
1 Harry Watt, *Don't Look at the Camera.*
2 Erik Barnouw, *Documentary*, p. 90.
3 *Adult Education*, Dec 1939.
4 Sir Stephen Tallents, *The Projection of England*
5 *Cinema Quarterly*, vol. 1, no. 4, summer 1933, pp. 203–8.
6 *Kine Weekly*, 2 April 1936, p. 3.
7 *Sight and Sound*, no. 27, autumn 1938.
8 *Kine Weekly*, 18 Dec 1930, pp. 35 and 40.
9 ibid., 10 Dec 1931, p. 23.
10 Arthur Calder-Marshall, *The Innocent Eye*, p. 136.
11 Shorter version *Shepherd's Watch* issued 1937.
12 *Cinema Quarterly*, vol. 1, no. 2, winter 1932, p. 117.
13 *Close Up*, vol. IX, no. 3, Sept 1932, pp. 161–2.
14 *Cinema Quarterly*, vol. 2, no. 1, autumn 1933, p. 37.
15 Copy in the N.F.A.
16 Elizabeth Sussex, *The Rise and Fall of British Documentary*, p. 39.
17 *Sight and Sound*, no. 7, autumn 1933, p. 105.
18 Richard Meran Barsam, *Non-fiction Film*, pp. 42 and 51.
19 *Sight and Sound*, no. 8, winter 1933/4, p. 144.
20 *Film Art*, no. 2, winter 1933, says it has a musical accompaniment.
21 The latter was referred to in *Sight and Sound* in the summer of 1933 as *Banana Symphony*.
22 *Film Art*, no. 2, winter 1933.
23 Paul Rotha, *Documentary Diary*, p. 90.
24 *Kine Weekly*, 3 Aug 1933, p. 15.
25 *Cinema Quarterly*, vol. 2, no. 1, autumn 1933, p. 47.
26 *Sight and Sound*, no. 23, autumn 1937, p. 159.
27 A reference in *Sight and Sound*, no. 8, winter 1933/4, p. 140, to 330 titles, only 13 of them in sound, in the new G.P.O. Film Library would seem to refer to this collection; the figure of 700 films used in *Kine Weekly*, 7 Sept 1933, p. 3, presumably does so as well, the apparent discrepancy being explained by their treating 35 mm. and 16 mm., as well as sound and silent, versions as separate items.
28 *Empire Film Library Catalogue*, 2nd ed. 1937, p. 4.
29 *Kine Weekly*, 27 May 1937, p. 51.
30 Sussex, *The Rise and Fall of British Documentary*, p. 24.
31 Letter in *New Statesman*, 14 March 1942, p. 177, and elsewhere.

(ii) *The Middle Years*
32 *Cinema Quarterly*, vol. 1, no. 4, summer 1933, p. 208.
33 Blackheath acquired R.C.A. sound later.
34 *Cinema Quarterly*, vol. 2, no. 4, summer 1934.
35 ibid., vol. 2, no. 4, summer 1934.
36 ibid., vol. 3, no. 2, winter 1935, pp. 70–4.
37 *Film Art*, no. 6, autumn 1935, p. 76.
38 *Sight and Sound*, no. 11, autumn 1934, p. 118.
39 The newspaper shown in the train sequence is dated July 1934.
40 *Cinema Quarterly*, vol. 3, no. 1, autumn 1934, pp. 18–19.

25 Gas *versus*
electricity (*New
Worlds for Old*,
1938).

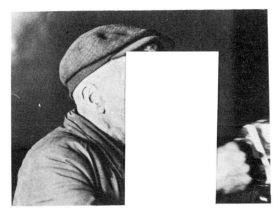

26 The details of life,
carefully observed
(*Spare Time*, 1939).

27 *The Times* reader
(*The Fourth Estate*,
1939).

41 See Sussex, *The Rise and Fall of British Documentary*, and the article by her in *Sight and Sound*, autumn 1975. We are indebted to her for her patient sifting of the recollections of her interviewees.
42 *Sight and Sound*, no. 16, winter 1935/6, p. 177.
43 *Cinema Quarterly*, vol. 3, no. 2, winter 1935, p. 119.
44 Both Paul Rotha's *Documentary Film* and the B.F.I. *Catalogue of Documentary Films* date it as 1933.
45 N.F.A. copy.
46 Paul Rotha, *Documentary Diary*, p. 129. *World Film News*, May 1936.
47 N.F.A. copy.
48 *Sight and Sound*, no. 8, winter, 1933/4, pp. 119–21.
49 At the Select Committee.
50 *Journey to a Legend and Back – The British Realistic Film* ed. Eva Orbanz, p. 40.
51 *Film Art*, no. 10, spring 1937, p. 34.
52 Paul Rotha, *Documentary Diary*, p. 97.
53 *Cinema Quarterly*, vol. 3, no. 1, autumn 1934, p. 37.
54 Rotha, *Documentary Diary*, pp. 98 and 107.
55 *Cinema Quarterly*, vol. 3, no. 3, spring 1935, pp. 177–8.
56 ibid., vol. 3, no. 4, summer 1935, pp. 194–6.
57 Rotha, *Documentary Diary*, p. 103.
58 *Documentary Diary* refers to this as *Death on the Roads*, but it was registered as *Death on the Road*.
59 Andrew Buchanan, *The Art of Film Production*, p. 16.
60 Rotha, *Documentary Diary*, p. 108.
61 Their *World Film News* advertisement in July 1936 mentions *Sixpenny Telegram*, but this is in the 1952 list as a G.P.O. film.
62 There are some title changes in connection with these films, but these are the names used by Rotha.
63 Rotha, *Documentary Diary*, p. 159.
64 *Sight and Sound*, vol. 5, no. 18, summer 1936, pp. 30–1.
65 Rotha, *Documentary Diary*, p. 146.
66 See *Sight and Sound*, no. 27, autumn 1938, pp. 116–17.
67 *The Spectator*, 11 Sept 1936.
68 *Life and Letters Today*, winter 1936, pp. 178–9.
69 *Night and Day*, 16 Dec 1937.
70 *Sight and Sound*, no. 23, autumn 1937, p. 155.
71 *Life and Letters Today*, winter quarter 1935/6, pp. 182–4.
72 ibid., spring 1936, pp. 164–9.
73 *Sight and Sound*, no. 19, winter 1936, p. 83.
74 *World Film News*, vol. 1, no. 9, Dec 1936, pp. 32–3.
75 *Film Art*, no. 10, spring 1937, p. 38.
76 *World Film News*, vol. 1, no. 9, Dec 1936, pp. 32–3.
77 *In Time with Industry* is listed separately in the 1952 list but both are 1937 and the subject sounds the same.
78 Both mentioned in *Life and Letters Today*, autumn 1937, pp. 152–3.
79 The whole verse may be found in Watt's autobiography.
80 Sussex, *The Rise and Fall of British Documentary*, p. 68.
81 Watt, *Don't Look at the Camera*, p. 80.
82 Sussex, *The Rise and Fall of British Documentary*, pp. 66–7.
83 Watt, *Don't Look at the Camera*, p. 96.

84 A shorter silent version, *Ship for Sale*, is in the 1952 list.
85 Rotha, *Documentary Diary*, p. 142.
86 *Kine Weekly*, 2 Jan 1936, p. 19.
87 ibid., 16 Jan 1936, p. 22; *World Film News*, April 1937.
88 He also wrote *Art and the Industrial Revolution*.
89 *Cinema Quarterly*, vol. 3, no. 1, autumn 1934, pp. 7–11.
90 ibid., vol. 1, no. 4, summer 1933, p. 207.
91 Watt, *Don't Look at the Camera*, p. 50.
92 *Life and Letters Today*, winter 1935/6, p. 191.

(iii) *Maturity*
93 Registered in June 1937, £100.
94 *Kine Weekly*, 27 May 1937, p. 51.
95 Rotha, *Documentary Diary*, p. 219.
96 Letter from Paul Rotha in *Sight and Sound*, vol. 8, no. 30, summer 1939, p. 81.
97 *Kine Year Book*.
98 *Factual Film* dates it as 1937 on p. 56 but refers to what seems to be the same report as 1938 on p. 180.
99 Reprint dated December 1939.
100 Rotha, *Documentary Diary*.
101 *Film Art*, no. 10, spring 1937, p. 40.
102 *The Spectator*, 26 Aug 1938.
103 Rotha, *Documentary Diary*, p. 151.
104 ibid.
105 N.F.A. copy.
106 *Kine Weekly*, 20 Jan 1938, p. 61.
107 In *Documentary Diary*, p. 59, Rotha gives titles which differ slightly from those registered.
108 *Sight and Sound*, no. 23, autumn 1937.
109 Sussex, *The Rise and Fall of British Documentary*, p. 100.
110 Rotha, *Documentary Diary*, p. 229.
111 ibid., pp. 225–8.
112 ibid., p. 228.
113 N.F.A. copy.
114 To confuse things even further, some published sources list *New Worlds for Old* as produced by John Taylor and directed by Frank Sainsbury.
115 Rotha, *Documentary Diary*, p. 260.
116 ibid., p. 261.
117 *Life and Letters Today*, autumn 1938, p. 99.
118 "Omnibus" programme on John Grierson, B.B.C. television, 25 Feb 1973.
119 Reviewed by *Sight and Sound* late in 1938, and dated 1938 in 1952 list.
120 Julian Symons, *The Thirties*, p. 101.
121 *Kine Weekly*, 7 Oct 1937, p. 38, 3 Feb 1938, p. 42.
122 The copy in the N.F.A. has no credits except that of Jennings as director, and the film figures twice in 1938, under both titles, in the 1952 list. But a shorter version, presumably altered to fit war conditions, was current in 1940 under the title *Cargoes*.
123 N.F.A. copy.
124 *Humphrey Jennings 1907–1950, a Tribute*.
125 Previously known as *Forty Million People*.

(iv)   *The End of the Decade*
126   *Kine Weekly*, 11 Aug 1938, p. 3.
127   *The Times*, 25 Nov 1938.
128   ibid., 26 Nov 1938.
129   *Kine Weekly*, 26 Oct 1939, p. 19.
130   ibid., p. 4.
131   *Kine Weekly*, 29 Dec 1938, p. 5.
132   "Omnibus" programme on John Grierson, B.B.C. television, 25 Feb 1973.
133   *Cinema Quarterly*, autumn 1933, p. 9.
134   *Searchlight on Democracy*, reprinted from *Adult Education*, Dec 1939.
135   *Sight and Sound*, winter 1975/6.
136   Watt, *Don't Look at the Camera*, p. 54.
137   *Life and Letters Today*, spring 1937, pp. 115–22.
138   ibid.
139   See *Journey to a Legend and Back – The British Realistic Film*, ed. by Eva Orbanz.
140   *Kine Weekly*, 18 March 1939.
141   *Cinema Quarterly*, autumn 1933, p. 8.
142   *Life and Letters Today*, winter 1936/7, pp. 157–61.
143   *Cinema Quarterly*, autumn 1934, pp. 7–9.

CHAPTER 4   REALITY AND THE DOCUMENTARY FILM

1   *Cinema Quarterly*, vol. 2, no. 2, winter 1933/4, p. 96.
2   Erik Barnouw, *Documentary*, p. 121.
3   *Sight and Sound*, winter 1975/6.
4   ibid.
5   Watt, *Don't Look at the Camera*, p. 77.
6   *Sight and Sound*, vol. 8, no. 32, winter 1939/40, pp. 136–7.
7   ibid.
8   ibid.
9   ibid.
10   *The Sunday Times*, 1 Feb 1976.

APPENDIX   THE BRITISH FILM INSTITUTE

1   R. S. Lambert, *Ariel and All His Quality*.
2   *The Film in National Life*, p. 1.
3   Arthur Vesselo, *Early Films*, p. 3.
4   *Kine Weekly*, 30 June 1932, p. 20, 7 July 1932, p. 23.
5   *Sight and Sound*, no. 9, spring 1934, pp. 3–4.
6   Walter Ashley, *The Cinema and the Public*, p. 16.
7   Payments into the Sunday Cinematograph Fund were £3,367 in 1933, £7,620 in 1934 and £9,117 in 1935.
8   Lambert, *Ariel and All His Quality*, from which much of the following account is drawn.
9   Renamed the National Film Archive in 1955.
10   Also published as a B.F.I. Leaflet, no. 4 of Aug 1934, *Report of a Special Committee Set Up by the British Kinematograph Society to*

Consider Means that Should Be Adopted to Preserve Cinematograph Films for an Indefinite Period.
11 Again, according to *Ariel and All His Quality*, p. 236.
12 In 1936 Sir Charles Cleland followed the Duke of Sutherland as Chairman, to be followed in turn by Sir George Clark in 1938 and Sir William Brass in 1939.
13 *Kine Weekly*, 12 May 1938, p. 5.

Bibliography

Arts Enquiry, The, *The Factual Film* (Oxford University Press, 1947).
Ashley, Walter, *The Cinema and the Public* (Nicholson & Watson, 1934).
Barnouw, Erik, *Documentary* (Oxford University Press, 1974).
Barsam, Richard Meran, *Non-fiction Film* (Allen & Unwin, 1974).
British Documentary Films 1929–1952, part I, *Films Controlled by the Central Office of Information* (Privately circulated, 1952).
British Film Institute, *Annual Reports*, 1934–9.
British Film Institute, *The British Film Institute: Its Aims and Objects* (1933).
British Film Institute, Leaflet No. 4, *Report of a Special Committee set up by the British Kinematograph Society to Consider Means that Should Be Adopted to Preserve Cinematograph Films for an Indefinite Period* (1934).
British Film Institute, *Report of the Conference on Films for Children* (November 1936; published 1937).
Calder-Marshall, Arthur, *The Innocent Eye* (W. H. Allen, 1963).
Cinema Quarterly, 1932–5.
Close Up, 1927–33.
Commission on Educational and Cultural Films, The, *The Film in National Life* (Allen & Unwin, 1932).
Consitt, Frances, *A Brief Abstract of a Report on the Value of Films in the Teaching of History* (Historical Association, 1931).
Curtis, David, *Experimental Cinema* (Studio Vista, 1971).
Educational Film Review, April–October 1935.
Empire Film Library Catalogue, 1937.
Empire Marketing Board Film Library Catalogue, 1932.
Field, Mary and Smith, Percy, *Secrets of Nature* (Faber & Faber, 1934).
Film Art, 1933–7.
Film Society Programmes, The, for seasons 5 (1929–30) to 14 (1938–9).
George, W. H., *The Cinema in School* (Isaac Pitman, 1935).
G.P.O. Film Library Catalogue, September 1937.
Grierson, John, 'The cinema', in *The Arts Today*, ed. Geoffrey Grigson (Bodley Head, 1935).
Grierson, John, *Searchlight on Democracy*, reprint from *Adult Education*, December 1939.
Hardy, Forsyth, *Grierson on Documentary* (Collins, 1946).
Huxley, Julian, *Africa View* (Chatto & Windus, 1931).
Huxley, Julian, *Memoirs* (Allen & Unwin, 1970).
International Review of Educational Cinematography, English edition published 1929–34 by International Institute of Educational Cinematography, Rome.

Kine Weekly 1929–39.
Kine Year Books 1929–40.
Kostelanetz, Richard, *Moholy-Nagy* (Allen Lane The Penguin Press, 1971).
Lally, William L. (ed.), *A National Encyclopaedia of Educational Films and 16 mm. Apparatus* (Central Information Bureau for Educational Films, 1937).
Lambert, Richard S., *Ariel and All His Quality* (Gollancz, 1940).
Lambert, Richard S. and Price, Harry, *The Haunting of Cashen's Gap* (1936).
Lauwerys, J. A. (ed.), *The Film in the School* (1935).
Life and Letters 1928–35.
Life and Letters Today 1935–9.
Lovell, Alan and Hillier, Jim, *Studies in Documentary* (Secker & Warburg with British Film Institute, 1972).
Marchant, Sir James (ed.), *The Cinema in Education* (Allen & Unwin, 1925).
Memorial booklet on Humphrey Jennings (Humphrey Jennings Memorial Fund Committee, 1951).
Memorial booklet on Richard Massingham (Richard Massingham Memorial Fund, 1955).
Monthly Film Bulletin (British Film Institute, 1934–9).
National Film Archive, *Catalogue of Viewing Copies* (1971) and *Catalogue of Viewing Copies Supplement* (1974).
National Film Archive Catalogue, Part II, *Silent Non-Fiction Films 1895–1934* (British Film Institute, 1960).
National Film Board of Canada. Film on the work of John Grierson.
National Film Library Catalogue, 2nd edn (British Film Institute, 1938).
Notcutt, L. A. and Latham, G. C. (eds), *The African and the Cinema* (Edinburgh House Press, 1937).
"Omnibus" B.B.C. Television programmes: on Humphrey Jennings, September 1970, and on John Grierson, February 1973.
Orbanz, Eva, *Journey to a Legend and Back – The British Realistic Film* (Edition Volker Spiess, 1977).
Ottley, D. Charles, *The Cinema in Education* (Routledge, 1935).
Political and Economic Planning, *The British Film Industry* (P.E.P., 1952).
Rotha, Paul, *Celluloid – The Film Today* (Longmans, Green, 1931).
Rotha, Paul, *Documentary Diary* (Secker & Warburg, 1973).
Rotha, Paul, *Documentary Film* (Faber & Faber, 1936; 2nd edn, 1939).
Sands, Pierre Norman, *A Historical Study of the Academy of Motion Picture Arts and Sciences (1927–47)* (Arno Press, 1973).
Sight and Sound (British Film Institute, 1932–9).
Some British and Foreign Documentary and Other Short Films (British Film Institute, January 1939).
Sussex, Elizabeth, *The Rise and Fall of British Documentary* (University of California Press, 1975).
Sussex, Elizabeth, 'Cavalcanti in England', in *Sight and Sound*, autumn 1975, p. 205.

Symons, Julian, *The Thirties* (Faber & Faber, revised edn, 1974).
Tallents, Sir Stephen, *The Projection of England* (Faber & Faber, 1932).
Vesselo, Arthur, *Early Films, a Selected Catalogue 1896–1934* (British Film Institute, September 1939).
Watt, Harry, *Don't Look at the Camera* (Paul Elek, 1974).
World Film News, 1936–8.

Film List

A complete list of documentary and educational films in Britain between 1929 and 1939 is hardly possible at this stage, but a preliminary list will be used, I hope, as a basis for further study by other people. It should be remembered that many such films were not registered with the Board of Trade, that standard and substandard versions as well as sound and silent versions of the same subjects might be made, and even given different titles, and that they might be cut up and re-used. This book includes most films made by mainstream documentary film-producers except the early E.M.B. editing jobs, and also the more interesting individual films of British Instructional Films, Gaumont-British Instructional, Visual Education and others. It would make the list very large, and the book very expensive, to include all the hundreds of films they made. Apart from these, I have put in such films as seemed interesting or likely to require identification. Thus no claim to be comprehensive is made. I have included such production details as date, length, company and personnel where they are available and reasonably reliable. In some cases where disagreement is known to exist I have tried, wherever possible, to use the credits as given on the film itself, but some other possibilities or claims have been noted in the main text of the book. The use of abbreviations in the Film List is in the interests of economy.

KEY TO ABBREVIATIONS OF PRODUCTION DETAILS USED IN THE FILM LIST

/	distributing company
alt.	alternative or working title
anim.	animated drawing or puppet film
assoc.	associate (producer or director, according to position in list)
asst.	assistant (the same)
c.	cameraman
comp.	compilation
cr.	commentator
cy.	writer of commentary
d.	director
des.	design or art direction
diag.	diagrams, usually animated
Dun.	Dunning colour
Dufay.	Dufaycolor
ed.	editor
f.	featuring
ft.	length in feet
Gasp.	Gasparcolor

m.   music
m.d.   musical direction
mins.   length in minutes
p.   producer
p.c.   production company or unit
p.m.   production manager
reels   length in reels
reg.   registered with Board of Trade (applies to length and date)
sc.   writing
sd.   sound recording
Spicer   Spicer colour
st.   silent film
sup.   supervision or consultation
synch.   synchronisation
Tech.   Technicolor
T.S.   date of trade show

Films are 35 mm. unless otherwise indicated, and are sound films unless otherwise indicated. If substandard and silent versions existed as well as standard and sound versions, this is not necessarily indicated.

ALPHABETICAL LIST OF ABBREVIATIONS OF PRODUCERS, DISTRIBUTORS, SPONSORS, ETC., USED IN FILM LIST

A.B.F.D.   Associated British Film Distributors
A.B.P.C.   Associated British Picture Corporation
Anglo-American   Anglo-American Film Distributors
A.R.F.P.   Associated Realist Film Producers
Assoc.   Associated
B.B.C.   British Broadcasting Corporation
B.C.G.A.   British Commercial Gas Association
B.F.I.   British Film Institute
B.I.F.   British Instructional Films
Brd   Board
Brit. Ind. Prod.   British Independent Productions
C.C.H.E.   Central Council for Health Education
Com.   Committee
Dev.   Development
Ed.   Education
E.F.L.   Empire Film Library
E.G.S.   Educational and General Services
E.M.B.   Empire Marketing Board Film Unit
E.T.M.(E.)B.   Empire Tea Marketing (Expansion) Board
Excl.   Exclusive Films
F.C.   Film Centre
F-N   First National Film Distributors

G.B.D.	Gaumont British Distributors
G-BE	Gaumont-British Equipments
G-BI	Gaumont-British Instructional
G.B.P.C.	Gaumont British Picture Corporation
G.F.D.	General Film Distributors
G.P.O.	General Post Office Film Unit
I.D.A.	Industrial Development Association
Imp. Rel. T.	Imperial Relations Trust
Imp. Air.	Imperial Airways
Jt	Joint
Kinograph	Kinograph Distributors
L.M.B.	L.M.B. Films
L.N.U.	League of Nations Union
M-G-M	Metro-Goldwyn-Mayer Pictures
Min.	Ministry
Nat.	National
New Era	New Era Films
N.F.L.	National Film Library
Pathé	Pathé Pictures
P.F.I.	Progressive Film Institute
P.O.	Post Office
Pub.	Publicity
Pub. F.	Publicity Films
Realist	Realist Film Unit
Shell	Shell Film Unit
Strand	Strand Film Company
Strand Zoo	Strand Films Zoological Productions
Techq.	Technique Distributors
T.I.D.A.	Travel and Industrial Development Association
U.A.	United Artists
Vis. Ed.	Visual Education
Wardour	Wardour Films
W.E.	Western Electric
Zeni	Zenifilms
Z.S.L.	Zoological Society of London

FILM LIST

Advance Democracy *p.c.* Realist for 4 London Co-operative Societies and Basil Wright/P.F.I. 1578 *ft.* *reg.* 7.39 Made 1938 *d.sc.* Ralph Bond *c.* Gerald Gibbs, A. E. Jeakins *m.* Benjamin Britten *f.* Fred Barker, Kathleen Gibbons.

Aerial Milestones *p.c.* Strand for Imp. Air. 2207 *ft.* 1939 *ed.* J. Martin-Jones, J. H. Stroud *sd.* Charles Poulton *cr.* Norman Shelley.

Aero Engine *p.c.* E.M.B. 4395 ft. 1932 *st. alt.* **Aeroplane Engine** *p.* John Grierson *d.sc.ed.* Arthur Elton *c.* George Noble.

Aeroplane Engine

See **Aero Engine**

African Skyways *p.c.* Strand for Imp. Air./A.B.F.D. 1939 *p.* Stuart Legg *d.* Stanley Hawes.

Aircraft Design *p.c.* G-BI/G-BD with Nat. Physical Laboratory 1 *reel* 1937.

Air Flow *p.c.* Strand for Air Min. 1936 *p.* Arthur Elton *d.* Stanley Hawes *c.* S. Onions, Dr Townend *Air Min.* Liaison Robert Fairthorne.

Air Outpost *p.c.* Strand for Imp. Air./A.B.F.D. 1500 *ft. reg.* 12.37 *d.* John Taylor, Ralph Keene *c.* John Taylor *ed.* Ralph Keene *cr.* Stuart Legg *m.* William Alwyn.

Airport *p.c.* Shell/A.B.F.D. 2 *reels* 1934 *p.* Edgar Anstey, Roy Lockwood.

Air Post *p.c.* G.P.O. 1058 *ft.* 1934 *p.* Arthur Elton *d.* Geoffrey Clark *c.* A. E. Jeakins, John Taylor.

Amoeba, The *p.c.* G-BI/G-BD 1 *reel* 1934 H. R. Hewer, Julian Huxley.

Animal Geography *p.c.* Strand Zoo/Techq. 950 *ft. reg.* 10.39.

Animal Legends *p.c.* Strand Zoo/Techq. 1520 *ft. reg.* 12.38.

Animals on Guard *p.c.* Strand Zoo/Techq. 1570 *ft. reg.* 7.39.

Annelid Worms *p.c.* G-BI/G-BD 1 *reel* 1935 *with* Scottish Marine Biological Station.

Around the Village Green *p.c.* T.I.D.A./M-G-M 1056 *ft. reg.* 8.38 *Made* 1937 *p.d.* Evelyn Spice, Marion Grierson *c.* Fred Gamage *cr.* John Watt *sd.* V. C. Sawyer *m.* Benjamin Britten.

A.R.P. Films *p.c.* G.P.O. 1938 3 *st.* one reel films.

At the Third Stroke *p.c.* G.P.O. 1939 *p.* Cavalcanti *d.* Richard Massingham *asst.* Stewart

McAllister *c.* H. Fowle *ed.* R. Q. McNaughton *des.* Joanna Macfadyen *sd.* Ken Cameron *f.* Russell Waters, Marjorie Lane.

Bag Net Fishing *p.c.* E.F.L. 325 *ft.* 1932 *st.*

Banking for Millions *p.c.* G.P.O. 2 *reels* 1935 *p.* John Grierson *d.* Raymond Spottiswoode.

Bassetsbury Manor *p.c.* Cyril Jenkins/A.B.F.D. 1589 *ft. reg.* 5.36.

B.B.C. – Droitwich *p.c.* G.P.O. for B.B.C./Zeni 1400 *ft. reg.* 4.35 *Made* 1934 *p.* John Grierson *d.* Harry Watt, Edgar Anstey *c.* William Shenton *cr.* Stuart Hibberd *sd.* E. A. Pawley.

B.B.C. – The Voice of Britain *p.c.* G.P.O. for B.B.C./A.B.F.D. 5035 *ft. reg.* 8.35 *T.S.7.35 p.* John Grierson, Stuart Legg *d.sc.ed.* Stuart Legg and others *c.* George Noble, J. D. Davidson, W. Shenton *sd.* E. A. Pawley *m.* Adrian Boult and B.B.C. Symphony Orchestra, Henry Hall and B.B.C. Dance Orchestra.

Behind the Scenes *p.c.* Strand Zoo/Techq. 1490 *ft. reg.* 5.38 *p.* Stuart Legg *d.* Evelyn Spice *c.* Paul Burnford *sd.edit.* Jack Ellit *cy.sup.* Julian Huxley.

Beside the Seaside *p.c.* Strand for T.I.D.A. 2300 *ft.* 1935 *p.* Marion Grierson *asst.* Alex Shaw *c.* F. Gamage, George Noble *m.* 43rd Light Infantry *conducted* D. J. Plater.

Big Money *p.c.* G.P.O./Techq. 1335 *ft. reg.* 9.38 *Made and Shown* 1937 *p.* Cavalcanti *d.* Harry Watt *c.* Jonah Jones, Chick Fowle *ed. and co-d.* Pat Jackson *sd.* George Diamond *m.* Brian Easdale.

Birth of the Robot *p.c.* Shell-Mex

B.P. 630 *ft.* 1936 Gaspar *anim. p.d.*
Len Lye *sc.* C. H. David *c.* Alex
Strasser *colour decor and prod.*
Humphrey Jennings *models* John
Banting, Alan Fanner *sd.* Jack
Ellit *m.* Gustav Holst.
Birth of the Year *p.c.* Strand Zoo/
Techq. 1340 *ft. reg.* 12.38 *p.* Stuart
Legg *d.* Evelyn Spice *c.* Paul
Burnford *ed.* Jack Ellit *sup.* Julian
Huxley *m.* William Alwyn.
Black Gold *p.c.* G.B.I./G-BI 1855
ft. reg. 8.39 *cr.* E. V. H. Emmett.
Black Nuggets *p.c.* Safety in Mines
Research Board/A.B.P.C. 1219 *ft.*
reg. 1.39.
Blowfly, The *p.c.* G-BI/G-BD 2
reels 1935 *d.* H. R. Hewer *sup.*
Julian Huxley.
Book Bargain *p.c.* G.P.O./Techq.
714 *ft. reg.* 8.38 *Made and shown*
1937 *d.* Norman McLaren *c.* H.
Jones *sd.* G. Diamond.
Britain's Countryside *p.c.* G.P.O.
for T.I.D.A. 1 *reel* 1933/4 *st. d.*
Marion Grierson.
British Made *p.c.* G.P.O. for
T.I.D.A. 1 *reel* 1939 *d.* George
Pearson *m.* E. H. Meyer.
British Navy, The *p.c.* Strand and
E.G.S./G.F.D. 1345 *ft. reg.* 3.39
p. Stuart Legg *c.* E.G.S. *ed.* Jack
Ellit.
Cable Ship *p.c.* G.P.O./New Era
1120 *ft. reg.* 7.34 *Made* 1933 *p.*
John Grierson *d.* Stuart Legg, Alex
Shaw *c.* A. E. Jeakins, John
Taylor.
Calendar of the Year *p.c.* G.P.O.
1519 *ft. Made* 1936 *Seen* 1937 *p.*
Cavalcanti *d.* Evelyn Spice *c.*
Jonah Jones, H. Fowle *sd.* E. K.
Webster *m.* Benjamin Britten.
Cambridge *p.c.* B.I.F./Wardour
1037 *ft.* 1932 *d.* Stuart Legg, G. F.

Noxon *c.* Jack Parker *sd.* D.
Howells *m.* Patrick Hughes.
Cargo for Ardrossan *p.c.* Realist
for Petroleum Films Bureau/
A.B.F.D. 2 *reels* 1939 *d.* Ruby
Grierson *asst.* G. Keen *c.* A. E.
Jeakins *sd.* H. G. Halstead *m.*
Alan Rawsthorne.
Cargo From Jamaica *p.c.* E.M.B.
1 *reel* 1933 *st. p.* John Grierson
d.c.ed. Basil Wright.
Cathedrals of England *p.c.*
T.I.D.A. 1 *reel* 1937 *st. d.* Marion
Grierson.
Cathode Ray Oscillograph *p.c.*
G-BI/G-BE 2 *reels* 1936.
Cause Commune, La *p.c.* G.P.O.
995 *ft.* 1939 *p.* Cavalcanti *ed.*
Robert Hamer *cy.* Robert Battefort
m. Brian Easdale *sd.* Ken Cameron.
Changes in the Franchise *p.c.*
G-BI/G-BE 1 *reel* 1937 p. Mary
Field *d.* A. Miller Jones *diag.* R.
Jeffryes.
Changing Year, The *p.c.* B.I.F./
Pathé 3160 *ft. reg.* 6.33 *d.sc.* Mary
Field *f.* Rene Ray, Eric Findon.
Chapter and Verse *p.c.* Strand for
Nat. Book Council/G-BE 32 *mins*
1936 *p.* Paul Rotha *d.* Stanley
Hawes *c.* George Noble.
Children at School *p.c.* Realist for
B.C.G.A./Techq. 2170 *ft. reg.* 3.38
First show 10.37 *p.* John Grierson
d. Basil Wright *c.* A. E. Jeakins,
Erik Wilbur *cr.* H. Wilson Harris.
Children's Story, The *p.c.* Strand
for Films of Scotland/M-G-M 1370
ft. reg. 5.39 *Made* 1938 *p.* Stuart
Legg *d.* Alex Shaw *c.* Jo Jago.
Orchestra of Trinity Academy
Edinburgh under George Reith.
Citizens of the Future *p.c.* Strand
and G-BI with Nat. Union of
Teachers/G-B.D. 1913 *ft. reg.*

10.35 *d.* Donald Taylor *c.* George Noble.

City, The *p.c.* G.P.O./Anglo-American 1742 *ft. reg.* 11.39 *Made* 1938 *p.* Cavalcanti *d.* Ralph Elton *c.* H. E. Fowle *cr.* Herbert Hodge *m.* Alan Rawsthorne.

City Prepares, A See **First Days, The**

Coal See **Mine, The**

Coalface *p.c.* G.P.O./A.B.F.D. 1016 *ft.* 1935 *p.* John Grierson *d.sc.* Cavalcanti *c.* archive material *Verses* W. H. Auden, Montagu Slater *ed.* William Coldstream *sd.* E. A. Pawley *sd. sup.* Cavalcanti *m.* Benjamin Britten.

Cocoa from the Gold Coast Cadbury Bros. for N.F.L. 1 *reel* 16 *mm. st.* 1938 *sup.* Geography Committee.

Colour Box, A *p.c.* G.P.O. 110 *ft. Made* 1936 *T.S.* 1.37 Dufay *anim. p.* John Grierson *d.* Len Lye.

Coming of the Dial, The *p.c.* G.P.O./New Era 1361 *ft. reg.* 7.34 *Made* 1933 *p.* John Grierson *d.* Stuart Legg *c.* Gerald Gibbs *abstract by* Moholy-Nagy.

Community Calls *p.c.* G.P.O. 1 *reel* 1937 *ed.* P. Brooke, R. Q. McNaughton.

Conga, 1936/7 Len Lye.

Conquering Space *p.c.* G.P.O. 985 *ft.* 1935 *p.* Stuart Legg *ed.* G. A. Shaw.

Conquest *p.c.* E.M.B. 31 *mins.* 1930 *st. ed.* John Grierson *asst.* Basil Wright.

Conquest of Natural Barriers, The *p.c.* E.M.B. 742 *ft.* 1930 *st.*

Conquest of the Air *p.c.* B.I.F./Wardour 2325 *ft. reg.* 12.31.

Conquest of the Air *p.c.* L.F.A./U.A. 6 *reels press show* 3.38 *p.*

Donald Taylor *d.* Alexander Shaw *c.* George Noble and others *ed.* R. Q. McNaughton *m.* Arthur Bliss *f.* Laurence Olivier, Margaretta Scott.

Contact *p.c.* B.I.F. for Imp. Air. and Shell-Mex BP/Wardour 2644 *ft. Made* 1932/3 *first shown* 7.33 *T.S.* 8.33 *d.* Paul Rotha *asst.* Ralph Keene *c.* Horace Wheddon, Jack Parker, Frank Goodliffe *m.* Clarence Raybould.

Copper Web, The *p.c.* G.P.O. 1 *reel Made* 1937 *shown* 1938 *d.* Maurice Harvey *c.* Henry Fowle *sd.* George Diamond.

Country Comes to Town, The *p.c.* E.M.B./G-B.D. ("Imperial Six") 2 *reels Made* 1931 *shown* 1933 *p.* John Grierson *d.* Basil Wright *c.* Basil Wright, James Burger.

Cover to Cover *p.c.* Strand for Nat. Book Council/A.B.F.D. 1855 *ft. reg.* 9.36 *alt.* **Preface to Life** *p.* Paul Rotha *d.* Alex Shaw *c.* George Noble *Verse cy.* Winifred Holmes *cr.* Ion Swinley, Leslie Mitchell *m.* Raymond Bennell.

Crafts of Hunza *p.c.* N.F.L. 1 *reel* 16 *mm. st.* 1936 *c.* Lt. Col. D. L. R. Lorimer *ed.* James Fairgrieve. (Also **Hunza Round the Year).**

C.T.O., The Story of the Central Telegraph Office *p.c.* G.P.O. 1357 *ft.* 1935 *p.* Stuart Legg *c.* J. D. Davidson, F. H. Jones.

Cyclone *p.c.* James Fairgrieve, Hubert Waley for Royal Geographical Association 97 *ft.* 1933.

Daily Round, The *p.c.* G.P.O. 1637 *ft.* 1937 *p.* Cavalcanti *d.* Richard Massingham *c. asst. d.* Karl Urbahn *sd.* George Diamond *m.* Herbert Murrill *f.* Russell Waters, etc.

Daisy Bell Comes to Town *p.c.*

Gas Industry with Nat. Milk Pub. Council *p.* Stuart Legg *d.* J. B. Holmes *c.* George Pocknall *cy.* V. C. Clinton-Baddeley *sd.* Micky Jay *m.* Walter Leigh *f.* Griffiths Brothers.

Dance of the Harvest *p.c.* E.T.M.B. 764 *ft.* 1934.

Dawn of Iran *p.c.* Strand for Anglo-Iranian Oil/U.A. 1285 *ft. reg.* 8.38 *Made* 1937 *p.* Arthur Elton *d.c.ed.* John Taylor *sd.* W. F. Elliott *m.* Walter Leigh.

Death on the Road *p.c.* G-BE with "News of the World" for Min. of Transport/G.B.D. 1500 *ft. reg.* 5.36 *d.* Paul Rotha.

Deferred Payment *p.c.* B.I.F. for C.C.H.E. 3 *reels* 1929 *st. d.* Mary Field.

Design for Spring *dist.* A.B.F.D. 20 *mins.* 1937 Dufay *d.* Humphrey Jennings.

Development of English Railways, The *p.c.* G-BI/G.B.D. 754 *ft. reg.* 11.36 *p.* Mary Field *d.* A. Miller Jones *c.diag.* R. Jeffryes.

Dinner Hour *p.c.* B.C.G.A./B.C.G.A. 2 *reels Made* 1935 *Shown* 1936 *p.* Arthur Elton *d.* Edgar Anstey *c.* Stanley Rodwell, T. R. Thumwood *sd.* L. G. Page.

Do It Now *p.c.* G.P.O. for Home Office/A.B.F.D. 996 *ft. reg.* 11.39 *alt.* **If War Should Come.**

Domesday England *p.c.* Maurice Browne/W.E. 2 *reels* 1934.

Domestic Science Films *p.c.* G-BI/ G-BE for H.M. Inspector of Domestic Science, Leeds, 4 *one-reel films* of 1934: **Making Rabbit Pies, Making Pork Pies, Frying in Batter, Baking Powder.**

Drifters *p.c.* E.M.B./New Era 3500 *ft. reg.* 12.29 *TS* 11.29 *st. p.* John

Grierson *c.* Basil Emmott.

Dry Dock *p.c.* G-BI/G-BE 969 *ft. reg.* 5.36 *d.* Stanley Hawes.

Earthworm, The *p.c.* G-BI/G.B.D. 2 *reels* 1935 *d.* H. R. Hewer *c.* F. Goodliffe *sup.* Julian Huxley *arranged* Dr G. Frankel.

Eastern Health Bureau at Singapore for L.N.U. 1937 *d.* Ralph Keene.

Eastern Valley *p.c.* Strand for an Order of Friends/Techq. 1500 *ft. T.S.* 12.37 *p.* Stanley Hawes *d.* Donald Alexander.

Edinburgh *p.c.* G.P.O. for T.I.D.A. 872 *ft.* 1934 *st. d.* Marion Grierson.

Eminent Scientists Series *p.c.* G-BI with National Physical Laboratory/ G-BE *half-reel each* 1935: Sir William Bragg, Col. Rookes Evelyn Bell Crompton, Sir Richard Glazebrook, Sir Oliver Lodge, Mr William Morday, Sir Joseph John Thompson, Lord Hirst of Witton, Lord Rutherford.

England Awake *p.c.* B.I.F./Wardour 3208 *ft. T.S.* 5.32 *d.* H. Bruce Woolfe, John Buchan *asst.* Stuart Legg *sd.* A. Birch *m.* W. E. Hodgson.

English Potter, The *p.c.* E.M.B. and T.I.D.A. 1 *reel* 1933 *st.*

Enough To Eat *p.c.* Gas Light and Coke Co./Kinograph 2018 *ft. reg.* 1.37 *T.S.* 10.36 *and* 2.37 *alt.* **Nutrition Film** *d.sc.* Edgar Anstey *asst.* Frank Sainsbury *c.* Walter Blakeley, Arthur Fisher *cr.* Julian Huxley *sd.* Charles Poulton (A.R.F.P. film).

Equation X+X=A Sin Nit, The *p.c.* B. G. D. Salt/B· G. D. Salt, Film Society 4 *mins.* 1936 *st. Notation by* Robert Fairthorne *anim.* Brian Salt.

Equation $\ddot{X}+X=0$, The *p.c.* B. G.

D. Salt/B. G. D. Salt, Film Society 4 *mins.* 1936 *st. Notation by* Robert Fairthorne *anim.* Brian Salt.

Eskimo Village *p.c.* E.M.B. for Admiralty 1 *reel* 1933 *st. p.* John Grierson *d.* Edgar Anstey.

Euclid. 1.32 *p.c.* B. G. D. Salt/B. G. D. Salt 1 *reel st.* 16 *mm.* 1936. *anim.* Brian Salt.

Expansion of Germany, The G-BI/ G.B.D. 1033 *ft. reg.* 11.36 *p.* Mary Field *d.* A. Miller Jones *c. diag.* R. Jeffryes.

Experiment in the Welsh Hills, An See **Shadow on the Mountain.**

Face of Britain, The *p.c.* G-BI/ G.B.D. 1730 *ft. reg.* 11.35 *d.sc.* Paul Rotha, *c.* George Pocknall, Frank Bundy *cy.* A. J. Cummings *sd.* W. F. Elliott.

Face of Scotland, The *p.c.* Realist for Films of Scotland/M-G-M 1209 *ft. reg.* 5.39 *Made* 1938 *p.* John Grierson *d.* Basil Wright *c.* A. E. Jeakins *sd.* W. F. Elliott *m.* Walter Leigh.

Fairy of the Phone, The *p.c.* G.P.O. 1 *reel* 1936 *p.* Basil Wright *d.* William Coldstream *c.* Jimmy Rogers *sd.* C. Sullivan *m.* Walter Leigh *f.* Charlotte Leigh.

Farm Factory, The *p.c.* G-BI/G.B.D. 1961 *ft. reg.* 11.36 *c.* G. Pocknall.

Farming in Spring, Summer, etc. See **Quiet of the Countryside, The**

Fens, The *p.c.* E.M.B. 1 *reel* 1933 *d.* Evelyn Spice.

Filter, The *p.c.* G-BI/G.B.D. 923 *ft.c.* Percy Smith *ed.* Mary Field with Metropolitan Water Brd.

Fingers and Thumbs *p.c.* Strand Zoo/Techq. 1534 *ft. reg.* 12.38.

First Days, The *p.c.* G.P.O./ A.B.P.C. 2110 *ft. reg.* 11.39 *alt.* A

City Prepares *p.* Cavalcanti, Humphrey Jennings, Harry Watt, Pat Jackson *cr.* Robert Sinclair *ed.* R. Q. McNaughton.

Fishing Banks of Skye See **On the Fishing Banks of Skye.**

Five Faces *p.c.* Strand for Federated Malay States 2851 *ft. reg.* 3.38 *d.* Alex Shaw.

Flag, The *p.c.* B.I.F./Pathé 1 *reel* 1933 *d.sc.* Mary Field *c.* Jack Parker.

For All Eternity *p.c.* Strand for T.I.D.A./M-G-M 1500 *ft. Made* 1934 *shown* 1935 *p.* Marion Grierson *m.d.* Walter Vale, Greville Cooke with All Saints' Choir.

Forty-eight Paddington Street *p.c.* B.I.F./Pathé 1 *reel* 1931/2 *sup.* Prof. A. Lloyd James.

Forty Million People See **Health for the Nation.**

Four Barriers *p.c.* G.P.O. with Pro Telephon, Zürich 732 *ft.* 1937 *p.* Harry Watt *c.* John Taylor *ed.* Pat Jackson, Ralph Elton *sd.* George Diamond.

Fourth Estate, The *p.c.* Realist for Times Publishing Co: 6 *reels Made* 1939/40 *Shown* 1970 *p.d.* Paul Rotha *unit man:* Patrick Moyna *c.* J. Rogers, H. Rignold, A. E. Jeakins *sc. consultant* Carl Mayer *speakers* Geoffrey Dell, Nicholas Hannen, Denis Arundell *sd.* L. G. Page *m.* Walter Leigh, Sadlers Wells Theatre Orchestra (F.C. film).

Free to Roam *p.c.* Strand Zoo/ Techq. 1349 *ft. reg.* 5.38 *p.* Stuart Legg *d.c.* Paul Burnford *sd.edit.* Jack Ellit *cy. and sup.* Julian Huxley *cr.* Norman Shelley *m.* William Alwyn.

French "U", The *p.c.* G-BI/G.B.D.

476 *ft.* 1934 *d.* Mary Field *c.* C. Van Enger.

Full Fathom Five Len Lye *f. voice of* John Gielgud. *Untraced.*

Future's in the Air, The *p.c.* Strand/A.B.F.D. 3321 *ft. reg.* 11.37 *p.* Paul Rotha *d.* Alex Shaw *unit man* Ralph Keene *c.* George Noble *cy.* Graham Greene *cr.* Ivan Scott *sd.* W. Elliott *m.* William Alwyn, Raymond Bennell *Maps* James Gardner.

Gap, The *p.c.* G-BI with Army and Air Councils/G.F.D. 3421 *ft. reg.* 4.37 *TS* 4.37 *d.* Donald Carter *Asst.* J. L. Bacon *c.* George Pocknall *des.* F. N. Bush *dialogue* E. V. H. Emmett *m.d.* Louis Levy *sd.* John Douglas *f.* G. H. Mulcaster, Patrick Curwen, Carleton Hobbs.

Gare, La *p.c.* G-BI/G.B.D. 536 *ft.* 1934 *d:* Mary Field *c.* C. Van Enger.

Give the Kids a Break *p.c.* Strand for Necessitous Children's Holiday Camp Fund 2 *reels* 1937 *p.d.* Donald Taylor *asst.* Ruby Grierson.

Glassmakers of England, The *p.c.* E.M.B. and T.I.D.A. 1 *reel* 1933 *st.*

Glittering Sword, The *p.c.* County High School for Boys, Altrincham 1800 *ft. reg.* 11.29 *st. d.sc.* Ronald Gow.

Glorious Sixth of June, The *p.c.* G.P.O. 1 *reel* 1934 *d.* Cavalcanti.

God's Chillun *p.c.* G.P.O. *half-reel* 1938 *Words* W. H. Auden *m.* Benjamin Britten *eds* Max Anderson, Rona Morrison, Gordon Hales *sd.* George Dewhurst *speech* J. Copland Grant.

Grain Harvests *p.c.* Carrick Classroom Films/G-BE 1 *reel* 1936 *p.* J. C. Elder, J. Blake Dalrymple.

Granton Trawler *p.c.* New Era for E.M.B./New Era 968 *ft. reg.* 11.34 *Made* 1933 *T.S.* 10.34 *p.* John Grierson *ed.* Edgar Anstey *sd.* E. A. Pawley.

Great Cargoes *p.c.* G-BI/G.B.D. 1953 *ft. reg.* 11.35 *p.* Paul Rotha *c.* George Pocknall, Frank Bundy.

Gullible Gull, The *p.c.* Strand Zoo/Techq. 1478 *ft. reg.* 10.39.

Happy in the Morning *p.c.* Pub F. for Gas Council 1 *reel* 1938 *p.sc.* Cavalcanti *assoc.d.* Pat Jackson *c.* Harry Waxman *sd.* Charles Poulton *m.* Henry Hall and his Band *song* Temple Abady *lyric* Stafford Byrne.

Health for the Nation *p.c.* G.P.O. for Min. of Health *with* B.B.C. 3207 *ft. T.S.* 5.39 *alt.* **Forty Million People** *p.* Cavalcanti *d.sc.* John Monck *c.* Jonah Jones *cy.* Hugh Gray *cr.* Ralph Richardson *sd.* Yorke Scarlett, Ken Cameron *m.* Marius Gaillard, B.B.C. Northern Orchestra.

Health in Industry See **Men in Danger.**

Heart of an Empire *p.c.* Strand for T.I.D.A./M-G-M 694 *ft. reg.* 1.36 *Made* 1935 *p.* Marion Grierson *d.* Alex Shaw *cr.* Laurence Gilliam *m.* 43rd Light Infantry Band.

Heavy Industry *p.c.* G-BI/G.F.D. 648 *ft. reg.* 8.37.

Hen Woman, The *p.c.* E.M.B. 1933 *d.* J. Norris Davidson. *Unfinished.*

Heredity in Man *p.c.* G-BI with Eugenics Society 1294 *ft. Shown* 8.37 *Sup.* Julian Huxley, H. R. Hewer *d.* J. V. Durden *cr.* Julian Huxley.

Here is the Land *p.c.* Strand for Land Settlement Assoc./Film Centre 1850 *ft. reg.* 3.38 *Made* 1937

T.S. 3.39 *p.* Paul Rotha *d.* Stanley Hawes *c.* Harry Rignold, S. Onions (F.C. film).

Her Last Trip *p.c.* G.P.O. 1838 *ft. alt.* **S.S. Ionian** *d.* Humphrey Jennings.

High Hazard *p.c.* Stanley Watson/ Zeni 1700 *ft. reg.* 3.35 *d.c.* Stanley Watson *sup.* John Gifford *cr.* F. Le Breton Martin *m.d.* John Reynders.

Honey Bee *p.c.* B.I.F./L.M.B. 943 *ft. reg.* 2.35.

Horsey Mail, The *p.c.* G.P.O. 770 *ft.* 1937 *p.* Cavalcanti *d.* Pat Jackson *c.* Fred Gamage *m.* Victor Yates *f.* Bob O'Brian, Claude Simmonds.

Housing Problems *p.c.* B.C.G.A. 1178 *ft.* 1935 *p.d.sc.* Arthur Elton, Edgar Anstey *asst.* Ruby Grierson *c.* John Taylor *sd.* Yorke Scarlett.

How Gas is Made *p.c.* B.C.G.A. 1 *reel* 1935 *p.* Arthur Elton *d.* Edgar Anstey *c.* John Taylor *sd.* L. G. Page.

How Plants Feed *p.c.* G-BI/G-BE 921 *ft.* 1934 *c.* Percy Smith *ed.* Mary Field with Prof. E. J. Salisbury.

How Stamps Are Made *p.c.* G.P.O. 685 *ft.* 1936 *st.*

How Talkies Talk G-BI/G-BE 1108 *ft. reg.* 2.36 *d.* Donald Carter *sup.* Dr T. Hafner.

How the Dial Works *p.c.* G.P.O. 507 *ft.* 1937 *p.* R. Elton.

How the Telephone Works *p.c.* G.P.O. with Research Section of P.O. Engineering Dept. 600 *ft.* 1938 *d.* Ralph Elton, J. Chambers *c.* Fred Gamage.

How to Cook *p.c.* Gas Industry/ B.C.G.A. 2 *reels* 1937 *p.* Arthur Elton *d.* J. B. Holmes *c.* George Pocknall *sd.* Micky Jay *f.* Marcel Boulestin.

How to Tell *p.c.* B.I.F. 1493 *ft.* 1931 *st.*

H.P.O. *p.c.* G.P.O. 340 *ft.* 1939 Dufay *anim.* Made *by* Lotte Reiniger *asst.* R. M. Harris *m.* Brian Easdale.

Hull Design G-BI/G.B.D. with Nat. Physical Laboratory 1 *reel* 1937.

Humber-Hillman See **Where the Road Begins.**

If War Should Come See **Do It Now.**

Industrial Britain *p.c.* E.M.B./ G.B.D. ("Imperial Six") 1980 *ft.* 1933 *Made* 1931 *p.* John Grierson *d.sc.* Robert Flaherty *ed.* Edgar Anstey *cr.* Donald Calthrop.

In Time With Industry *p.c.* G.P.O. *half-reel* 1937 Len Lye.

Introducing the Dial *p.c.* G.P.O. *half-reel* 1934 *p.* John Grierson *d.* Stuart Legg *c.* Gerald Gibbs.

Islanders, The *p.c.* G.P.O./A.B.F.D. 1519 *ft.* 1939 *p.* J. B. Holmes *d.* Maurice Harvey *asst.* Stewart McAllister *c.* Harry Rignold, Jonah Jones *cr.* Jack Livesey *sd.* Ken Cameron *m.* Darius Milhaud.

Job in a Million, A *p.c.* G.P.O. with London Postal Region 1466 *ft.* 1937 *p.* John Grierson *d.* Evelyn Spice *c.* S. Onions *ed.* Norman McLaren *sd.* G. C. Diamond *m.* Brian Easdale.

John Atkins Saves Up *p.c.* G.P.O. 2 *reels* 1934 *d.* Arthur Elton *c.* J. D. Davidson *cy.* V. C. Clinton-Baddeley *f.* Leslie Higgins, Eileen Lee.

Kaleidoscope *p.c.* Len Lye for Churchman's Cigarettes 1 *reel* 1935 Spicer *anim. painted and designed* Len Lye *charted and synch.* Jack Ellit *m.* Don Baretto and his Cuban Orchestra.

Kensal House *p.c.* B.C.G.A. 2 *reels*

1937 *d*. Frank Sainsbury.
Keyboard Talks *p.c.* G-BI/G-BE 990 *ft. reg.* 2.36 *f*. Mark Hambourg.
Key to Scotland, The *p.c.* Strand for T.I.D.A. 1244 *ft. reg.* 3.36 *Shown* 10.35 *p*. Marion Grierson *m. arranged* Ursula Greville and Leighton Lucas.
King Log *p.c.* E.M.B./G.B.D. ("Imperial Six") 2 *reels* 1933 *Made* 1932 *p*. John Grierson *d.ed.* Basil Wright.
King's Breakfast, The *p.c.* Facts and Fantasies/A.B.F.D. 970 *ft. reg.* 12.37 *Made by* Lotte Reiniger *asst.* Martin Battersby; from *poem by* A. A. Milne *decoration* E. H. Shepherd *m*. H. Fraser-Simson *m.d.* Ernest Irving *singers* Olive Groves, George Barker.
King's English *p.c.* B.I.F./Pathé 2 *reels* T.S. 1.33 *d*. Mary Field *c*. J. Parker.
Kings in Exile *p.c.* G-BI/G.F.D. 1020 *ft. reg.* 3.38 *c*. G. Pocknall, G. W. MacPherson.
King's Stamp, The *p.c.* G.P.O. 1 *reel* 1935 part-Dufay *d*. William Coldstream *c*. Jonah Jones, H. E. Fowle *sd.* E. A. Pawley *m*. Benjamin Britten *f*. Barnett Friedmann.
Lancashire at Work and Play *p.c.* T.I.D.A. for Lancashire I.D.A./ Zeni 3 *reels* 1933/4 *st. p*. John Grierson *d*. Donald Taylor *c*. George Noble.
Lancashire Home of Industry *p.c.* T.I.D.A. 1 *reel* 1933/4 *st. p*. John Grierson *d.sc.* Donald Taylor *c*. George Noble.
League at Work, The *p.c.* Realist for L.N.U. 2 *reels* 1937 *p*. Basil Wright *d*. Stuart Legg.
Life Cycle of a Plant, The *p.c.* G-BI/G.B.D. 1 *reel made* 1934 *ed.*

Mary Field *c*. Percy Smith.
Liner Cruising South *p.c.* E.M.B. for Orient Line/New Era 1578 *ft.* 1933 *st. p*. John Grierson *d.c.* Basil Wright.
Line to Tschierva Hut *p.c.* G.P.O. and Pro Telephon, Zürich 868 *ft.* 1937 *p*. John Grierson *d.sc.ed.* Cavalcanti *c*. John Taylor *m*. Maurice Jaubert.
Liquid History *p.c.* E.M.B. for Shell-Mex B.P. 1 *reel.*
Locomotives *p.c.* G.P.O. 793 *ft.* 1934 *d*. Humphrey Jennings *m.d.* John Foulds.
Londoners, The *p.c.* Realist for B.C.G.A./Techq. 3300 *ft. reg.* later 2058 *ft. reg.* 4.39 *T.S.* 3.39 *p*. John Grierson, Basil Wright *d.sc.* John Taylor *asst.* Philip Leacock *c*. A. E. Jeakins *cr*. Howard Marshall *verse* W. H. Auden *ed*. Alan Gourlay *sd.* H. G. Halstead *m*. E. H. Meyer.
London On Parade *p.c.* T.I.D.A./ F-N 1014 *ft. reg.* 1.39 *d*. Marion Grierson.
London Town *p.c.* E.M.B. for T.I.D.A. 2 *reels* 1933 *st. d*. Marion Grierson *c*. William Shenton.
London Wakes Up *p.c.* Strand/ Techq. 1035 *ft. reg. Made* 1936 *reg.* 8.38 *p*. Paul Rotha *d*. Ruby Grierson.
Love on the Wing *p.c.* G.P.O. 157 *ft.* 1938 Dufay *anim. d*. Norman McLaren *c*. Fred Gamage *m*. Jacques Ibert.
Lubrication of the Petrol Engine *p.c.* Shell 1181 *ft.* 1936/7 *p*. Arthur Elton *d*. Grahame Tharp *c*. Stanley Rodwell *diag.* Francis Rodker.
Lumber *p.c.* E.M.B./New Era 1089 *ft. reg.* 12.31 *p*. John Grierson *d.ed.* Basil Wright.

Man Who Changed His Mind, The *p.c.* County High School for Boys, Altrincham 2696 *ft. reg.* 12.28. **Mediaeval Village** *p.c.* G-BI/G.B.D. 1703 *ft. reg.* 11.36 *d.* J. B. Holmes *c.* Frank Bundy, Frank Goodliffe *advisers* H. L. Beales, R. S. Lambert. **Mediterranean Island, A** *p.c.* B.I.F. with Geographical Association/ Pathé 1 *reel* 1933 *ed.* James Fairgrieve.

Men Behind the Meters *p.c.* B.C.G.A. 1836 *ft.* 1935 *d.* Arthur Elton *c.* John Taylor *sd.* L. G. Page.

Men In Danger *p.c.* G.P.O. 2091 *ft.* Made 1938/9 Shown 5.39 *Alt.* **Health in Industry** *p.* Cavalcanti *d.* Pat Jackson *c.* H. Fowle *cr.* Sir Henry Bashford *sd.* Ken Cameron *m.* Brian Easdale.

Men of Africa *p.c.* Strand for Colonial E.M.B. 1940 *p.sc.* Basil Wright *d.* Alex Shaw *c.* Jo Jago, Harry Rignold *cr.* Leslie Mitchell *location sd.* Leevers Rich Ltd.

Men of the Alps *p.c.* G.P.O. and Pro Telephon, Zürich 917 *ft.* 1937 *p.* Harry Watt *c.* John Taylor *ed.* Maurice Harvey, R. Stocks *sd.* E. K. Webster.

Message from Geneva *p.c.* G.P.O. and Pro Telephon, Zürich 792 *ft.* 1937 *d.sc.* Cavalcanti *c.* John Taylor.

Midsummer Day's Work *p.c.* G.P.O. 1100 *ft.* 1939 *p.d.sc.* Cavalcanti *asst.* D. Knight *c.* Jonah Jones, James Rogers *cr.* Robin Duff *ed.* R. Q. McNaughton *sd.* Ken Cameron *m.d.* J. E. N. Cooper.

Milling Machine *p.c.* Steuart Films and G-BI/Steuart 1 *reel* 1934 *d.* R. Steuart *technology* Alex Francis.

Mine, The *p.c.* G-BI/G.B.D. with Safety in Mines Research Brd. 1612 *ft. reg.* 9.36 *alt.* (theatrical version) **Coal** *d.* J. B. Holmes *c.* F. Bundy *diag.* R. Jeffryes.

Mites and Monsters *p.c.* Strand Zoo/Techq. 1523 *ft. reg.* 5.38 *p.* Stuart Legg *d.* Donald Alexander *c.* Paul Burnford, Jo Jago *sup. and cy.* Julian Huxley.

Modern Orphans of the Storm *p.c.* Realist and Victor Saville for Nat. Jt. Com. for Spanish Relief 972 *ft.* 1937 *p.d.* Basil Wright, Ian Dalrymple *cr.* E. V. H. Emmett.

Monkey Into Man *p.c.* Strand Zoo/Techq. 1400 *ft. reg.* 5.38 *p.* Stuart Legg *d.* Stanley Hawes *c.* George Noble *sup. and cy.* Julian Huxley *tech. assistance* Dr Zuckerman *m.* William Alwyn.

Monsoon Island *p.c.* E.T.M.(E.)B. 917 *ft.* 1934 *st. d.* Basil Wright.

Mony a Pickle *p.c.* G.P.O. 1 *reel* 1938 *p.d.* Cavalcanti, Richard Massingham.

Mystery of Marriage, The *p.c.* B.I.F./Wardour 3119 *ft. reg.* 9.31 *d.sc.* Mary Field *sd.* A. Birch *m.d.* W. E. Hodgson *f.* Rene Ray, Eric Findon.

Mystery of Stonehenge, The *p.c.* A. Moncrieff Davidson/Reunion 1000 *ft. reg.* 5.35 *p.d.* A. Moncrieff Davidson *c.* James Hodgson *cr.* Gerald Heard.

Negombo Coast *p.c.* E.T.M.(E.)B. 1 *reel* 1934 *st. d.* Basil Wright.

Negombo Coast, From Colombo *dist.* E.F.L. 1 *reel* 1934.

Netting Salmon *p.c.* Carrick Classroom Films 225 *ft. st.* 1935 *p.* J. C. Elder-Dalrymple Productions.

New Generation, The *p.c.* New Era for Chesterfield Educational Authority/New Era 2300 *ft.* 7.32 *st. p.* John Grierson *d.* Stuart Legg *c.* Gerald Gibbs.

New Operator, The *p.c.* E.M.B. for G.P.O. 750 *ft.* 1932/3 *st. p.* John Grierson *d.* Stuart Legg *c.* Gerald Gibbs.

News for the Navy *p.c.* G.P.O. 1938 *d.* Norman McLaren *c.* Chick Fowle, Fred Gamage *sd.* George Diamond *f.* Evelyn Corbett, J. F. Haggard.

New Worlds for Old *p.c.* Realist for Gas Industry 2 *reels* 1938 *p.d.* Paul Rotha *assoc. d.* Frank Sainsbury *c.* Harry Rignold, S. Onions, A. E. Jeakins *cr.* Alistair Cooke *m.* William Alwyn *Victorian decor* Vera Cuningham.

Nightmail *p.c.* G.P.O./A.B.F.D. 2115 *ft. reg.* 3.36 *p.* John Grierson *d.* Basil Wright, Harry Watt *asst.* Pat Jackson *c.* Jonah Jones, Chick Fowle *sc.* John Grierson, Basil Wright, Harry Watt *Verses* W. H. Auden *sd.* A. E. Pawley *sd. sup.* Cavalcanti *m.* Benjamin Britten *ed.* Basil Wright, R. Q. McNaughton.

N. or N.W. *p.c.* G.P.O. 719 *ft.* 1937 *p.* Cavalcanti *d.sc.ed.* Len Lye *c.* Jonah Jones *sd. edit.* Jack Ellit *f.* Evelyn Corbett, Dwight Godwin.

Northern Summer *p.c.* Orient Line/Zeni 1567 *ft. Made* 1934 *shown* 1935 *d.* Alex Shaw *c.* George Noble *m.* Raymond Bennell.

North of the Border *p.c.* G.P.O. 1937 *p.* Cavalcanti *d.* Maurice Harvey.

North Sea *p.c.* G.P.O./A.B.F.D. 2924 *ft. reg.* 7.38 *p.sc.* Cavalcanti *d.sc.* Harry Watt *asst.* Brian Pickersgill *c.* Jonah Jones, H. Fowle *ed.* R. Q. McNaughton *sd.* George Diamond *m.* Ernest Meyer.

Nutrition Film See **Enough to Eat.**

O'er Hill and Dale *p.c.* E.M.B./ G.B.D. ("Imperial Six") 1414 *ft. Made* 1932 *shown* 1933 Shorter version in 1937 **Shepherd's Watch.** 868 ft. *p.* John Grierson *d.c.* Basil Wright *cr.* Andrew Buchanan.

Of all the Gay Places *p.c.* T.I.D.A./ M-G-M 1082 *ft. reg.* 8.38 *d.* Donald Taylor *c.* W. B. Pollard.

Oh Whiskers! *p.c.* G.P.O. for Min. of Health 807 *ft.* 1939 *anim.* Brian Pickersgill *rhymes* Winifred Holmes *c.* Fred Gamage *sets* J. L. Forsyth, J. M. Bryson *sd.* Ken Cameron *m.* J. E. N. Cooper.

Oil from the Earth *p.c.* Shell/ Techq. 1667 *ft. reg.* 12.38 *T.S.* 9.38 *p.* Arthur Elton *d.* D'Arcy Cartwright *m.* Ernest Meyer.

One Family *p.c.* E.M.B. (B.I.F.)/Pro Patria 6208 *ft. reg. first show* 7.30 *d.* Walter Creighton *f.* Lady Keble, Lady Ravensdale, Lady Carlisle, Lady Lavery, Phyllis Neilson-Terry, Sam Livesey, etc.

On Harmonic Motions: Result-ants and Ellipses *p.c.* Steuart Films 50 *ft. or loop st.* 1933 *p.d.* H. E. Dance, Max Kaufmann with F. A. Meier.

On the Fishing Banks of Skye *p.c.* G.P.O. 1 *reel* 1935 *p.* John Grierson *c.* J. D. Davidson *m.* J. Foulds *cy.* John Grierson.

On the Way to Work *p.c.* Strand for Min. of Labour/Min. of L. 1908 *ft. reg.* 3.37 *Made* 1936 *d.* Edgar Anstey *c.* George Noble.

Order of the Bath See **Taking the Plunge.**

Outline of the Working of Money, An *p.* Prof. M. Polyani 25 *mins.* *16 mm. st.* 1938.

Paraffin Young, Pioneer of Oil *p.c.* Realist for Scottish Oils 1241 *ft.* 1938(?) *p.* Arthur Elton *d.* Ralph Bond *c.* A. E. Jeakins *sd.* W. F. Elliott *f.* Don Gemmell.

Parks and Palaces See **People in the Park.**

Party Dish *p.c.* Gas industry for B.C.G.A. 2 *reels* 1937 *f.* Marcel Boulestin.

Passport to Europe *p.c.* Realist for Workers' Travel Association about 1937 *d.* Ralph Bond *c.* Chick Fowle *m.* Montague Brearly.

Peace Film See **Peace of Britain.**

Peace of Britain *p.c.* Freenat Films/Dofil 290 *ft.* 4.36 *p.* Paul Rotha and others *m.* Benjamin Britten.

Penny Journey *p.c.* G.P.O. 1 *reel* 1938 *d.* Humphrey Jennings *c.* Henry Fowle, W. B. Pollard.

People and Places *p.c.* Orient Line 880 *ft.* *Made* 1934 *shown* 1935 *d.* Alex Shaw *c.* George Noble.

People in the Park *p.c.* Strand/ M-G-M 1250 *ft.* 1936 *p.* Paul Rotha *d.c.* Donald Alexander, Paul Burnford.

Pepys' England *p.c.* Vis. Ed. 1 *reel* 1934 *st.* *c.* Eric Spear *ed.* C. A. Radley.

Pett and Pott *p.c.* G.P.O. 2059 *ft.* 1934 *p.* John Grierson *d.sc.ed.* Cavalcanti *assoc.d.* Basil Wright, Stuart Legg *c.* John Taylor *sets* Humphrey Jennings *sd.* John Cox *m.* Walter Leigh.

Plan for Living *p.c.* G-BI for B.C.G.A. 12 *mins.* 1938 *d.sc.* Donald Carter *c.* George Pocknall *des.* William Hodgson, *costumes* Cyrano *ed.* Paul Grun *sd.* A. Birch *diag.* R. Jeffryes *m.* J. Beaver *lyrics* J. Davies *dances* Beaumont *f.*

Julian Huxley, Kenneth Lindsay.

Plums That Please *p.c.* E.M.B. 1 *reel* 1931.

P.M.G. on a Post Office Problem, The *p.c.* G.P.O. 573 *ft.* 1936.

Port of London *p.c.* E.M.B. 1) 25 *mins.* 2) 30 *mins.* 1930.

Post-Haste *p.c.* G.P.O. 933 *ft.* 1934 *p.* John Grierson *ed.* Humphrey Jennings.

Pots and Plans *p.c.* Gas Industry for B.C.G.A. 1 *reel* 1937 *p.* Arthur Elton *d.* J. B. Holmes.

Power in the Highlands *p.c.* G-BI/G.B.D. 860 *ft.* *reg.* 5.36.

Power Unit *p.c.* Shell 1899 *ft.* 1936 *p.* Arthur Elton *d.* D'Arcy Cartwright, Grahame Tharp *c.* Stanley Rodwell *diag.* Grahame Tharp, Francis Rodker.

Preface to Life See **Cover to Cover.**

Prelude to Flight *p.c.* Savoy Film for Shell/Techq. 1500 *ft.* *reg.* 1.39 *Made* 1938 *p.c.* D'Arcy Cartwright *d.* Grahame Tharp *asst.* Geoffrey Bell.

Progress *p.c.* G-BI/G.B.D. 1667 *ft.* *reg.* 11.35

Propeller Making *p.c.* G-BI/G.B.D. 738 *ft.* *reg.* 5.36 *c.* G. Pocknall, F. Bundy *ed.* D. Chambers.

Quiet of the Countryside, The *p.c.* G-BI/G.B.D. 4 *one-reel films* on The Farm in Spring, Summer, Autumn and Winter *reg.* 9.35 *and* re-registered *as* Farming in Spring, Summer, Autumn and Winter *in* 12.36.

Rainbow Dance *p.c.* G.P.O. for P.O. Savings Bank 357 *ft.* *TS* 1.37 *made* 1936 Gaspar *anim.* *p.* Basil Wright, Cavalcanti *d.* Len Lye *c.* Jonah Jones *colour and sd. synch.* Jack Ellit *dance* Rupert Doone *m.*

Rico's Creole Band.
Rate of Change *p.* A. D. Segaller/ Vis. Ed. 9 *mins.* 16 *mm. st.* 1937.
Raw Materials G-BI/G.F.D. 792 *ft. reg.* 8.37.
Red Army, The *p.c.* G-BI/G.B.D. 972 *ft.* 1936 *d.* Andrew Miller Jones *c.* Jack Rose.
Rice Cultivation for N.F.L. *half-reel* 16 *mm. st. ed.* Committee under James Fairgrieve.
Rising Tide *p.c.* G-BI and Southern Railway/G.B.D. 3 *reels T.S.* 8.34 *p.* Harry Bruce Woolfe *d.* Paul Rotha *c.* Jimmy Rogers, George Pocknall, Frank Goodliffe *m.* Clarence Raybould.
Roads Across Britain *p.c.* Realist/ A.B.P.C. 1269 *ft. reg.* 7.39 *p.* John Taylor *d.* Sidney Cole *c.* Arthur Graham *crs.* Stuart Legg, Herbert Hodge, Kent Stevenson *m.* William Alwyn. American section by American Documentary Films Inc.
Roadwards *p.c.* Brit. Indep. Prods. for B.S.A. and Daimler 2200 *ft.* 1933 *p.d.* Paul Rotha *c.* Jack Parker.
Roadways *p.c.* G.P.O./Techq. 1319 *ft. reg.* 9.38 *Made* 1937, *shown* 10.37 *p.* Cavalcanti *d.* William Coldstream, Stuart Legg *asst.* Ralph Elton *c.* Jonah Jones, Chick Fowle *ed:* R. Stocks *sd.* George Diamond *m.* E. H. Meyer.
Romance of a Lump of Coal, The *p.c.* B.C.G.A. *half-reel* 1935.
Rooftops of London *p.c.* Strand/ M-G-M 1254 *ft. reg.* 11.36 *p.* Paul Rotha *d.c.* Ralph Keene, Paul Burnford.
Roots *p.c.* G-BI/G.B.D. 1135 *ft.* 1934, *p.* Percy Smith *ed.* Mary Field *sup.* Prof. F. Salisbury.
Sailing 1,000 Miles up the Amazon *p.c.* Blake Dalrymple 2 *reels* 1936.

Salmon Leap See **Upstream.**
Saving of Bill Blewitt, The *p.c.* G.P.O. 3 *reels* 1937 *p.* John Grierson *assoc.p.* Cavalcanti *d.sc.* Harry Watt *asst.* Pat Jackson *c.* Jonah Jones, S. Onions *m.* Benjamin Britten.
Savings Bank, The *p.c.* G.P.O. 1 *reel* 1935 *p.* Stuart Legg *ed.* Raymond Spottiswoode.
Scotland for Fitness *p.c.* G-BI for Films of Scotland/A.B.P.C. 993 *ft. reg.* 5.38 *d.* Brian Salt.
Scratch Meal, A *p.c.* Gas, Light and Coke Co:/A.B.F.D. 1108 *ft. reg.* 1.37 *T.S.* 11.36 *d.* Arthur Elton *f.* Marcel Boulestin (A.R.F.P. film).
Sea Change *p.c.* Orient Line/Zeni 1690 *ft.* 1935 *d.* Alex Shaw *c.* George Noble *m.* Raymond Bennell.
Sea Urchin, The *p.c.* G-BI/G-BE *d.* J. V. Durden *sup.* Julian Huxley *c.* Frank Goodliffe, H. R. Hewer *diag.* R. Jeffryes.
Secrets of Nature 1930
Set 1) **Peas and Cues, Sundew, Bathtime at the Zoo, Down Under, Merlin, Aphis.**
Set 2) **Sea Level, Safety in Hiding, Plants of the Underworld, Marine Models, Flight Machine, Daily Dozen at the Zoo.**
Set 3) **Springtime at the Zoo, The Frog, The Iris Family, Scarlet Runner and Co:, Phantoms, Hold-all.**
Set 4) **Starting in Life, Mitey Atoms, A Spoon in his Mouth, Special Messengers, The Strangler, Playtime at the Zoo.**
Secrets of Nature 1931
Set 1) **In All His Glory, Magic Myxies, Light of Love, A World in a Wineglass, Friendly Flies,**

War in the Trees.
Set 2) **Water Folk, Dream Flowers, The Great Crested Grebe, The Short-Eared Owl, The Bittern, Two-Pounder.**
Secrets of Nature 1932
Set 1) **Romance in a Pond, The Nightingale, Froth-Blower, Springtime in the Scillies, Raiders of the Fens, Orphans of the Wood.**
Secrets of Nature 1933
Set 1) **Fit to Boil, Brewster's Magic, Amazing Maize, Nature's Double Lifers, Gathering Moss, Brock the Badger.**
Seven Til Five *p.c.* Glasgow School of Art Kinecraft Society 16 *mm.* 1935 *d.* Norman McLaren.
Shadow on the Mountain *p.c.* E.M.B./G.B.D. ("Imperial Six") 1833 *ft. Made* 1931 *shown* 1933 *alt.*
Experiment in the Welsh Hills, An *p.* John Grierson, *d.* Arthur Elton *c.* Jack Miller.
Shakespeare *p.c.* G-BI/G.B.D. 1064 *ft.* 1934 *d.* J. B. Holmes *sup.* Dr G. Harrison.
Sheltered Waters *p.c.* •Orient Line/ Zeni 824 *ft. Made* 1934 *shown* 1935 *p.* Alex Shaw *d.* Evelyn Spice *c.* George Noble *m.* Raymond Bennell.
Shepherd's Watch See **O'er Hill and Dale.**
Shipcraft *p.c.* G-BI/G.B.D. 748 *ft. reg.* 5.36.
Ship for Sale *p.c.* G.P.O. 1937 *st.*
Shipyard *p.c.* G-BI for Vickers Armstrong and Orient Line/G.B.D. 2233 *ft. reg.* 10.35 *Made* 1934/5 *shown* 5.35 *d.* Paul Rotha *c.* George Pocknall, Frank Bundy, Harry Rignold, Frank Goodliffe

sd. W. Elliott.
Simple Magnetism and Electricity *p.c.* G.P.O. 1250 *ft.* 1936 *p.* A. G. Highet *d.* Ralph Bond *c.* A. E. Jeakins *sd.* E. K. Webster.
Six-Thirty Collection *p.c.* New Era for G.P.O./New Era 1453 *ft. reg.* 11.34 *Made* 1933 *shown* 10.34 *p.* John Grierson *d.* Edgar Anstey, Harry Watt *c.* J. D. Davidson, S. Onions *sd.* Jack Cox.
Skye High *p.c.* Stanley Watson/Excl. 1650 *ft. reg.* 6.38.
Smoke Menace, The *p.c.* Realist for B.C.G.A./Techq. 1215 *ft. reg.* 3.38, *first show* 10.37 *p.* John Grierson, Basil Wright *d.* John Taylor *cr.* Peter Hine *cy.* J. B. S. Haldane (F.C. film).
Some Aspects of the Coal Industry *p.c.* G-BI/G-BE 12 *mins.* 1937 *p.* Mary Field *d.* Andrew Miller Jones *diag.* R. Jeffryes.
Song of Ceylon, The *p.c.* G.P.O./New Era 3585 *ft. reg.* 8.35 *Made* 1933/4 *p.* John Grierson *d.c.ed.* Basil Wright *asst.* John Taylor *sc.* John Grierson, Basil Wright and others *cr.* Lionel Wendt, *sd.* E. A. Pawley *sd. sup.* Cavalcanti *m.* Walter Leigh.
Sorting Office *p.c.* G.P.O. 1 *reel* 1935 *st. d.* Harry Watt.
S.O.S. (Radio Service) *p.c.* G.P.O. 1934 *st. p.* Cavalcanti *Possibly unfinished.*
So This Is Lancashire *p.c.* New Era for T.I.D.A./Zeni 1964 *ft. reg.* 4.35 *Made* 1933 *d.* Donald Taylor *c.* George Noble *m.* J. Foulds.
So This Is London *p.c.* T.I.D.A./ Zeni 1263 *ft. Made* 1933 *T.S.* 5.35 by Strand *p.* John Grierson *d.* Marion Grierson *r.* William Shenton *m.* J. Foulds.
Southern April, A *p.c.* B.I.F. for

•

E.M.B./New Era 1 *reel* 1930 *d.* Walter Creighton.

Spare Time *p.c.* G.P.O. 1368 *ft.* *T.S.* 4.39 *p.* Cavalcanti *d.sc.* Humphrey Jennings *asst.* D. V. Knight *c.* H. Fowle *cr.* Laurie Lee *sd.* Yorke Scarlett *Music:* Steel, Peach and Tozer Phoenix Works Band, Manchester Victorians' Carnival Band, Handel Male Voice Choir.

Speaking from America *p.c.* G.P.O. 925 *ft.* 1938 *p.* Cavalcanti *d.* Humphrey Jennings *c.* W. B. Pollard, Fred Gamage *cr.* Robin Duff *diag.* J. Chambers *sd.* Ken Cameron.

Speed the Plough *p.c.* Strand/ A.B.F.D. 1928 *ft. reg.* 6.39 *p.* Arthur Elton *d.* Stanley Hawes, *sup.* Professor Scott Watson.

Spring Comes to England *p.c.* E.M.B. for Min. of Agriculture and Fisheries/A.B.F.D. 1437 *ft.* *Made* 1933 *shown* 1934 *p.* John Grierson *d.* Donald Taylor *c.* Jonah Jones, Jimmy Rogers *m.* J. Foulds.

Spring Offensive *p.c.* G.P.O. 2 *reels* 1939 *alt.* **An Unrecorded Victory** *p.* Cavalcanti *d.* Humphrey Jennings *c.* H. E. Fowle, Eric Cross, *sc.* Hugh Gray, *cy.* A. G. Street, *des.* Edward Garrick (sic, on film), *ed.* Geoff Foot *Music* by Liszt arranged Brian Easdale *m.d.* Muir Mathieson *sd.* Ken Cameron.

Spring on the Farm *p.c.* New Era for E.M.B./New Era 824 *ft. reg.* 11.34 *Made* 1933 *p.* John Grierson *d.* Evelyn Spice *c.* A. E. Jeakins *m.d.* J. E. N. Cooper.

S.S. Ionian See **Her Last Trip.**

Statue Parade *p.c.* Strand/M-G-M 1260 *ft. reg.* 1.37 *Made* 1936 *p.* Paul

Rotha *d.c.* Ralph Keene, Paul Burnford.

Steel *p.c.* G-BI/G.B.D. 1 *reel* 1936 *d.* Paul Rotha.

St. James's Park *p.c.* T.I.D.A. 664 *ft.* 1935 *st. d.* Marion Grierson.

Story of a Disturbance, The *p.c.* G-BI/G.B.D. 1 *reel* 1936 *p.d.* Donald Carter *c.* Frank Goodliffe *sup.* R. A. Watson Watt.

Story of the Wheel, The *p.c.* G.P.O. 1 *reel* 1934/5 *ed.* Humphrey Jennings.

Story of Watling Street, The *p.c.* Vis. Ed. 2 *reels* 1934 *d.* C. A. Radley, Eric Spear *c.* Eric Spear *ed.* C. A. Radley.

Strand Animal Films 1, q.v. (*reg.* 5.38) *p.c.* Strand with Z.S.L. **Behind the Scenes, Free to Roam, Mites and Monsters, Monkey into Man, Zoo and You, Zoo Babies.**

Strand Animal Films 2, q.v. (*reg:* 12.38 – 10.39) *p.c.* Strand with Z.S.L. **Animal Geography, Animal Legends, Animals On Guard, Birth of the Year, Fingers and Thumbs, The Gullible Gull, Time of Your Life.**

Streamline *p.c.* G-BI/G.B.D. 1005 *ft. reg.* 5.36.

Success *p.c.* Steuart Films for Willesden Ed. Com. 15 *mins.* 16 *mm. st.* 1933 *d.* J. B. Holmes *c.* Ronald Steuart.

Surface Tension, Parts I & II *p.c.* B.I.F./Pathé 2 *reels* 1932 Louis Anderson Fenn.

Swinging the Lambeth Walk *p.c.* T.I.D.A. 330 *ft. shown* 3.40 Dufay *anim. Colour accompaniment by* Len Lye *m.d.* Ernest Meyer.

Sydney Eastbound *p.c.* Strand/

Anglo-American 1682 *ft. reg.* 11.39.
Taking the Plunge *p.c.* Strand/Zeni 881 *ft. reg.* 7.35 *alt.* **Order of the Bath** *d.* Donald Taylor *c.* George Noble *cr.* Ivan Samson.
Telephone Workers *p.c.* G.P.O./ New Era 1673 *ft. reg.* 7.34 *p.* John Grierson *d.* Stuart Legg *c.* Gerald Gibbs.
Tell the World *p.c.* G.P.O. 1938 *d.* Ralph Elton.
Test for Love, A *p.c.* G-BI/G-BE 1034 *ft.* 16 *mm.* 1937 *d.* Vernon Sewell.
Theorem of Pythagoras, The *p.c.* B.G.D. Salt 1 *reel* 16 *mm. st.* 1936 Brian Salt.
These Children Are Safe *p.c.* Strand for T.I.D.A. 1776 *ft.* 1939 *p.* Donald Taylor *d.* Alex Shaw *asst.* Michael Law *c.* Jo Jago *cr.* John Hilton *sd.* Charles Poulton *m.* William Alwyn.
They Made the Land *p.c.* G-BI for Films of Scotland/M-G-M 1774 *ft. reg.* 4.39 *d.* Mary Field *c.* George Stevens *cr.* E. V. H. Emmett.
This Was England *p.c.* G-BI/G.B.D. 1844 *ft. reg.* 10.35 *d.* Mary Field *c.* G. Pocknall, F. Bundy.
Thistle, The *p.c.* G-BI/G-BE 1 *reel* 1934 *d.* Percy Smith *ed.* Mary Field.
Thunderstorm *p.c.* James Fairgrieve and Hubert Waley for Royal Geographical Society 97 *ft.* 1933.
Time of Your Life *p.c.* Strand Zoo/Techq. 1487 *ft. reg.* 3.38 *d.* Stanley Hawes *sup.* Julian Huxley.
Tocher, The *p.c.* G.P.O. 455 *ft.* 1938 *p.* Cavalcanti *Made by* Lotte Reiniger *m.* Rossini *arranged by* Benjamin Britten.
Today and Tomorrow *p.c.* Strand

for Nat. Council of Social Service 2 *reels* 1937 *d.* Ruby Grierson *cy.* Howard Marshall.
Today We Live *p.c.* Strand for Nat. Council of Social Service/A.B.F.D. 2150 *ft. reg.* 12.37 *Made* 1936/7 *T.S.* 7.37 *p.* Paul Rotha *cr.* Stanley Hawes *d.* Ruby Grierson, Ralph Bond *c.* S. Onions, Paul Burnford *sc.* Stuart Legg *cr.* Howard Marshall *m.* Raymond Bennell.
Tough'Un, The *p.c.* G-BI/G.F.D.939 *ft. reg.* 12.38.
Town Settlement *p.c.* G-BI/G.B.D. 1104 *ft. reg.* 10.35.
Trade Tattoo *p.c.* G.P.O. *half-reel* 1936/7 Tech. *anim. p.* John Grierson *d.* Len Lye *musical ed.* Jack Ellit *m.* Lecuona Band.
Transfer of Power *p.c.* Shell 1810 *ft.* 1939 *p.* Arthur Elton *d.* Geoffrey Bell *c.* Sydney Beadle *sd.* A. Birch *diag.* Francis Rodker.
Uncharted Waters *p.c.* E.M.B. for Admiralty 1 *reel* 1933 *st. p.* John Grierson *d.c.ed.* Edgar Anstey.
Under the City *p.c.* G.P.O./New Era 1300 *ft. reg.* 7.34 *p.* Arthur Elton *d.* Alex Shaw *c.* J. D. Davidson, John Taylor.
Unrecorded Victory, An *See* **Spring Offensive.**
Upstream *p.c.* E.M.B./G.B.D. ("Imperial Six") 2 *reels Made* 1931 *shown* 1933 *p.* John Grierson *d.* Arthur Elton *c.* Jack Miller *cr.* Andrew Buchanan.
Voice of the World *p.c.* New Era for Gramophone Co 3 *reels* 1932 *p.* John Grierson *d.* Arthur Elton *c.* George Noble.
Watch and Ward in the Air *p.c.* Strand for Imp.Air./Techq. 1498 *ft. reg.* 6.38 *Made* 1937 *p.* Stuart

Legg *d.* Ralph Keene *c.* George Noble, Jo Jago.

Way to the Sea, The *p.c.* Strand for Southern Railway/A.B.F.D. 1470 *ft. Made* 1936 *T.S.* 2.37 *p.* Paul Rotha *d.* J. B. Holmes *c.* George Noble, John Taylor *crs.* Geoffrey Tandy, Norman Wooland *end cy.* W. H. Auden *m.* Benjamin Britten.

Wealth of a Nation *p.c.* Strand for Films of Scotland/M-G-M 1480 *ft. reg.* 5.39 *Made* 1938 *p.* Stuart Legg *d.* Donald Alexander *asst.* Bladon Peake *c.* Harry Rignold, Jo Jago *cr.* Harry Watt.

Weather Forecast *p.c.* New Era for G.P.O./New Era 1526 *ft. reg.* 11.34 *T.S.* 10.34 *p.* John Grierson *d.* Evelyn Spice *c.* George Noble *sd. sup.* Cavalcanti.

We Live in Two Worlds *p.c.* G.P.O. and Pro Telephon, Zürich/ Techq. 1194 *ft. reg.* 7.38 *Made* 1936/7 *p.* John Grierson *d.* Cavalcanti *c.* John Taylor *sc. and cr.* J. B. Priestley *ed.* R. Q. McNaughton *sd.* E. K. Webster *m.* Maurice Jaubert.

Welsh Plant Breeding Station, Aberystwyth, The *p.c.* G-BI for Imp. Rel. T. 1 *reel* 1939 *d.c.* J. V. Durden.

What's On Today *p.c.* G.P.O. 1094 *ft.* 1938 *d.* R. Q. McNaughton *c.* Jonah Jones *ed.* Brian Pickersgill *cr.* Robin Duff *sd.* Ken Cameron.

Where the Road Begins *p.c.* Steuart Films for Humber-Hillman Car Co 1000 *ft.* 1933 *alt.* **Humber-Hillman** *d.* J. B. Holmes *c.* Jimmy Rogers *m.* Clarence Raybould.

White Flies and Tomatoes *p.c.* G-BI/G-BE 1 *reel* 1934 *c.* Percy Smith *sup.* Professor F. Salisbury.

White Horses *p.c.* A. Moncrieff Davidson/Reunion 801 *ft. reg.* 7.35 *p.d.* A. Moncrieff Davidson *c.* Ronald Anscombe.

Who Writes to Switzerland? *p.c.* G.P.O. 1 *reel* 1937 *st. d.sc.* Cavalcanti *c.* John Taylor.

Windmill in Barbados *p.c.* New Era for E.M.B./New Era 900 *ft. reg.* 11.34 *Made* 1933 *p.* John Grierson *d.c.ed.* Basil Wright *sd.* E. A. Pawley *sd.sup.* Cavalcanti.

Wings Over Empire *p.c.* Strand/ Anglo-American 2380 *ft. reg.* 10.39 *TS* 7.39.

Winter on the Farm *p.c.* G.P.O. 2 *reels* 1933 *p.* Stuart Legg *d.* Evelyn Spice.

Workers and Jobs *p.c.* Arthur Elton for Min. of Labour/A.B.F.D. 1013 *ft. Made* 1934/5 *shown* 1935 *p.d.* Arthur Elton *c.* Osmond Borrodaile *sd.* R. A. Smith.

Work Waits For You *p.c.* Strand for Min. of Labour/Min. of L. 3200 *ft.* 1936 *st. d.* Alex Shaw *c.* H. Fowle.

Zoo and You *p.c.* Strand Zoo/ Techq. 1500 *ft. reg.* 5.38 *p.* Stuart Legg *d.* Ruby Grierson *c.* Harry Rignold, S. Onions *cy. sup.* Julian Huxley *m.* William Alwyn *f.* Mabel Constanduros.

Zoo Babies *p.c.* Strand Zoo/Techq. 1440 *ft. reg.* 5.38 *p.* Stuart Legg *d.* Evelyn Spice *c.* Paul Burnford, Jo Jago *cy. sup.* Julian Huxley *m.* William Alwyn *cr.* Leslie Mitchell.

Index